THE
STUDENT
EQEDGE

THE STUDENT EQ EDGE

EMOTIONAL INTELLIGENCE
AND YOUR ACADEMIC
AND PERSONAL SUCCESS

Steven J. Stein • Howard E. Book • Korrel Kanoy

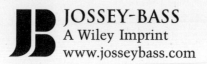

JOSSEY-BASS
A Wiley Imprint
www.josseybass.com

Cover design: Michael Cook

Copyright © 2013 by John Wiley & Sons, Inc. All rights reserved.
Published by Jossey-Bass
A Wiley Imprint
One Montgomery Street, Suite 1200, San Francisco, CA 94104-4594—www.josseybass.com

Jossey-Bass books and products are available through most bookstores. To contact Jossey-Bass
directly call our Customer Care Department within the U.S. at 800-956-7739, outside the U.S.
at 317-572-3986, or fax 317-572-4002.

Wiley publishes in a variety of print and electronic formats and by print-on-demand. Some
material included with standard print versions of this book may not be included in e-books or
in print-on-demand. If this book refers to media such as a CD or DVD that is not included in
the version you purchased, you may download this material at http://booksupport.wiley.com.
For more information about Wiley products, visit www.wiley.com.

Library of Congress Cataloging-in-Publication Data

Library of Congress Cataloging-in-Publication Data has been applied for and is on file with
the Library of Congress.
ISBN 978-1-118-09459-4 (paper); ISBN 978-1-118-48220-9 (ebk);
ISBN 978-1-118-48221-6 (ebk); ISBN 978-1-118-48223-0 (ebk)

Printed in the United States of America
FIRST EDITION

PB PRINTING   10 9 8 7 6 5 4 3 2 1

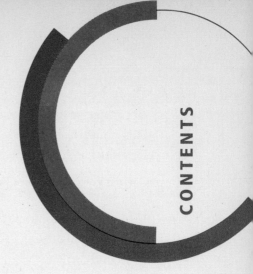

Times have certainly changed since we were students. Technologies that we only imagined have become realities in today's world. Personal devices and services such as those once depicted only in futuristic comics (think of Dick Tracy's 2-Way Wrist Radio)—enabling us to speak from anywhere across distances to people elsewhere, magically call up information as wide-ranging as who starred in some obscure movie and what food reviewers say about the closest ten restaurants, instantly video conference with people across the hall or around the globe, and so much more—are now here.

However, some things have not changed very much. We still need to interact with other people. And we need to self-regulate our behaviors and our emotions. Of course, there have always been people who poorly manage these skills. They tend to be more socially isolated, perform worse in their academic courses, and generally wind up with fewer choices in their lives. What *has* changed is that we've come a long way in better understanding the importance of being aware of and managing our impulses, emotions, and behaviors.

In this book, we hope to share with you some of what we've learned about emotional and social intelligence. We've reworked our internationally successful book for general audiences into this version, specifically adapted for older teens and young adults pursuing their secondary and post-secondary education. Our goal is to provide examples and learning opportunities that can make a difference in your academic as well as your personal life. The book is organized into sixteen areas of functioning—skills that you can learn—that our research has found to be important aspects of emotional intelligence. As psychologists and a psychiatrist, we have found this model to be extremely useful in helping people to both understand their own behavior and that of those around them, as well as be a better manager of both their own and others' behavior.

We welcome your feedback about how we can make this book more accessible to you and your peer group.

We each came to writing this book from a different path, but we share gratitude for those who have made this book possible. Our families, who displayed infinite patience with the "need to write"; our friends and colleagues, who supplied heavy doses of encouragement; and certainly the people who have told us their stories. Steven thanks the great people at Multi-Health Systems (MHS), who have worked hard to help provide the data and research used throughout this book. Korrel would like to thank the many students she taught during her career at Peace College; working with them provided self-actualization that made work fun, challenging, and meaningful. We also recognize our editor, Erin Null, who demonstrated her own emotional intelligence, balancing constructive suggestions with positive comments.

Steven J. Stein, Ph.D., is a psychologist and CEO of Multi-Health Systems (MHS), a leading international test publishing company. He has authored several books on emotional intelligence, including the original *The EQ Edge: Emotional Intelligence and Your Success* (coauthored with Dr. Howard Book); *Make Your Workplace Great: The Seven Keys to an Emotionally Intelligent Organization*; and *Emotional Intelligence for Dummies*. He has shared information on emotional intelligence with audiences throughout the United States, Canada, Mexico, Europe, Asia, and Africa. As well, he has appeared on hundreds of TV, radio, online, and print media productions.

For over a dozen years, **Dr. Howard E. Book's** area of expertise has been benchmarking and enhancing the emotional intelligence of individuals and groups, as well as developing training programs to enhance the strength of this ability. Dr. Book has also written, lectured, and offered workshops on the importance of emotional intelligence and success in the real world internationally. He is a member of the Consortium for Research in Emotional Intelligence in Organizations, part-time faculty at the INSEAD School of Business in France and Singapore, and a former board member of the International Society for the Psychoanalytic Study of Organizations, and with Dr. Steven Stein he coauthored the book *The EQ Edge: Emotional Intelligence and Your Success.* Dr. Book holds the rank of associate professor, Department of Psychiatry, Faculty of Medicine at the University of Toronto.

Korrel Kanoy, Ph.D., is a developmental psychologist who served as a professor of psychology at William Peace University (formerly Peace College) for over 30 years, where she won the McCormick Distinguished Teaching Award and the Excellence in Campus Leadership Award before being named Professor Emeritus in 2012. She has taught college-level courses in emotional intelligence since 1998. Korrel designed a comprehensive approach to infusing emotional intelligence into first-year experience courses, senior capstone courses, and college and university service offices. She has worked with over 200 college students to help them improve their EI and trains people from all over North America to use emotional intelligence instruments such as the EQ-i 2.0 and EQ-i 360. She has published a children's book, *Annie's Lost Hat,* which teaches preschoolers lessons about emotional intelligence through the story. She is a coauthor of *Building Leadership Skills in Adolescent Girls.*

PART 1

Introduction

Joe had a lot of book smarts but was lacking some key skills that kept him from getting the grades that he deserved. First, he didn't like asking for help, so he never sought clarification about assignments he did not understand. Second, he almost always underestimated how long it would take him to complete big projects, which often left him cramming to finish most of it the last night. And finally, he often got very impatient when he could not figure out how to do an assignment and quickly gave up.

As he was growing up, Joe's impatience had contributed to other difficulties in his life. His driver's license was suspended a year after he got it because of the seriousness of his speeding offenses. Also, when it came time to choose a college, he had started off applying to only one because of what he had heard about their fraternity parties, but that college had very high acceptance standards and Joe didn't get in. He had to scramble late in the year to get into a college that he didn't really want to attend. All of these challenges Joe faced relate to his emotional intelligence.

The publication in 1995 of Daniel Goleman's *Emotional Intelligence: Why It Can Matter More Than IQ* (Goleman, 1995) generated a flood of interest in the role that emotional intelligence plays in our lives. Goleman elegantly surveyed years of research into psychological functioning and interpersonal skills, presenting his case to general readers in a coherent and accessible way. The response was seismic. At long last, the so-called soft skills that do so much to determine our success were rescued from the fringe and seriously considered by mainstream educators, business people, and the media.

CHAPTER 1

Emotional Intelligence: Here to Stay

E motional intelligence is not a fad or a trend. Nor is it quite as new as many people believe. It seems novel only because it was shuffled aside, sent into hibernation by the 20th century's fixation on "hard" data and rationalism at any cost. Only now, in the 21st century, are the social sciences catching up and coming to grips with those aspects of personality, emotion, cognition, and behavior that were previously judged incapable of being identified, measured, and fully understood. Now they're increasingly recognized as crucial to effective functioning at school, in the workplace, and in our personal lives. Good relationships and coping strategies are keys to our success in every area of human activity, from the initial bonding between parent and child to the ability of teachers to bring out the best in their students.

In fact, one of a number of emotional intelligence breakthroughs took place in the 1980s, when the American-born Israeli psychologist Dr. Reuven Bar-On (1988) began his work in the field. He was perplexed by a number of basic questions. Why, he wondered, do some people possess greater emotional well-being? Why are some people better able to achieve successful relationships? And—most important—why do some people who are blessed with superior intellectual abilities seem to fail in life, whereas others with more modest intellectual gifts succeed? By 1985, he thought he'd found a partial answer in what he called a person's emotional quotient (EQ), an obvious parallel to the long-standing measure of cognitive or rational abilities that we know as IQ, or intelligence quotient.

But what exactly makes up one's emotional quotient (also called emotional intelligence)? Bar-On's original definition (1997) has been revised to the current definition we use: "A set of emotional and social skills that influence the way we perceive and express ourselves, develop and maintain social relationships, cope with challenges, and use emotional information in an effective and meaningful way" (Multi-Health Systems, 2011, p. 1). EQ covers everything from how confident we feel, to our ability to express emotions constructively instead of destructively, to our skills in forming successful relationships, to our ability to stand up for ourselves, to setting and achieving goals, to handling the stress we all face.

The EQ Explosion

What is it about emotional intelligence that has made it so popular all over the world? First, people are excited and relieved to receive confirmation of what they've instinctively known all along—that factors beyond just IQ are at least as important as intelligence when it comes to success in life. In fact, one can make the argument that in order for us to take advantage of and flex our cognitive intelligence to the maximum, we first need good emotional intelligence. Why? Because regardless of how brainy we may be, if we turn others off with abrasive behavior, are unaware of how we are presenting ourselves, or cave in under minimal stress, no one will stick around long enough to notice our high IQs. One day—ideally sooner rather than later—we will assess EQ in schools at least as often as we test IQs.

Second, emotional intelligence is important in navigating the challenges of life, whether you're a teenager, young adult, or grandparent.

Remember Joe? His lack of emotional intelligence hurt his academic performance, and it also contributed to some questionable decisions as a teenager. Joe was more likely to take unnecessary risks without weighing the consequences and to act impulsively, often getting himself into serious trouble. And he wasn't very realistic about which colleges he could get into, so he ended up getting into only one college that he really didn't want to attend.

Emotional intelligence is essential for personal happiness and well-being. It affects your relationship skills and your ability to deal successfully with others. Consider Suzy. Her emotional intelligence helped her to build strong friendships. She was skilled at listening to her peers and made an effort to get to know others and let them get to know her. She always worked effectively on teams and as a result was often asked to lead or serve as captain. Suzy's success in the interpersonal area of her life made her very happy. Even when bad things happened, Suzy was able to maintain a positive attitude because of all the support she got from friends.

Although not all students show the more extreme ends of emotional intelligence as Joe and Suzy do, we all fall somewhere within a continuum. Some of us find it easier to navigate our emotions and social behaviors than others do. The good news is that we can all learn to improve ourselves in these areas.

Young people like Suzy are the ones who will most likely emerge as leaders in their professional careers. Why? Because so much of what we do in the professional world involves working effectively with other people. Leaders who are well-liked and know how to motivate others will get higher productivity levels from people they supervise. Professionals who are good problem solvers, have clear goals, and do their fair share of work on projects get noticed by leaders. Colleagues who elevate the work morale by their positive attitude and cheerful disposition get along better with their peers. So, as you mature, learn more, and develop personally, it's just as important to pay attention to your emotional intelligence development as to your knowledge development.

● Redefining Intelligence, Achievement, and Success

Most of us can remember the smartest person in our class—the class brain, the person who got straight A's and seemed destined to follow a path of uninterrupted triumph. Some of those class brains will be highly successful adults. But others won't.

Now think about other classmates and guess which one or two of them will go on to chalk up major life success. Perhaps they will create and lead companies of their own or become prominent and well-respected leaders in their communities. These future stars in the professional world may be honing their teamwork skills through athletics, learning how to lead a diverse group by serving as a club president, or gaining empathy by engaging in lots of community service. They may not, however, be making straight A's because EQ and IQ are two different things.

It is scarcely a revelation that not everyone's talents fit most school systems' rather restrictive model for measuring achievement. History is full of brilliant, successful men and women who underachieved in the classroom, sometimes dropping out of formal education; this list includes Bill Gates, American astronaut and U.S. Senator John Glenn, and Whoopi Goldberg, among many, many others. But despite these well-known individuals and a growing body of research evidence (which you'll read about in Chapters 19–22), many people believe that success in school equals success in life—or, at the very least, in the workplace. Now that assumption is being overturned, and schools like yours are taking on the challenge of teaching emotional intelligence.

What Is Success?

Let's define it as the ability to set and achieve your personal and professional goals, whatever they may be. That sounds simple, but of course it's not. An individual's definition of success will quite naturally ebb and flow over time. We want different things and pursue different goals simply because we grow older, accumulate experience, and shoulder new responsibilities. What is our main concern at any given moment? Maybe it's to get into or graduate from the most prestigious college, to make terrific grades, to be the star of the team, to become a famous pianist, or to have a great romantic relationship. Perhaps we're faced with a serious illness, beside which all else pales in comparison, and success becomes a matter of survival. So much for supposedly simple definitions. But most of us would agree that to succeed on our own terms (or on terms acceptable to us) in a wide variety of situations remains a constant goal.

If you stop to think about your friends and family members—in fact, about many of the students, teachers, and the people you encounter in all sorts of day-to-day settings—which ones do you consider to be the most successful? Which of them seem to enjoy the fullest and happiest lives? Are they necessarily the most intellectually gifted, with the most prestigious job title or the highest income? It's more likely they have other characteristics, other skills, which underlie their capacity to achieve what they desire. And some of those with the highest positions, such as a chief executive officer (CEO) of a company, don't always succeed in that role.

Why CEOs Fail

In the June 21, 1999, *Fortune* cover article, authors Ram Charan and Geoffrey Colvin indicated that unsuccessful CEOs put strategy before people. Successful CEOs shine—not in the arena of planning or finances, but in the area of emotional intelligence. They show integrity, people acumen, assertiveness, effective communication, and trust-building behavior.

In the late 1990s the CEO of a major corporation, a man who had been groomed for this position for a number of years, was fired after being at the helm for a short time. Although he was an excellent accountant and a first-rate strategist, he lacked people skills. His arrogance alienated workers, his method of dismissing a top-ranking executive was an embarrassment to the board, and his strategies—particularly for a company that sees itself as people-friendly—appeared ruthless and greedy.

Paul Wieand, CEO of a leadership development program in Pennsylvania, was profiled in *Fast Company* at a turning point in his career (Kruger, 1999). He had a resignation letter written, but instead of resigning, he took stock of himself, and he came to understand that strong leadership begins with self-awareness: knowing who you are and what your values are. He accentuated the importance of communication, authenticity, and the capacity for nondefensive listening—nothing to do with strategic planning or budgetary knowledge, but everything to do with emotional intelligence. Wieand's emphasis on self-awareness can be traced back to Peter Drucker, a seminal thinker on management who, in his book *Management Challenges for the 21st Century* (Drucker, 1999), stresses that self-awareness and the capacity to build mutually satisfying relationships provide the backbone of strong management.

Those most familiar with the business world agree that a new CEO has about 90 days to make an impression. According to them, an incoming CEO, having first obtained boardroom backing, should hit the road and hold face-to-face meetings; explain his or her vision and seek the advice of employees at every level; state the company's new goals and find out what stands in the way of their implementation; get a three-ring binder and take lots of notes; deliver bad news quickly and in person, thus putting a cap on lingering doubts; ensure needed political support by cultivating contacts with the appropriate level of government; and be available to and open with the media.

As you can see, not one of these activities involves the evaluation of assets and liabilities, the development of strategic planning exercises, the analysis of financial statements, or an all-consuming focus on the bottom line. Rather, each one depends on—indeed, constitutes—emotional intelligence: listening to and understanding people's concerns, fostering meaningful dialogue, building trust, and establishing personal relationships with all the parties involved.

Your Best and Worst Teacher

Here's a real-life example from your current world. Take a moment to think about the worst teacher, coach, or supervisor you have ever experienced—the person who brought dread into your heart at the thought of returning to school, practice, or work the next day. The person that made you—or almost made you—want to quit school, the team, your piano lessons, or your job. Jot down half a dozen of the characteristics that made this person so unbearable.

Now think of the best teacher, coach, or supervisor you ever had—someone you learned from, who understood you and made you want to do better. On the same piece of paper, write down a list of six or seven attributes of that person.

Were the ogre's qualities related to poor knowledge of the subject matter, lack of knowledge of the sport, or bad budgeting skills? We bet not. We bet that most—if not all—of the qualities of the teacher, coach, or supervisor you dreaded did not reflect limitations in his or her IQ, but rather shortcomings in EQ. Here's how you can tell. If you wrote down things like "Yelled at me," "Didn't care about my opinion," "Didn't know my name," "Didn't care if I understood the instructions," or "Was always negative," then you've identified characteristics of a low EQ person.

As for the teacher, coach, or supervisor you might "take a bullet for," chances are your commitment to him or her was also not on basis of IQ, but on EQ. A high EQ teacher, coach, or supervisor would listen to you, show concern about your development, set high goals and communicate them calmly and clearly (and then give you the support needed to achieve them), create a positive environment, and so on.

What Are the Differences Between IQ and EQ?

Simply put, IQ is a measure of an individual's intellectual, analytical, logical, and rational abilities. As such, it's concerned with verbal, spatial, visual, and mathematical skills. It gauges how readily we learn new things; focus on tasks and exercises; retain and recall objective information; engage in a reasoning process; manipulate numbers; think abstractly as well as analytically; and solve problems by the application of prior knowledge. If you have a high IQ—the average is 100—you're well equipped to pass all sorts of examinations with flying colors and (not incidentally) to score well on IQ tests.

All that's good—in fact, it's terrific! Yet everyone knows people who could send an IQ test score sky-high, but who can't quite make good in their personal, educational, or working lives. They rub others the wrong way; success just doesn't seem to pan out. Much of the time, they can't figure out why.

The most probable reason is they're sorely lacking in emotional intelligence.

Some people equate emotional intelligence with street smarts or common sense, but EQ is so much more than street smarts or common sense. It has to do with our capacity to objectively assess our strengths, as well as be open to viewing and challenging our limitations, mistaken assumptions, unacknowledged biases, and shortsighted or self-defeating beliefs. Emotional intelligence also encompasses our ability to react appropriately to facts, to solve problems effectively, and to control impulses that could create problems for us. Those high in EI grasp what others want and need and what their strengths and weaknesses are and then work effectively with those people in teams. High EI people remain unruffled by stress; they create meaningful goals and then accomplish them. They are engaging and positive, the kind of person that others want to be around.

Cognitive intelligence, to be clear, refers to the ability to concentrate and plan, to organize material, to use words effectively, and to understand, assimilate, and interpret facts. In essence, IQ is a measure of an individual's personal information bank—one's memory, vocabulary, mathematical skills, and spatial-relations skills. Some of these skills obviously contribute to doing well in life. That is why EQ's detractors are barking up the wrong tree when they claim that anyone who promotes emotional intelligence is out to replace IQ, or to write off its importance altogether. The fact remains, however, that IQ does not and cannot solely predict success in life or in the workplace. EQ, across several studies (Bar-On, 1997, 2004; Bar-On, Handley, & Fund, 2005; Handley, 1997; Ruderman & Bar-On, 2003), accounted for an average of 30 percent of variation in work performance. When compared with Wagner's (1997) extensive meta-analysis that revealed that cognitive intelligence accounts for approximately 6 percent of occupational performance, the findings presented here suggest that EQ accounts for much more variance than IQ when explaining work performance, especially within a given career. And researchers investigating the relative predictability of IQ and EQ for specific occupations found that EQ accounted for the three most significant predictors, followed by IQ and then three additional EQ skills (Aydin, Dogan, Mahmut, Oktem, & Kemal, 2005).

Millionaire's Opinions about EQ and IQ

In the book *The Millionaire Mind* by best-selling author Thomas Stanley (2001), he reported the findings of a survey of 733 multi-millionaires throughout the United States. When asked to rate the factors (out of 30) most responsible for their success, the top five were:

- Being honest with all people
- Being well disciplined
- Getting along with people
- Having a supportive spouse
- Working harder than most people

All five are reflections of emotional intelligence. You may wonder how having a supportive spouse relates to emotional intelligence. Good marital relations are heavily influenced by emotional intelligence, as will be demonstrated in the final chapters of this book.

Cognitive intelligence, or IQ, was twenty-first on the list and endorsed by only 20 percent of the multimillionaires. In fact, it ranked even lower when the responses of attorneys and physicians were taken out of the analysis. SAT scores, highly related to IQ, were, on average, 1190—higher than the norm, but not high enough for acceptance to a top-rated college. And what about grade point averages? They came in at an average of 2.92 on a 4.0 scale for these multimillionaires.

IQ Is Stable; EQ Can Develop

Another major difference between cognitive and emotional intelligence is that IQ is pretty much set. IQ tends to peak when a person is about 17, remains constant throughout adulthood, and wanes during old age. EQ, however, is not fixed. EQ, like IQ, can be measured with a population average of 100 and a range that most people fall between—from 70 to 130. A study of almost 4,000 people in Canada and the United States concluded that EQ—which can range from below 70 to above 130—rises steadily from an average of 95.3 (when

Figure 1.1 EQ-i over the Age Span

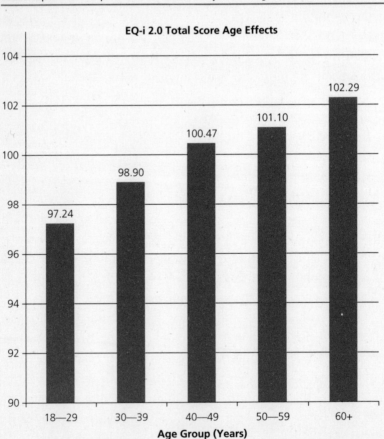

you're in your late teens) to an average of 102.3 when you're in your sixties (Multi-Health Systems, 2011).

Now you know the major differences between IQ and EQ. But one or two misconceptions remain. For example, some people persist in confusing EQ with other psychosocial concepts that have made their way into other tests and surveys of human potential. To understand what makes EQ distinct, let's look at some of the things that EQ is not.

What EQ Is Not

First of all, EQ isn't a measure of academic or other achievement, which concerns specific sorts of performance—as, for that matter, does a report card. It isn't a measure of vocational interest, which centers on a person's natural inclination toward or predilection for a particular field of work: vocational testing might show, for example, that you have an interest in work that involves looking after the emotional needs of others, such as psychology, social work, ministry, or counseling.

Nor is EQ the same as personality—the unique set of traits that help form a person's characteristic, enduring, and dependable ways of thinking, feeling, and behaving. Imagine someone's personality as the way he or she meets and greets the world, or as the capsule answer to the question: What is he or she like? A reply might be "Well, he's shy and thoughtful, a real straight-shooter." Or "She's kind of soft-spoken, but she's got a great sense of humor once you get to know her."

Personality is the concept most often confused with emotional intelligence, but it differs in two important ways. First, like IQ, the traits that our personalities comprise are relatively fixed. If we're by inclination honest, introverted, or loyal, we're unlikely to significantly change these characteristics, especially the older we get. As a result, people can become rather too neatly pigeonholed: witness the so-called Type A personality (hard-driving and prone to anger) versus Type B (relaxed and less ambitious). People tend to feel stuck with the hand they were dealt. EQ, on the other hand, concerns behaviors and skills—things we can always change, especially as we become more aware of which behaviors and skills contribute the most to our success and well-being. With practice, someone can become more assertive (an EQ skill) even though the person remains an introvert or fairly cautious—both personality characteristics. Second, emotional intelligence, unlike personality, is made up of short-term tactical skills that can be brought into play as the situation warrants. Thus the individual building blocks of emotional intelligence—and its overall structure—can be improved by means of training, coaching, and experience.

● Where in the Brain Is Your Emotional Intelligence?

Although there is most likely no single point in the brain that is responsible for emotional intelligence, we are getting a better understanding of which parts of the brain may play a role. Neuroscientist Damasio (1994) proposed a theory in which a neural array in the brain called the "somatic marker" is the location for a lot of what we call emotional intelligence.

Damasio proposed that a number of sections of the brain—the ventromedial prefrontal, parietal, and cingulate areas—all contribute to emotional intelligence, as well as the right amygdala and insula. The work, based on studying people with lesions in these areas, demonstrated that they had emotional and social deficits. For example, they had problems reading social and emotional cues in other people (Damasio, 1994).

In some fascinating research carried out at the Walter Reed Army Institute of Research and McLean Hospital at Harvard Medical School, brain imaging was used in normal subjects to get a better picture of emotional functioning. The researchers, William Killgore and Deborah Yurgelun-Todd (2007), administered the EQ-i Youth Version (EQ-i YV) to 16 adolescents. They chose adolescents because that age is a prime time for the development of emotional and social competencies. Each of these teenagers was subjected to functional magnetic resonance imaging (fMRI), in which their brain waves were carefully monitored while they were exposed to a series of fearful faces.

The researchers were able to find significant relationships between the EQ scores and brain activity. Specifically, the EQ scores were related to activity in the cerebellum and visual association cortex. The level of emotional intelligence on the EQ-i YV was inversely related to the efficiency of neural processing within the somatic marker circuitry during the emotional stimulation (Killgore & Yurgelun-Todd, 2007). Here's a quote from their study that summarizes these findings:

> During the perception of fearful faces, higher levels of EQ in adolescent children were associated with greater activity in the cerebellum and visual association cortex, as well as with decreased activity in a variety of emotion-related limbic and paralimbic regions, including the insula, cingulate, ventromedial prefrontal cortex, amygdala, hippocampus, and parahippocampal gyrus. These findings suggest that EQ in adolescent children may involve greater neural efficiency of these key emotional-processing structures and, therefore, may lead to reduced reactivity in response to emotional provocation within the somatic marker circuitry believed to mediate the integration of somatic states and cognition during decision making. (Killgore and Yurgelun-Todd, 2007, p. 149)

Interestingly, these areas of the brain are quite distinct from the areas where most of the functions of cognitive intelligence are triggered.

Another study looking at emotional intelligence and the brain focused on people undergoing temporal lobe resections, which is a surgical procedure used on people suffering from certain types of epilepsy who are not benefitting from medication. The research was carried out at Dalhousie University in Canada by Gawryluk and McGlone (2007). They administered a battery of tests to 38 patients who underwent this type of surgery in the temporal lobe area of the brain.

The EQ-i scores of patients were affected after the surgery. The EQ-i scores were also related to the patient's psychosocial adjustment, in that higher EI scores reflected better postsurgical coping in these areas. The EQ-i scores were not differentially affected by which side of the brain where the operation occurred (Gawryluk & McGlone, 2007).

● What Are the Building Blocks of EQ?

Reuven Bar-On (1988, 1997) arrived at a way to capture emotional and social intelligence by dividing it into five general areas or realms and 16 scales. Continued research with the team at Multi-Health Systems created the current EQ-i version 2.0, shown in Figure 1.2 (Multi-Health Systems, 2011).

Figure 1.2 Emotional Intelligence Model

Source: Reproduced with permission of Multi-Health Systems. All rights reserved. www.mhs.com

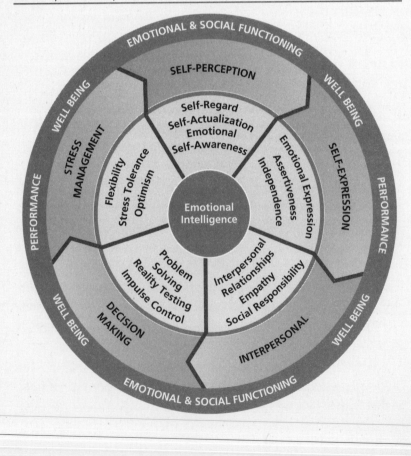

Model of Emotional Intelligence (EI)

The **Self-Perception** Realm concerns your ability to know and manage yourself. It includes *emotional self-awareness*—the ability to recognize how you're feeling and why you're feeling that way and the impact your emotions have on thoughts and actions of yourself and others; *self-regard*—the ability to recognize your strengths and weaknesses and to feel good about yourself despite your weaknesses; and *self-actualization*—the ability to persistently try to improve yourself and pursue meaningful goals that lead to a richer life.

The **Self-Expression** Realm deals with the way you face the world. *Emotional expression* involves the ability to express your feelings both in words and nonverbally; *independence* involves the ability to be self-directed and self-controlled, to stand on your own two feet; and *assertiveness* involves the ability to clearly express your thoughts and beliefs, stand your ground, and defend a position in a constructive way.

The **Interpersonal** Realm concerns your "people skills"—your ability to interact and get along with others. It is composed of three scales. *Interpersonal relationships* refers to the ability to forge and maintain relationships that are mutually beneficial and marked by give-and-take and a sense of trust and compassion. *Empathy* is the ability to recognize, understand, and appreciate what others may be feeling and thinking. It is the ability to view the world through another person's eyes. *Social responsibility* is the ability to be a cooperative and contributing member of your social group and society at large.

The **Decision-Making** Realm involves your ability to use your emotions in the best way to help you solve problems and make optimal choices. Its three scales are *reality testing*—the ability to see things as they actually are, rather than the way you wish or fear they might be; *problem-solving*—the ability to find solutions to problems where emotions are involved, using the right emotion at an optimum value; and *impulse control*—the ability to either resist the temptation to act rashly or to delay that action.

The **Stress Management** Realm concerns your ability to be flexible, tolerate stress, and control impulses. Its three scales are *flexibility*—the ability to adjust your feelings, thoughts, and actions to changing, challenging, or unfamiliar conditions; *stress tolerance*—the ability to remain calm and focused, to constructively withstand adverse events and conflicting emotions without caving in; and *optimism*—the ability to maintain a realistically positive attitude, particularly in the face of adversity.

There is one additional indicator of your EI. *Happiness* is the ability to feel satisfied with life, to enjoy yourself and others, and to experience zest and enthusiasm in a range of activities. Happiness is related to four other areas of EI: self-regard, self-actualization, interpersonal relationships, and optimism.

Throughout this book, we'll be demonstrating how much emotional intelligence impacts your success as a student, in relationships, and in life. For starters, take a look at Table 1.1, which describes some of the key ways your EQ can influence your academic performance.

Measuring Emotional Intelligence in Students

There are many measures of emotional intelligence, but only a handful of them have been assessed for reliability and validity as has the Emotional Quotient Inventory (EQ-i) 2.0 (MHS, 2011). The research you will read in this book and the EI skills you will learn are based on the EQ-i 2.0. Steven, the CEO of MHS (the company that publishes the EQ-i 2.0), has been involved in the development and research of the EQ-i versions since its publication. Howard and Korrel are active practitioners and trainers with the EQ-i 2.0, and Korrel has assessed and taught emotional intelligence to college students for 15 years.

The EQ-i 2.0.

The EQ-i 2.0 is composed of 133 items and is self-reporting. You fill it out, responding to how each item applies to you, with one of five possible answers ranging from "never/rarely" to "always/almost always." Each of the 16 scales is individually scored, as is each of the five realms.

Table 1.1 The EQ-i 2.0 Scales, What They Assess, and How They Relate to Students

EQ-i 2.0 Scales	Definition	Application to Students
Self-Perception		
Emotional Self-Awareness	Ability to be aware of and understand one's feelings and their impact	Emotional self-awareness is the foundation of EI; self-awareness allows a student to identify an emotion and how it is influencing behavior and interactions. A student without self-awareness is captive to his or her emotions, reacting without an accurate understanding of why.
Self-Regard	Ability to respect and accept one's strengths and weaknesses; self-acceptance; resultant level of confidence	A lack of confidence could hinder performance; very low scores could indicate a mental health problem or a history of harsh criticism. Accepting one's limits allows one to seek improvement; acknowledgment of strengths builds confidence.
Self-Actualization	Ability to improve oneself and pursue meaningful objectives; goal oriented	There is a strong body of literature demonstrating that students perform better once they have definitive goals for their education or for pursuing the major they've chosen.
Self-Expression		
Emotional Expression	Ability to express one's feelings verbally and nonverbally	Those who can verbally express emotions in a constructive way will have more meaningful relationships and will resolve conflict more effectively; congruence between your verbal and nonverbal emotions results in better communication and less conflict.
Independence	Ability to be self-directed and free of emotional dependency on others	Students who lack independence may have trouble separating effectively from parents or handling independent living; conversely, independence that is too high may cause a student to not seek help from others (tutors, counselors, faculty) when needed.
Assertiveness	Ability to express feelings, beliefs, and thoughts in a nondestructive way	A base level of assertiveness is necessary to approach a professor for help, confront a roommate problem, say no to someone who is trying to take advantage of you, or just speak up in class.

(Continued)

Table 1.1 The EQ-i 2.0 Scales, What They Assess, and How They Relate to Students (Cont'd)

EQ-i 2.0 Scales	Definition	Application to Students
Interpersonal		
Interpersonal Relationships	Ability to develop and maintain mutually satisfying relationships	Maintaining existing friendships, making new friends, and becoming integrated into social groups helps students have meaningful relationships and avoid isolation; for college students, it is part of making a successful transition to living on campus; however, too much focus on relationships can hinder academic performance.
Empathy	Ability to recognize, understand, and appreciate the feelings of others	Students who do not try to understand others' perspectives will experience more conflict and less satisfying relationships; they are also likely to be less tolerant of differences.
Social Responsibility	Ability to contribute to society, one's social group, and the welfare of others	Students are members of numerous groups, from athletic teams to teams on a class project; students with social responsibility will do their share to make the team successful, cooperating and collaborating for the best outcomes. Those without this skill may be more likely to violate norms that could lead to rejection or perform ineffectively on teams and thus experience more conflict.
Decision Making		
Reality Testing	Ability to remain objective by seeing things as they really are	Students with good reality-testing skills can accurately judge academic situations (How long will it take to write this paper? How well am I doing in this class?), social issues (Is this environment safe? Can I trust this person?), or financial situations (Can I afford this?).
Problem Solving	Ability to solve problems where emotions are involved; using a systematic process	Students face many problems from friendship issues to financial concerns; students who realize a problem exists and can accurately identify the real problem can more effectively solve it. Part of problem solving is making sure emotions don't drive us to false conclusions, quick answers, or "analysis paralysis."

Impulse Control	Ability to resist or delay an impulse, drive, or temptation to act	The ability to resist temptations to overindulge in food, drink, spending, and partying and the ability to control rash decisions—such as dropping a required class or sending a harsh email or text—protect a student from making bad choices that often lead to greater stress.
Stress Management		
Flexibility	Ability to adapt one's feeling, thinking, and behavior to change	The transition to college involves many adjustments (shared living space, shared baths, managing money, and so on). Those who do not adapt well to change will not fare as well. Also, students with too much flexibility may have difficulty making big decisions.
Stress Tolerance	Ability to effectively cope with stressful or difficult situations	Students face both positive (graduation) and negative (huge project due) stressors. Managing stress well results in better cognitive functioning (less disorganization) and less inner turmoil that can distract from goals.
Optimism	Ability to remain hopeful and resilient despite setbacks	Optimism is predictive of many beneficial outcomes throughout life, such as better health; students will inevitably face some adversity (bad grades, difficult roommate situation), and the ability to stay positive while also persisting to overcome the obstacle is a key to success.
Additional Scale		
Happiness	Ability to feel satisfied with oneself, others, and life in general	Emotions are contagious—an unhappy student can negatively affect the mood of those around him/her; also, very low scores on this dimension could signal depression and the need for counseling.

Finally, a total score is obtained. Rather like an IQ test, this ranges up or down from 100—as do scores in each of the realms and scales.

The EQ-i 2.0 has been designed to contain a great many nuances and shadings. It is not a test that spits out a measure of one's emotional intelligence. Rather, it must be administered and interpreted by a trained professional skilled in understanding these nuances and the interrelationships among the scores of the 16 scales that constitute emotional intelligence. In addition, they must be able to give feedback to the person being tested to confirm or question the accuracy of the test results.

Higher Education and Youth Versions

There are special interpretations of the EQ-i 2.0 for students (aged 18 and up; high school, college, university students) and a different version for youth aged from 7 to 18. The youth version covers five general areas of emotional intelligence but doesn't get into the specific scales.

If you're interested in the EQ-i 2.0, you can have it administered by a qualified professional in your area, such as at your college counseling center. For the moment, the aim of this book is to enable you to enhance your emotional intelligence on your own, whether or not you choose to take the EQ-i 2.0 itself. For additional information about the EQ-i 2.0 assessment, visit www.mhs.com and select "emotional intelligence."

Gender and Race as Measured by the EQ-i: Are There Differences?

Earlier in this chapter, we pointed out that EQ does increase with age and eventually levels off before beginning to decline slightly in our seventies. But what about cultural, racial, or gender differences in EQ—do those exist?

First, it's heartening to learn that emotional intelligence cuts across the gender gap. Over and over again, we have found that males and females have remarkably similar overall scores on the EQ-i 2.0, the world's most widely used test of emotional intelligence (Bar-On, 1997; MHS, 2011). This holds true in a number of diverse countries and cultures worldwide. However, in the interpersonal relationships realm females do score higher than males. There are some small, but statistically significant differences in the scales as well, with males scoring higher in independence, problem solving, and stress tolerance. Females, on the other hand, score higher in emotional self-awareness, emotional expression, and empathy. In sum, males and females have small differences in emotional intelligence, but nothing that gives either gender a distinct advantage.

It's equally heartening to discover that emotional intelligence transcends race. Particularly in the United States, heated controversy has long surrounded the discrepancies (which arise for a number of complex and arguable reasons) that have been found between the average IQ scores for groups of Caucasians, African-Americans, and Asian-Americans.

This is one reason MHS attempted to compile the world's first data analysis of racial differences (if any existed at all) when it came to the components of emotional intelligence. Our first study was based on approximately 1,000 people located throughout North America who had completed the EQ-i. We compared the results obtained by members of the three races just mentioned, as well as those obtained by Hispanic-Americans (Bar-On, 1997). As you can see in Figure 1.3, the average overall scores varied by less than 5 percent—a difference so small it might have arisen by chance. Nor were there any significant differences among average scores for each of the EQ-i's five realms. In short, there seem to be no emotional advantages or disadvantages whatsoever based on race. Thus members of any ethnic group can confidently take and benefit from the EQ-i, and emotional intelligence itself remains a measure that can be applied in good conscience throughout a range of multicultural settings.

These results were replicated in our 2010 study with the new EQ-i 2.0. This time we included a sample almost four times larger (3,888 people) in the testing from throughout North America. The results, shown in Figure 1.4, parallel what we found 17 years earlier, but the gaps were a bit wider this time, with African Americans averaging 106 and Asian Americans averaging 95 (MHS, 2011).

Figure 1.3 Racial Groups and Emotional Intelligence

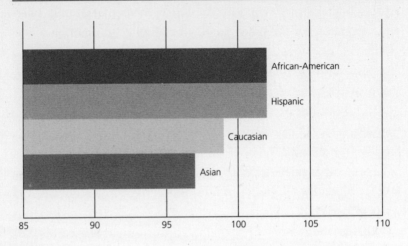

Figure 1.4 Racial Groups and Emotional Intelligence, 10 Years Later

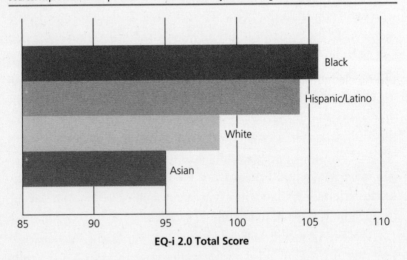

EQ-i 2.0 Total Score

Increasing Your Emotional Intelligence

Last, and perhaps the most important point in this first chapter, people are buoyed by the knowledge that EQ is not permanently fixed. You can learn to be more emotionally intelligent. Increasing EQ in youths may help reduce the risk of harmful behaviors related to drug and alcohol misuse, aggression, and other self-defeating behaviors. Developing emotional intelligence at an early age gives individuals an edge well into adulthood (Mischel et al., 2011).

Now you know that age, sex, and ethnic background do not deter you from enhancing your EQ. The stronger your emotional intelligence, the more likely you are to be successful as a student, working professional, parent, leader, partner to your significant other, or candidate for a workplace position. It's never too early or late to make a change for the better.

No matter what comes of the world you call your own, it's in your own best interest to open your mind to new possibilities and new ways to change. Those changes will not come easily; there's no such thing as a quick fix. Old habits, old modes of behavior are like old clothes—comfortable, broken-in, reassuring, and predictable. Building unfamiliar skills requires awareness, dedication, and practice on your part. As well, any change involves an element of risk— there's no guarantee of success. Nor, even when you achieve a higher level of emotional intelligence, will you deal with each and every situation in the best possible way. But you will possess a new level of knowledge that will enable you to chart new ways to behave in response to the conditions you encounter. Based on our knowledge and experience, we believe that by reading and putting into practice the materials in this book, you can and will gain new insights into yourself and others that will enable you to change for the better and achieve greater success in your life.

Class Closed and the ABCDE Model

Before we begin to examine and work with the 16 scales of emotional intelligence, as defined by the EQ-i 2.0, let's look at a couple of examples that show EQ in action. You may even recognize some things you have done—or a friend has done.

Class Closed

Let's consider the case of two students, Brett and John, who faced the same dilemma. Both students were on track to graduate at the end of that semester, and both needed to earn credit for an interdisciplinary seminar that semester. Only a few of those courses were offered, and the classes filled quickly. So both Brett and John found themselves in the same situation when they went to register—all of the interdisciplinary classes offered conflicted with their chemistry classes except for one class, which was already full.

Neither Brett nor John wanted to delay their graduation, so they contacted their advisor, who suggested they go talk to Professor Smart, explain their situation, and ask whether he would allow them to register for the class he was teaching. Here's where the story gets interesting.

Brett arrived first to talk with Professor Smart. John arrived just minutes later. While standing in the hallway waiting to talk with the professor, he overheard Brett's conversation.

Brett began by telling the professor that he was supposed to graduate that spring and had to be let into the professor's interdisciplinary course titled The Media: Economic, Political, and Social Effects on American Society. The professor indicated that he had already allowed some additional students into the class and there was no room to add others.

Brett countered with "I'm a senior and it's a requirement, so you've got to let me in. Please, sir, I just need this class to graduate on time."

Professor Smart suggested that Brett attend the next class period; if anyone dropped out of the class, he would let Brett into the class.

"But what happens if no one drops?" Brett asked. "I can't risk not graduating because you won't guarantee me a spot in the class. My parents have paid a lot for my education and even donated money to the school, so it seems to me the school should guarantee me a spot in every class that I need to graduate."

Professor Smart repeated his offer to Brett. Brett flushed and said, "I can't believe this! You've let other students into the class, and I need the class just as much as they do. I'm going to contact the department chair and tell her you're being unfair."

With that, Brett stomped out of Professor Smart's office.

Seeing John in the hallway, Brett warned him, "If you're trying to get him to let you into the class, don't waste your time. He won't do it."

John knew that he wouldn't get in the class if he *didn't* ask. So he knocked softly on Professor Smart's office door and was invited in. John offered his hand to the professor and said, "Hi, I'm John. Do you have about five minutes? I need to talk with you about adding your media class."

Professor Smart motioned for John to sit down. John continued, "I know you get a lot of requests from students to overenroll your course. Everybody who takes the class really likes it. I should be honest, though. Part of the reason I want to take it is that I am trying to graduate this semester. I'm a chemistry major, and my required chemistry courses and labs conflict with all of the other interdisciplinary courses offered this semester. It's my fault for not meeting this requirement earlier, but I honestly didn't think it would be so hard to fit the interdisciplinary course into my schedule."

Professor Smart nodded and asked, "What do you plan to do after graduation?"

John explained that he was interviewing with a pharmaceutical company and that the job would start in June if he was offered it. He told Professor Smart about how much he loved doing chemistry experiments and that the job involved a lot of lab work.

Professor Smart paused and then said, "Well, you probably heard the offer I gave to the other young man about coming to class for a few days and waiting to see if anyone drops the class."

John replied, "Thanks! I'll come to the next class."

On the way back to his residence hall, John went by the bookstore and bought the book for the media class. Back at his room, John began reading the first chapter. Brett walked in and saw John with the media book.

"Did that guy let you in after he told me no?" Brett asked in an angry voice.

"No, he offered me the same thing he offered you. I can come to class for a few days and wait to see if anyone drops."

Brett laughed, "Do you realize how popular that course is? No one is going to drop it. My parents are going to call the president of the university to see what can be worked out for me to graduate this semester. You better hope your parents will do the same thing."

The first day John went to media class, the room was packed, and the last person to come in ended up sitting on the floor. A few minutes into class, Professor Smart asked for a volunteer to view a media clip and give a reaction to it. Everyone was quiet, so John raised his hand and said, "I'll do it."

After watching the clip, Professor Smart asked John's opinion. After John gave his opinion, Professor Smart asked, "How did the information in the first chapter of the textbook influence your opinion?"

John explained how information about stereotyping in the media he had read in the first chapter had influenced his response to the clip. Professor Smart nodded and asked for other comments.

A class discussion ensued about how much stereotyping occurs in the media.

After the next class, Professor Smart asked John to stay for a few minutes.

"Well, John, it looks like someone has dropped my course. I value your contributions to class, so you can stay in the course if you want to."

John stayed in his class and graduated on time. His friend Brett ended up going to summer school to take the required interdisciplinary class.

Why do we tell this story? Simply put, these two students' experiences cover almost every component of emotional intelligence, from emotional self-awareness and empathy to impulse control and optimism. Note that their respective success and failure had virtually nothing to do with IQ or grades or family connections. John's dilemma had a happy ending in large part because he made good use of his EI skills, whereas Brett failed because he had no EI skills to speak of. Bear this scenario in mind—we will return to it from time to time as we work our way through the following chapters.

● The ABCDEs

Next, let's take a look at one of the fundamental frameworks that underpin many of the vignettes and exercises we'll encounter throughout this book. It's known as ABCDE (or the A-E model)—a system for altering your perceptions, attitudes, and behavior that was pioneered by the late Dr. Albert Ellis, internationally recognized as the father of the theory and practice of Rational Emotive Behavior

Therapy (REBT) (Ellis, 1955). Ellis's great contribution to 20th-century psychology was his insistence that you can modify and change your feelings by means of logical and deductive reasoning, rather than allowing your feelings to get the better of you. He developed the A-E model to help individuals challenge irrational beliefs (Ellis, 2004).

To illustrate how it works, let's look at another scenario, this one involving young love.

Brian and Brittany had been dating since her family moved into the neighborhood a year or so earlier. But after about nine months, Brittany had left to attend college in another state. They'd stayed in touch by phone, text, and e-mail, but had enjoyed only one brief visit, when she'd flown back for her sister's birthday. So Brian was eagerly awaiting her return for Christmas. Imagine his surprise when he looked out the window on December 20 and saw her car parked in the driveway of her house. "Gee, she's home already," he thought. "Why didn't she text or call?"

Later that evening, at the dinner table, Brian's father couldn't help but notice his son's unaccustomed silence.

"You seem a bit preoccupied," his dad said. "It's like you're not even here."

"I don't feel like eating," Brian sighed. "Brittany's been home for hours and she hasn't called. She's probably found some other guy—someone at the college." With those words, he stood up and slouched off.

How can we understand Brian's sudden downward spiral? At first glance the answer seems obvious: Brian was upset simply because Brittany didn't call or text him after she got home. Using the A-E model, Brittany's failure to call is labeled the *activating event* (A) and Brian's reaction the *consequence* (C). In this scenario the consequence was twofold: Brian felt demoralized, sad, and pessimistic, and he withdrew by rising from the table and seeking refuge in his room. A—Brittany's not calling—appeared to lead directly to C.

However, this reading of what transpired leaves out a crucial, often overlooked, intermediate step: *beliefs* (B)—in this case, Brian's beliefs, triggered by the sight of Brittany's parked car (A). The morose and *unsubstantiated beliefs*, or negative self-talk, that filled Brian's mind were what actually caused his depression and withdrawal (C).

The critical lesson is that if A leads to B and B to C, Brian can change the consequences by identifying and defusing his self-defeating beliefs and replacing them with different, more adaptive and realistic beliefs.

And what works for Brian can work for you.

Before we explain the A-E model, which will help you identify and defuse your beliefs, we need to define what we mean by beliefs. *Beliefs* (B) are shorthand for the silent self-talk we engage in throughout the day. Our internal dialogue is ongoing and continuous, but we are usually unaware of it. It is the "boy, it's cold outside, I'm going to be miserable today" we mutter inside our heads when we step out into a bitter winter day. Or the "my boss is going to be so mad if I show up late again" that runs through our mind as we approach a red traffic light. Or the more damaging "I can't do that" when faced with a tough math problem.

Some of your undermining self-talk may be caused by "dated tapes": the automatic replay of frequent and harsh statements made to you when you were a child. Often these take the form of "Can't you do anything right?" or "You'll never get ahead" or "People won't like you if you do that." Identifying these dated tapes can help defuse their power.

Central to the completion of the ABCDE chart is the ability to tune in to this inner dialogue, this belief system that causes emotional and behavioral *consequences* (C). When you sense an irrational belief, your next task is to actively debate, dispute, and discard (D) these maladaptive, self-defeating beliefs that give rise to your emotional and behavioral consequences (Cs). Submit every element of your internal monologue to rigorous examination by asking yourself the following key questions and writing down your answers.

○ *Where's the proof?* List the objective, verifiable evidence that supports each belief, or the lack thereof. Brian had no objective proof that Brittany had lost interest in him. Had they been fighting recently? No. Had she been calling him less frequently? No. When she did call, had she seemed less loving? No.

○ *Are there alternative, more logical explanations to explain the activating event?* Brian wrote down alternative explanations for why Brittany might not have called him: she was tired after the long drive and fell asleep, or she was busy talking to her folks. And there could be explanations Brian didn't think of, such as her sister waiting at her house to see her.

○ *If someone asked me for advice about this scenario, what might I say that could help alter the person's perspective?* For Brian, it was helpful to imagine how he might respond if his good friend Jake came to him after seeing his girlfriend Kathy's car in her driveway and voiced concern that she no longer loved him and had probably found another boyfriend. Brian found himself thinking: "Hold on, Jake; you and Kathy have been dating for a long time. You have a good relationship, and she's very up front about any concerns she has. I think you are overreacting. There's no evidence at all that she no longer wants to be with you. And, Jake, I think you're making things worse for yourself just sitting around worrying. Why don't you text her? Maybe you'll find out she's not home, or she's asleep, or she was just about to call you. Do something! Don't just sit there."

○ *Have I ever been in a similar situation before and held a similar belief, only to find out that it was wrong?* Brian remembered that he often "catastrophizes" in relationships with a girlfriend. When Carmine—the girl he had dated two years ago—was 15 or 20 minutes late meeting him, he always overreacted. And it never turned out that she had lost interest in him. It was just another example of her lack of attention to detail. In fact, ultimately it was he who broke up with her.

○ *If so, did I learn anything from that outcome, and can I apply that knowledge to this situation?* Brian realized, "I tend to think the worst when it comes to girlfriends. I imagine the worst possible outcome—they've lost interest and are seeing someone else. That belief turns out to be a reflection of my own lack of confidence."

As you can imagine, successfully disputing the irrational belief leads to new, more rational beliefs, which in turn produce new *effects* (E). Brian is no longer worried; he becomes excited about seeing Brittany later, eats dinner with his father, and sends Brittany a text telling her he's glad she's home.

The ABCDE chart in Table 2.1 shows how Brian applied this method to his situation.

The power of the ABCDE approach is that defusing illogical, maladaptive beliefs allows more rational and adaptive beliefs to emerge, shifting your emotions and behaviors to be more adaptive and effective.

Table 2.1 Learning the ABCDEs

A Action or event	B Beliefs (which may be irrational)	C Consequences: Emotional, behavioral	D Dispute: Facts, other reasons, and past events that contradict the irrational belief. Ask yourself what could explain the action in column A: Where's the proof? Are there more logical explanations? and so on	E Effects: Different emotions, different behaviors
Seeing Brittany's car in the driveway and knowing she was home and hadn't called	She should have called! She's probably lost interest in me. I bet she's dating a guy at school. I'll never find anyone like her again.	Emotions: Feeling sad, worried, and pessimistic Behaviors: Withdrawing, not contacting Brittany	We haven't had a fight lately; she's been calling me a lot; she texted me that she was tired and might want to take a nap before getting together; maybe she's talking with her parents.	Emotions: Calm, excited about seeing her later, hopeful about the relationship Behaviors: Eat dinner, send her a text

● Changing Hot Feelings to Cool Feelings

Another method of addressing your self-defeating belief system is by identifying and moving away from "hot" feelings to "cool" feelings. Hot feelings have a spiraling effect on mood and thoughts, whereas cool feelings tend to have a less intense effect. Although cool feelings may still be unpleasant to some degree, they are less incapacitating.

Cool feelings are responses to adverse situations, such as a bad grade or trouble in a relationship, that are less harmful and far healthier than hot feelings, and far easier to deal with. So try to change your hot, maladaptive feelings to their cool, adaptive counterparts.

Hot feelings	Cool feelings
Rage, fury, and anger	Annoyance and irritation
Despondency, despair, depression, and pessimism	Sadness
Severe guilt, intense remorse	Regret
Self-worthlessness, self-hate	Self-disappointment
Severely hurt feelings	Mildly bruised feelings
Anxiety, fear, and panic	Concern

Only by replacing unhealthy emotions with less volatile substitutes can we better manage our feelings and address our real problems in the outside world. Brian successfully changed his anxiety to concern and then was able to think more rationally about Brittany.

● The Major Musts and the Absolute Shoulds

Many factors conspire to produce unwarranted "hot feelings," but the prime offenders are Major Musts and Absolute Shoulds. Each can be broken down into what we demand of ourselves and others, and what we expect of the world at large.

Here are some examples of Major Musts in action:

- I must always make an A (in order for me to feel okay).
- You (he/she/they) must like me and include me in your group (in order for me to feel okay).
- My school or home or the world must make sure nothing bad happens to me (in order for me to feel okay).

And here are a few examples of the Absolute Shoulds:

- I absolutely should not gain any weight (in order for me to feel okay).
- You (he/she/they) absolutely should make me a starter on the team (in order for me to feel okay).
- My school (or home or living conditions) absolutely should make sure I am successful (in order for me to feel okay).

These demands make no sense. There's no law stating that any of us must behave in certain ways or attain certain goals. Nor must others behave in accordance with our wishes. As for the world at large or maybe just your school, things don't always go the way you want them to go. (And sometimes it's what you did or didn't do that makes things happen or not happen!) These sweeping and unrealistic expectations, when they aren't fulfilled, lead straight to a full plate of red-hot feelings.

In our scenario, the idea that Brittany must or should call Brian the second she comes home is irrational. There may be all sorts of valid reasons why she *doesn't* call, but at any rate, why *must* she call? Brian would certainly prefer that she do so, but Brittany might well prefer that he call her to see whether she's arrived.

If Brian were able to replace his musts and shoulds with far more appropriate *prefers*, which give everybody room for negotiation and compromise, he'd be well on the way to cooler, more sensible feelings.

🔵 Thinking Errors

As you might imagine, all these musts and shoulds lead inescapably to even more irrational and erroneous conclusions. These conclusions are what we call "hot links" to hot emotions because they inevitably make matters worse. Fortunately, they too can be cooled off by means of very simple techniques. The five main conclusions—or "thinking errors"—and their preferred substitutes are as follows:

○ *"This is awful."* Instead of wallowing in despair and telling yourself, "This is 100-percent, irredeemably awful," try using moderating or mitigating terms that will serve to tone down the sense of catastrophe. Whatever's bugging you may be inconvenient, a real hassle, a pain in the neck, or anything else you choose to call it. However, it probably isn't the end of the world.

○ *"I can't stand it."* Instead of falling into this trap, remind yourself that you have in fact stood—and will continue to stand—all manner of difficult situations. They're a part of life, and life has a habit of going on.

○ *"I can't do anything right, and others are against me."* Heaping criticism on yourself, or always blaming others and wishing ill fortune on them, can only lead to anger and fury. That directs your anger two ways—ways that are equally wounding. First, blaming yourself for everything that goes wrong or viewing what has happened as well-merited punishment for your sins and shortcomings—real or imagined—is not going to make your situation any better. Second, blaming others may make you feel better temporarily, but it does little good to get you out of any hole you have dug for yourself. Remind yourself that blame and condemnation—directed at yourself or others—are not constructive; look for ways to resolve the problem instead.

○ *"I'm worthless."* If this were true, there'd be no point in you or anybody else doing anything to aid a lost cause. We all carry enough of a load at the best of times, without saying things like "I'm no good—a complete and utter screw-up. That's why I always fail. I don't deserve good things." Thoughts and expressions of self-worthlessness lead straight to depression and despair. Remind yourself that, even if you have made a mistake or an error in judgment, you have more good qualities than bad, you often do things right, you can learn from your mistakes, and you are still a good person who deserves good things.

○ *"Always" and "Never."* Statements along the lines of "Everyone always dumps on me; they never give me a hand" or "Things will never get better, never change" are plainly self-defeating and invite feelings of hopelessness and helplessness. So avoid "always" and "never" and put your feelings into perspective: there is always hope for change, and although some people may sometimes dump on you, many people do, in fact, give you a hand.

● Tune In to What Your Body Is Telling You

A skeptic might say: Why not wallow in the worst and get it over with, perhaps achieving some sort of catharsis? Not so long ago, this was the popular wisdom in certain circles. Letting it all hang out was considered preferable to suppressing strong emotions; venting one's anger or despair was deemed healthier than bottling it up.

There's a degree of truth in that point of view, but psychological truths often come with more subtle shadings than popular catch-phrases would have us believe. More recent research indicates that, paradoxically, "venting" magnifies angry feelings rather than relieving them (Lerner, Gonzalez, Dahl, Hariri, & Taylor, 2005; Palarmis, Allred, & Block, 2010).

The time to detect and weed out your irrational beliefs is when your emotions are running hot—when you're upset, anxious, irate, defensive, depressed, or stressed out. Because feelings and bodily responses are so closely linked, when you are uncertain as to *what* you are feeling (other than the fact that it is unpleasant), you can begin to obtain a more accurate fix on that feeling by becoming aware of how your body is behaving. Here are several examples:

Feelings	Physical signs
Anger	Hands-on-hips posture, pounding heart, sweating, and rapid breathing
Rage	Clenched fists *
Fury	Cold-focused stare, loud and rapid speech
Depression	Fatigue
Despair	Weighed-down posture
Despondency	Slouching; staring into space; a slow, hesitant voice; frequent sighing
Anxiety	Restlessness, pounding heart, rapid breathing
Fear	Tense muscles, rapid heartbeat, and sweating
Panic	Aching muscles and headaches, tension in neck and shoulders, rapid heartbeat, and sweating

Focusing on our bodies' manifestations of these and many other feelings allows us to classify those feelings as belonging to one of the four basic emotional families: Anxiety, Anger, Sadness, or Contentment. Contentment presents no problem. As for the rest, identifying and labeling them afford us a degree of control. We can begin to talk ourselves out of them, detecting and disputing the irrational beliefs that set them in motion and achieving new, more desirable effects.

● A Happy Ending

Filling in the chart helped Brian master the art of ABCDE instead of succumbing to gloom, as demonstrated by his new, improved self-talk: "Look at what I've been saying to myself. This is no way to behave. Who says that Brittany has to do anything, let alone call me the minute she gets back? Okay, she didn't call or text. There are all sorts of logical explanations. What isn't logical is my dreaming up some guy she's thrown me over for. That's nonsense—there's no evidence of that at all." With that, Brian picks up the phone to call her.

As you can see, Brian's ability to identify and overcome his irrational beliefs enabled him to move from hot to cool emotions, discover alternative and more plausible reasons for Brittany's actions, admit to and confront his feelings of rejection, conquer them, and behave in a logical and positive manner. And even if, despite his efforts, the events should prove to be a worst-case scenario—that is, if Brittany actually wants to dump him and is waiting to tell him so—he'll still be better prepared to deal with that reality in a truthful and honest way.

By the way, when Brian texted Brittany, he found out that, tired from the long drive home, she had taken a nap and just woken up. Now, well rested, she was eager to see him.

The Self-Perception Realm

This realm of emotional intelligence concerns what we generally refer to as the "inner self." It determines how in touch with your feelings you are and how good you feel about yourself and about what you're doing in life. Success in this area means that you are aware of your feelings, feel confident, and have direction and meaning in pursuing your life goals.

Figure Part 2 Self-Perception and Emotional Intelligence

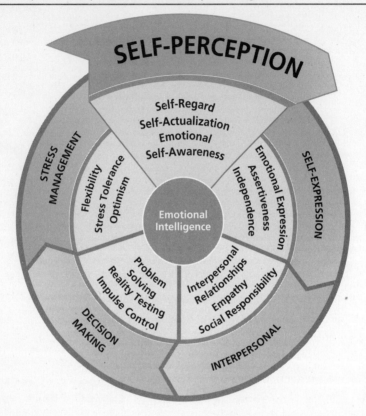

CHAPTER 3

Emotional Self-Awareness

He who knows the universe and does not know himself knows nothing.
—Jean de La Fontaine, 1679

Definition: "Emotional self-awareness includes recognizing and understanding one's own emotions. It involves the ability to differentiate between subtleties in these emotions, while being aware of their causes and the impact they have on thoughts and actions of oneself and others. At the core of emotional self-awareness is the ability to know what one is feeling and why, while being able to recognize and understand the source of those feelings" (Multi-Health Systems, 2011, p. 4).

Don't Bother Me

Sarah came home one evening after getting a D on a major test in her biology class. When she walked in, her mother asked her whether she had remembered to go get the oil changed in her car. Sarah blasted her mother, "Quit nagging me. I said I'd get that done, and I will."

Her mom replied, "But you promised you'd do it today, and it's already overdue."

"I don't care," Sarah yelled over her shoulder as she went up to her room. She stayed in her room fuming for the rest of the evening.

She came downstairs around 10 and fixed herself a sandwich. When her mother asked her why she was so upset, Sarah replied, "I just don't like you bugging me about everything. You treat me like a kid."

Do you think the question about getting the car's oil changed was the major cause of Sarah's emotions?

Chances are, she was disappointed in her grade and possibly mad at herself. But instead of acknowledging those feelings to herself, she lashed out at the first person who tried to interact with her. She did not have the capacity to take her emotional temperature and recognize the feelings of anger, bitterness, and disappointment that swirled within her. Nor was she aware of how these feelings had pushed her to take out her anger and bitterness inappropriately on her mother.

How might Sarah have responded if she had had a stronger ability to be emotionally self-aware? First, she would have recognized her internal turmoil, perhaps by noticing the tension in her neck, the way she uncharacteristically swore to herself when she got caught in slow traffic on the way home, or the force with which she slammed the car door when she got home. By asking herself what had occurred that day that could have upset her, she would also have been conscious of how her anger related to the disappointing grade in her biology class. She would have recognized that these feelings of anger and bitterness put her at risk for behaving with uncharacteristic anger toward other people.

As a result of her emotional self-awareness, Sarah might have entered her home and told her mother, "Sorry, Mom, I had a bad day at school. I'm sorry I didn't stop to change the oil on the way home. Just give me some time to cool down. I'll look after the car as soon as I can. I need to go take a run to work off some stress."

In this scenario, Sarah knows that she feels angry, recognizes why she is in this state, and is aware that she is at risk of behaving angrily toward her mother. She communicates this to her mother immediately, and she offers suggestions about what will help her calm down.

This kind of communication, blended with her real attempts to not behave too irritably, will allow her mother to support her in her attempts to settle down.

● Know Thyself

Emotional self-awareness is the foundation on which most of the other elements of emotional intelligence are built, the necessary first step toward exploring and coming to understand yourself, enabling you to make positive changes. Obviously, what you don't recognize, you cannot manage. If you aren't aware of what you're doing, why you're doing it, and the way it's affecting others, you can't change. If you think there's nothing wrong, then there's no need or reason to change. That's why emotional self-awareness is key and basic to our emotional intelligence. Mastering this one overarching skill will empower you to work toward improvement in all the other areas of emotional intelligence. Without it, you'd get no feedback from yourself, you'd be unable to monitor your progress, and your chances of achieving your goals would be impeded.

Individuals with a strong sense of emotional self-awareness (1) *recognize when they feel out of sorts, irritable, sad, or frustrated* and (2) *understand how these feelings alter their behavior in a way that may alienate others*. Usually they can also figure out (3) *what incident precipitated their feelings*. The capacity to know what they are feeling and how they are behaving allows them a degree of control over their potentially alienating behavior.

● Why Emotional Self-Awareness?

The goal of emotional self-awareness isn't to overanalyze our emotions, to unduly suppress them, or to do away with them altogether. We all behave in inappropriate ways some of the time. Nor will we ever be rid of unpleasant feelings; they're entirely natural after disappointment, criticism, or loss. But we must strive to be conscious of what we feel and why we feel the way we do, so that we aren't driven blindly by internal forces or pushed into self-defeating behavior by default, for want of the requisite information.

Being emotionally self-aware also has a preventative benefit. Remember the ABCDE technique described in the previous chapter and the debilitating self-talk? If we learn to interpret correctly the events that stimulate this self-talk, we can, with practice, learn to alter what we tell ourselves when we see the activating event coming. Thus emotional self-awareness serves to protect us.

Let's say that you are aware of your "hot buttons"—those deep-seated sore spots that others unknowingly prod. Suppose you're about to get back a big English term paper at school, which is bound to entail at least some degree of constructive criticism. If criticism is a hot button for you, you can prepare yourself by remaining on the lookout for irrational beliefs. Say, for example, that in times past your self-talk has been instinctively defensive after getting a lower grade than you wanted, something along the lines of "Who does she think she is? I'll never get a good grade from this teacher." You could dispute this tendency by reminding yourself of other classes in which your grades on writing assignments improved throughout the semester. Or you could remember what your older sister said about how much her writing improved in this teacher's class.

Knowing what blind alleys you've strayed into before, you can work to reprogram your self-talk, that harmful inner monologue. You can also be alert to tangible signals that your anger or frustration is rising: body signs such as shoulder tension and a raised voice. Knowledge is power—and self-knowledge is premium power that leads to successful emotional management.

So, even though you've prepared yourself to respond more rationally, let's suppose you're in English class; you get back that paper, and you've received a C grade. The teacher marked all over your paper and wrote a summary note at the end: "Your writing is well organized but lacks spark. Use different sentence patterns, more descriptive language, and unexpected twists to capture the reader." Irrational beliefs would sound something like this: "Who does she think she is? She ought to be dealing with my strengths, not tearing me down."

But perhaps you could temper your irritation long enough to replace it with the following thinking: "Wait a minute! What's this about 'tearing me down'? Where's the evidence that she wants to tear me down? Is that her style? Are there other explanations? After all, she is my teacher, so of course she wants to point out how I can better myself. If I do better, she looks better. I realize I do have some difficulty hearing negative feedback, but I can learn from her and use that feedback to my advantage.

"So my *response* of feeling torn down does not mean she *intended* to tear me down. There is a difference. It's more likely that she wants to be helpful. I need to remember not to get so upset, particularly when it comes to feedback about how to improve my writing."

With these examples you can see the advantage of being aware of your hot buttons, challenging irrational beliefs when your emotions get triggered, and using your self-awareness to create a better outcome for yourself (for example, less anger about your grade and more willingness to take the teacher's suggestions about how to improve). But if you are thinking, "That sounds too hopeful; I could never respond to a grade like that," you've just engaged in more negative self-talk! The more you tune into your negative self-talk and the emotions that cause it, the better you'll be able to shut it down.

● The Tyrannical Instructor

All the students at the college knew better than to challenge Professor Cross. He had a bad habit of embarrassing students in front of their peers; sometimes he yelled and slammed his book shut when someone gave an incorrect answer. He didn't bother to learn students' names.

Professor Cross was in charge of running the chemistry labs. Today, as usual, he was barking orders and glaring at people. One of the students, Kelly, walked up to him and asked, "Why are you always so mad?"

"I'm not mad!" protested Professor Cross. His face reddened, and he glared at Kelly with folded arms. "I'm just trying to get you all to follow the proper safety procedures!"

The students standing nearby turned away, muffling their laughs of disbelief.

This scenario is extreme, but scarcely unique. Anger is perhaps the prime offender in the emotional spectrum. It skews our judgment, making us oblivious to our surroundings and to ourselves. Its extreme physiological manifestations make it even harder for us to escape its grip long enough to register what's happening, let alone correct our behavior. Quite often angry people are unaware that they're angry. They're dimly aware that something's happening, but they don't know what it is, and whatever it is, it must be someone else's fault or they wouldn't be so mad. Obviously their actions are having an effect on them and on those around them, but they can't grasp the extent of the negative impact. If Professor Cross had emotional self-awareness, he'd be able to do three things: first, he would be able to notice that he is indeed angry or at least frustrated, instead of denying it. Second, he would understand why he's feeling that way. Maybe he's tired of grading, or he resents the pressure to do research and teach at the same time, or he's frustrated with the lower-level classes he's assigned while others get to teach more advanced classes. Finally, he'd be able to recognize that his grouchiness makes it less likely students will connect with him or learn as much—two things that will contribute to even greater dissatisfaction on everyone's part!

Just like Professor Cross, who denied his anger, we're often the last to see ourselves or our moods with any degree of clarity. Yet being aware of any emotion is the first step toward controlling it.

Out-of-control emotions always work against us. If you're angry and sarcastic and belittling, and you don't even know it, two things are bound to follow. First, physiologically speaking, you will release more stress hormones, which eventually wear down the body and make you more likely to get sick. Second, you'll turn people off without understanding why. They'll flee from you, or at the very least view you in a highly negative light. No matter how strong your other abilities—the knowledge you possess or the skills you've acquired—you won't get a chance to demonstrate them. Key relationships will sour before they can be forged.

● Hot Buttons

In our example, a hot button about criticism on a paper led to negative self-talk and not taking a teacher's comments as constructive help. Hot buttons are those issues that cause us to be alert, that trigger our deepest emotions and send us spiraling out of control. The funny thing is, hot buttons can be useful—they serve as a warning that someone has violated one of our basic values or that we've stumbled into an area of our life where we are raw or sensitive.

How do you deal with getting your hot buttons pushed? Part of self-awareness is knowing yourself and understanding how you react to others. For example, a certain comment, such as "Wow, your hair looks bad," may trigger an angry retort from you in response. This may be even more likely if you were frequently insulted by your brother or sister related to appearance. We all have certain triggers or hot buttons that cause us to react without thought or control. We're usually more sensitive around people we know well—people who either know just how to push our buttons or simply stumble into that area accidentally. Usually we regret the knee-jerk response that we make in these situations, but we're not quite sure how to stop it.

Instead of overreacting, we can become reflective. So when we experience the impulse to hit back, retreat, or get upset, we can learn to stop, reflect, and then react. Our first response could be to stop and think something like, "What did she mean by that?" In other words, "Is it something about me or something about her that caused the insult? Maybe she's having a bad day, or she feels inferior about something, or she just has no self-control. Well then, why should I get angry about her problems?"

Then we should quickly focus on our own reactions. Why should we upset ourselves over someone else's thoughtless remarks? Being self-aware enables you to reflect on your own emotions with a series of questions and to use the ABCDE model to better understand your reaction.

Why am I reacting to her comments?
What are my irrational beliefs?
Does she matter that much that I need to upset myself?
Am I strong enough to manage my own emotions?
Can I just relax and let it pass for now?
If I relax, maybe I can figure out what's really going on with her.
What does it mean that I let myself get upset over a remark like that?
Am I that sensitive about my hair? Do I really care whether she likes my hair?

By taking a two-pronged approach—(1) focusing on your reaction and your emotions and (2) exploring the cause of your reaction—you can become more self-aware of the way you approach these high-impact situations. This increased awareness will enable you to better handle these events as they happen.

● Emotional Self-Awareness Gone Missing in Action

Five years after he graduated from college, Rick set up his own company. Retail chains contract with his company to send young mystery shoppers into branches of their stores to evaluate their salespeople and customer service. One of his largest clients was Xecutive Xtreme Sportz, an extreme sports company focusing on athletes involved in high-effort sports like heli-skiing, mountain climbing, and Ironman competitions.

As part of the training on how to act like a customer with frontline sales people, Rick invited Luke, a recent college grad and expert skier, to accompany him to one of the Xecutive Xtreme Sportz megastores.

At the store, they were approached by Lindsay, an attractive sales-person in her mid-twenties.

"Hi," she said with a smile. "May I help you?"

"This store must have a policy of only hiring women who are helpful and beautiful!" Rick responded, adding, "Don't they, Luke?"

Luke nodded half-heartedly, quickly stating, "We're looking for skis that adapt well in extreme skiing conditions, like very deep and powdery snow."

"Great," Lindsay said, looking at Luke. "We've got a fabulous selection. What size are you looking for?"

"He needs 195s," Rick interjected, and then asked Lindsay, "Do you like to ski?"

At this point, Luke, perplexed and uncomfortable with Rick's apparent flirting with the salesperson, attempted to refocus on their task of assessing how this employee deals with customers. After all, Rick had hired Luke to do just that, so Luke tried one more time. "I'm interested in these two different styles of skis—can you tell me which one will work best for really deep and powdery snow?"

Before Lindsay had an opportunity to reply, Rick turned to Luke and jokingly interjected, "You are one serious dude, Luke!" Luke replied: "I guess." Then he grew silent.

Rick had little capacity for self-awareness. He was oblivious to how inappropriate his flirtatious behavior was—especially since he was the boss, and he was there to work, not to find a date. He was also unaware of the discomfort he had caused Luke and possibly the sales-person. At a deeper level, Rick was also oblivious to the competitive feelings he had toward his younger employee, and his need to bolster his own ego and come across as cool to Lindsay. The problem was not Luke's behavior; it was Rick's.

How do you respond when someone you're with starts to make you uncomfortable in a situation? Do you first become aware of your feelings? Are you inclined to say something or just grin and bear it? Being aware of our feelings helps us better manage these situations. Once we understand our emotions, we can better decide what steps to take. Knowing when and how to speak up in difficult situations will be further discussed in Chapter 8, Assertiveness.

● Become Aware of Others' Reactions to Your Behavior

So far we've talked about two key parts of self-awareness: (1) knowing what emotion you're feeling at the moment it begins and (2) knowing what triggered that emotion. There's a third part, though, that's equally important. We must be aware of how others respond to our emotions. Another seemingly simple vignette illustrates how a little self-awareness can have significant effects. Consider this anecdote of a conversation between a student government leader and her best friend.

> My friend told me that everyone knows I want to be a good leader, but I was making everyone anxious by the way I approached the meetings. I often came rushing into meetings with a stack of handouts piled on top of my notebook. I'd begin by telling everybody how much we had to get accomplished that day and that we couldn't waste any time. Usually I was sorting through all the papers I had brought to the meeting when I was making these statements. And then, whenever anyone began talking about something I didn't think was important, I would start shifting around in my chair and sometimes even interrupt.
>
> It wasn't until another member of student government pointed out all of this that I became aware of my anxiety level just before meetings. Now I make sure to plan well ahead so that I won't be rushing around right before a meeting begins. And I prepare an agenda so that everybody can see what we need to discuss and know what's most important.

Learn to take your "emotional temperature"—what causes you to run hot or cold, and how you react (and others react to you) when your emotions are triggered. You've heard the phrase "knowledge is power"; accordingly, start gaining insight about your emotions (knowledge) so that you'll have more choices about how you want to react.

Reflection Questions

You can repeat the following exercise, substituting a different emotion word for "embarrassed," such as "angry," "sad," or "excited." By answering these questions for each of the major emotions, you can go a long way toward developing better emotional self-awareness.

Think of the last time you were embarrassed about something:

1. What were you embarrassed about?
2. What did you say to yourself about the situation?
3. What was the worst that could have happened under the circumstances?
4. Were there alternative things you could have said to yourself?
5. Was there any emotion other than embarrassment that you could have felt?
6. How did you behave after getting embarrassed? How did your behavior or emotions affect others?

For more help developing emotional self-awareness, consult *The Student EQ Edge: Student Workbook* to help improve your skills in this area.

Self-Regard

CHAPTER 4

No one can make you feel inferior without your consent.
  —Eleanor Roosevelt, 1937

Definition: "Self-regard is respecting oneself while understanding and accepting one's strengths and weaknesses. Self-regard is often associated with feelings of inner strength and self-confidence. Self-acceptance is the ability to accept one's perceived positive and negative aspects as well as one's limitations and possibilities. The component of emotional intelligence is associated with general feelings of security, inner strength, self-assuredness, self-confidence, and self-adequacy" (Multi-Health Systems, 2011, pp. 3–4).

Setting the Bar Too High

Marcie was frequently concerned that she didn't make a good enough impression on others: "I don't think I was dressed up enough" or "Maybe I talked too much and hogged the conversation." An objective observer would disagree with both, but Marcie set the bar for her everyday social interactions so high that it was impossible for her to live up to her expectations of herself. She was unable to recognize her strengths: that she was both fashionable and engaging in her interactions.

Ishmail, on the other hand, could not forgive himself for any perceived failures: "I got an 85 on the exam. It should have been a 95. What is the matter with me? I lost 10 points on stupid mistakes. Geez, I'm dumb." Ishmail's self-talk reflects the severe criticism he rains upon himself for not being perfect and his lack of tolerance for making any mistakes. He cannot accept his "warts."

Natasha was quite the opposite; she presented herself as an expert on everything. Clothes, music, shopping, guys—she seemed to have an answer to every question. She bragged about being the smartest student in her media class. She believed that the only reason she didn't get the highest grade was that her professor had it in for her and showed favoritism to other students. Natasha seems to have high self-regard, but actually she lacked any awareness of her weaknesses—a key part of self-regard. She was so high on herself, but unrealistically so, that few people could stand to be around her for very long. She may have had high self-esteem, but she did not have high self-regard.

Self-Regard Is Not Self-Esteem

You want to like and think highly of yourself, but what's really important is to know your strengths and weaknesses and then *still* like yourself! Self-esteem, as we know, has become a buzz-phrase in both the classroom and the workplace, not to mention a multi-billion-dollar industry. There are a multitude of books, audio and video tapes, software programs, and Internet sites devoted solely to increasing it. Some of them, alas, are way off target.

We certainly aren't minimizing the idea of feeling good about yourself. After all, self-esteem is defined as a person's overall evaluation of his or her worth. But people have been taught, like Natasha, to focus on inflating their worth as an endpoint or goal. The problem is that an undue emphasis on self-esteem leads to blindly pumping yourself up. Telling yourself how great you are may or may not be a valid part of an approach to repairing a damaged ego, but it's not an end in itself.

Self-regard, on the other hand, has more to do with our ability to accurately know our strengths and weaknesses. Being high in self-regard has more to do with being in touch with who you really are, what areas you really excel at, and what attributes are more challenging for you. Also, as we'll soon see, it encompasses the ability to accept yourself as you are and to feel confident.

Low self-esteem may indeed be dysfunctional, but artificially high self-esteem may be almost as problematic. The child who learns the "I am special" mantra without the ability to recognize weaknesses and to want to correct them is done a tremendous disservice. Ladling out lavish and indiscriminate praise without making sure that you're helping the child actually achieve something that merits approval can lead to devastation when the world fails to continue to pat the child on the back for success that wasn't earned. Real self-esteem is built up gradually, layer by layer, through taking justifiable pride in real accomplishment, not through a third party's weaving a cocoon of unrealistic positivity.

● Like Yourself, Warts and All

Of course, you don't want to fixate on weaknesses, either, which is every bit as unbalanced as denying shortcomings (out of fear that they somehow cancel out your strengths, no matter how demonstrable those may be). Nor do you want to either blow your strengths out of all proportion or fall into the trap of fearing that they'll never be strong enough. The idea is to like yourself as a total—and sometimes contradictory but always developing—package.

Sometimes those who think too highly of themselves without knowledge of their warts end up on shaky ground. Let's think back to the classroom scene described in Chapter 2, and Brett's pleading with his professor and then getting angry. His opening gambit was to tell him why he *had* to be admitted into his course. What were the odds that this would advance his cause—that is, to get into an already full class? Did he really believe that his professor would be convinced by his personal demands? The only result of his self-puffery was to turn the professor off. Among his other mistakes, Brett tried to pull rank on the professor by threatening to involve his parents, who donate money to the university. Informing people how rich and famous and powerful you are, especially in the middle of a crisis during which you need to enlist their support, is bound to work against you. But Brett had no ability to recognize this as a weakness; instead, he believed it helped his cause. He was wrong.

Brett's behavior also gave a very strong message that he cared not a bit about the professor or his course—a message that certainly alienated the professor and undercut any chance of his making it into his class. In fact, this behavior of only thinking about ourselves is often a sign of deep insecurities. Brett quite probably has inflated his own worth in many other circumstances. If, on the other hand, he had high self-regard, he'd also have the wit to behave politely and further his ends—as did John, the next student in line to be enrolled in the class. In sum, then, self-regard means that you feel comfortable enough about yourself that you don't have to go around attempting (and usually failing) to bowl people over with how important you are or the other trappings of oversized egos. If you've really got it, you don't need to flaunt it.

● Don't Bite Off More than You Can Chew

Consider the thousands of would-be entrepreneurs who set wildly unrealistic goals, declaring that they're going to be "the next Bill Gates." By this, they mean not only that they'll do it their way but that they'll do it all themselves. They inevitably fail because they don't acknowledge their blind spots and shortcomings—those areas where others could give them a hand. If they do get a business up and running, they very often can't delegate or collaborate effectively because they are, at root, insecure.

In fact, they haven't been paying attention to what made Bill Gates so successful. He's one of the world's richest self-made billionaires. He arouses strong and not always positive reactions, but no one denies that he built a uniquely successful company from scratch, at the same time serving as a pioneer in the transition to personal computers. His enormous contribution to the information and communication age may not be fully appreciated for many years to come.

Surely someone as intelligent and accomplished as Gates must be extremely self-absorbed, conceited, and full of himself. Anyone who could make that much money that quickly would be entirely justified in thinking that he or she is exceptional. His ego must be boundless, as big as the moon.

On the contrary, Gates, like most truly successful people, isn't like that at all. Those who know him reveal that he always flies economy class, not business or executive class—in part because he doesn't feel the need to advertise who, and how great, he is. Besides, as he sees it, he's pretty thin and doesn't need the wider seat that you get up front.

Those who know Gates well and work closely with him verify that he's not egotistical. Although he's very confident, and he may appear cocky to some, Gates acknowledges that others know more about certain aspects of the business than he does; thus, he surrounds himself with people who are experts in technology, marketing, and business. And, as you'll read about in a later chapter, he admits when he is wrong. We suspect that Gates, if he took the EQ-i, would score rather high when it came to self-regard.

● Confidence, Not Cockiness

Much importance—perhaps too much—is attached to projecting an air of all-encompassing confidence in the workplace. But there's a fine line involved. People who act like know-it-alls are more likely headed for a rough landing. By thinking that they've got a handle on everything, they overextend themselves. The more they venture into unfamiliar areas, the more vulnerable they become. It's knowing what you don't know, finding out who knows it, and capitalizing on that knowledge that separates the successes from the could-have-beens, should-have-beens, and almosts.

In the business world we often see leaders who fail because their self-regard is shaky, that is, they cannot tolerate having any "warts," and certainly cannot tolerate having their warts visible publicly. They cover up their fragile self-regard by never admitting when they are wrong, by blaming others for their own mistakes, and overemphasizing their "strengths" in order to make sure that nobody inadvertently notices their "warts." They present themselves as know-it-alls who need to surround themselves with "yes men," who cannot tolerate any suggestion of criticism, and who never allow that they are responsible for an error but rather deal with a mistake by finding someone else to blame.

The Components of Self-Regard: Awareness, Acceptance, and Attitude

Self-regard can be an important tool in helping you be successful academically. In fact, it might be as important as IQ. But how? First, let's look at the three major components of self-regard (see Figure 4.1). It begins with your awareness of your strengths and limitations (let's call this the *awareness* phase of self-regard). Then you can either accept yourself as you are—both the wonders and the warts—or you can become overly self-critical (let's call this the *acceptance* phase). And third, depending on your awareness and acceptance levels, you'll either exude confidence or you won't (let's call this the *attitude* phase of self-regard).

Now let's look at how these components affect David, a student with a moderate learning disability who still makes all As and Bs because of his well-developed self-regard. Whenever David is assigned a major paper, one of the first things he does is to look at the elements of the assignment. Does the paper involve finding outside sources? David is good at this. Does it involve coming up with his own theory or position? David knows he struggles with this. Is the

Figure 4.1 The Components of Self-Regard

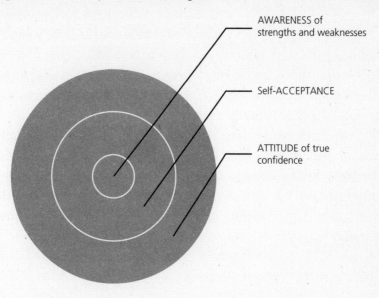

topic assigned to him or does he get to pick the topic? David knows that when he gets to choose his own topic he wastes lots of time searching for the perfect topic.

In order to complete the steps of preparing for and writing the paper, David had to be aware (AWARENESS) of his strengths and weaknesses as a writer and accept those. Based on how he answers the three questions, David then plans how he will approach the assignment. If he does have to choose his own topic, he will set up a meeting with the librarian, who is good at helping him brainstorm ideas. And if he has to come up with his own theory, he always writes a draft and asks for feedback from the faculty member. He doesn't get overly obsessive about this, and he can ACCEPT the feedback and use it to produce a version he is satisfied with. So no matter what type of paper David is assigned—one that makes use of his strengths or challenges his weaknesses—he feels confident about his ability to be successful (ATTITUDE).

● Why Self-Regard?

What makes self-regard important for life success? People who are satisfied with their life and accomplishments often score high in self-regard when they take the EQ-i. Once again, this *doesn't* mean they inflate their self-worth. Rather, they are accurate at gauging and appreciating their strengths and weaknesses.

A 360° assessment compares a person with how others who know him or her well—managers, peers, subordinates, spouse—would complete the same ratings on that person. Those with the highest self-regard score themselves closer to how others view them. In other words, they—the individual and all of the raters—all agree on what the person's strengths and weaknesses are. People with high self-regard don't have "blind spots." A simple way to carry out an informal 360° assessment is to ask the people you know well—friends, roommate, coach, teacher, parents—what they see as your strengths and the areas in which you could improve. Then see whether their list matches yours. The closer the match, the higher the AWARENESS part of your self-regard.

The more you can like (ACCEPT) yourself as you are, and the more AWARENESS you have of your strengths and weaknesses, the more confident (ATTITUDE) you will be in your short- and long-term interactions and assignments. Getting a handle on your strengths helps you build them even more. Suppose you discover that you are pretty good at math. Manipulating numbers comes easily to you, and you enjoy solving mathematical problems. By doing more work in this area, practicing with increasingly difficult problems, you get even better at it.

Many people who are highly proficient in math really enjoy working with numbers. They also have an accurate sense of what kinds of problems they are good at. The same holds true with your emotional skills. Knowing your strengths and working to develop them even more can really help you excel.

On the other hand, we've often seen people fail at some things because they thought they could do everything. They overestimate their capabilities. Really successful people know what they're *not* good at. They decide whether to work at improving themselves in those areas or to surround themselves with others who can compensate for their weaknesses. Think of some of the most happily married people you know. Although they may have similar interests and tastes, do they have complementary skills? Is one partner more cool and collected under stress, one better at managing household finances? Does one better discipline the children and is one more socially extroverted with friends? An important key to success is being aware of your limitations and knowing how you will deal with them.

Self-regard can be viewed like a seesaw. You want to balance your ability to acknowledge your strengths while addressing your weaknesses, your expressions of confidence with your requests for help, all the while exuding a sense of peace about who you are right now. Answer the following questions to help you gauge your self-regard.

Reflection Questions

Write down your top three strengths (for example, make friends easily, compassionate):

1.

2.

3.

What do you see as three important areas in which you could improve? (For example, could be a better listener, become less self-centered):

1.

2.

3.

How have you become aware of your strengths and weaknesses? (For example, asked others, just know from other people's reactions to me):

1.

2.

3.

How do you feel about yourself right now? Choose the number that most closely describes it.

1. I wish I had more strengths. I just seem to make too many mistakes.
2. What's not to like? I've got all the skills and qualities I want.
3. I know I'm not perfect, but I like myself and know that I can improve.

Answer 3 demonstrates the highest self-regard.

How confident are you in general? Choose the number that most closely describes it.

1. Maybe a bit too confident; sometimes others may see me as cocky.
2. Just right; I feel confident.
3. A bit too self-conscious about myself.

Answer 2 demonstrates the highest self-regard.

Consult *The Student EQ Edge: Student Workbook* to further develop your self-regard.

CHAPTER 5

Self-Actualization

Whereas the average individuals often have not the slightest idea of what they are, of what they want, of what their own opinions are, self-actualizing individuals have superior awareness of their own impulses, desires, opinions, and subjective reactions in general.
  —Abraham Maslow, American professor of psychology (1908–1970); created Hierarchy of Needs (Maslow, 1987) to explain human behavior

Definition: "Self-actualization is the willingness to persistently try to improve oneself and engage in the pursuit of personally relevant and meaningful objectives that lead to a rich and enjoyable life. Striving to actualize one's potential involves engaging in enjoyable and significant activities and making a lifelong and enthusiastic commitment to long-term goals. Self-actualization is an ongoing, dynamic process of striving toward the maximum development of one's abilities, capacities, and talents. This component of emotional intelligence is associated with persistently trying to do one's best and improve oneself in general. Self-actualization is associated with feelings of self-satisfaction" (Multi-Health Systems, 2011, p. 4).

● Many Interests

Roya and Jason were best friends in high school. Jason was the class valedictorian with a perfect grade point average. Roya was only 0.1 of a point lower as a result of earning two Bs during her high school career. They both wanted to attend Duke University on a Robertson scholarship, one of the most prestigious at Duke.

The week of the interviews came. When asked about what gave her fulfillment, Roya talked about the volunteer work she did at Duke Children's Hospital and her role as editor of her high school student newspaper. She also talked about being a member of the swim team and the camaraderie of the group. She mentioned her love of theatre and talked about the most recent play she had attended. When she was asked what she wanted to major in at college, Roya indicated that she didn't know yet. She wanted time to explore multiple disciplines and careers before deciding.

When Jason was asked the same questions, he talked about the joy of solving a tough problem in physics, the excitement of his family that he had earned the valedictorian role, and the fact that he was nominated by his school for so many academic scholarships. He talked about reading everything he could about engineering because that was his career goal. He mentioned that he joined the engineering club at school because they often went to job sites to understand local engineering projects for their club meetings. His fascination with and aptitude for engineering indicated he would be very successful in the field.

Several weeks later when Robertson scholarship offers were made, Roya received one and Jason did not. Maybe that's surprising to you, but not to us. Whereas all of Jason's interests and activities were focused on one thing—academic and career success—Roya was much more balanced in her life. She was active in the arts and sports and edited the school paper. She was involved in volunteer work. She received meaning from many things and mastered academics even though she did not yet have a career goal. She exuded a zest for learning and exploration that signaled she would excel at whatever she chose. She was self-actualized in many dimensions of her life.

● Set Action-Oriented Goals

We admit that *self-actualization* sounds a bit like psychological jargon, but the concept is really quite integral to individual well-being. Abraham Maslow was the first to coin the term, in the 1940s, as part of his "hierarchy of needs" theory (Maslow, 1987). He believed that there are five basic needs that must be satisfied if we're to survive and then go on to live happy and fully realized lives.

First, we need air to breathe, water to drink, food to eat, and a tolerable temperature. Then we must achieve safety, so that we aren't in pain or peril. Next comes love—the need to belong, to be wanted and cared about by friends, relatives, and family. Fourth is esteem—the need to achieve self-respect, to take pride in our accomplishments and know that they're recognized by others. Then comes self-actualization, a pinnacle of self and other acceptance at which we are characterized by fulfillment and meaning (Maslow, 1987).

Based on this framework, we developed something we call the Life Map (shown in Figure 5.1), to help you chart your own course of self-actualization. We've used this with many different people, from students to senior citizens, to self-check at various life phases. Self-actualization involves being satisfied with where you are on life's highway—satisfied with all your achievements, at school, at work, at play, and in relationships.

The idea is to strive for a healthy balance among the many activities that make up your life. For example, how much time do you spend in Relationship County? How quickly do you speed through School Responsibilities to reach Traveltown, Fitness Junction, or Funville? How often do you want to put your feet up in Relax Village?

Your own personal life map would reflect other interests: maybe Sports City or Workville. Workville may take on greater meaning when you come to that time in your life to buy your first house or a brand-new

Figure 5.1 The Life Map

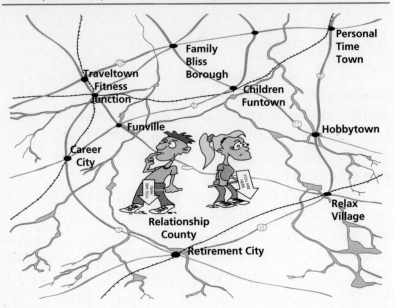

car, not your parents' hand-me-down or the used clunker. And what about the quality of the time spent at each location? Each should be important and meaningful in itself. Take a moment now to see what you accomplish as you move along the pathways of your life. What goals would you like to reach in each area, in return for the time and effort you devote to them? How many hours per week or month are you willing to commit to those goals? Of course we know you're not thinking about retirement yet, but one of the things we've learned from people in the process of retiring is that those who developed hobbies in college—playing a musical instrument, painting, tennis, photography—have a much easier and happier time adjusting to retirement in later life.

● Do What You Love

Career counselors often bemoan the fact that too many people who are seeking a direction in life begin (and quite often continue) an interview by dwelling on how much money they can make in a given field. They may know or sense they're good at something totally different, but they shun their natural inclination because it won't pay off. They'll hate working with computers all day; they can barely sit still for an hour at a time. But that's where, in their minds, the future is. "The" future becomes—out of economic necessity—their future also. As a result, they may learn about computers and become employable. They'll also become extremely unhappy, and not nearly as successful as someone who's legitimately drawn to the wonders of technology.

Career success is very seldom based on career duress or pressure—what a person believes he or she must do in order to make a living. That's not a very shining prize. It may get you a paycheck, but it won't get you where you want to (and ought to) go. We don't suppose that Bill Gates set out with the specific goal of becoming the world's richest self-made business magnate. He set out to gratify his personal passion for computers and pursued that passion with vigor. Everything else flowed from this well-founded decision.

Or take Michael Dell, the founder of Dell Computers, whose family urged him to become a physician. Dell actually enrolled in a premed course at the University of Texas, but he spent most of his time selling the computers he'd cobbled together while studiously neglecting his classes. As we know, he then very wisely followed his true inclination, his true calling in life. Thanks to Dell's innovative marketing techniques, his firm grew into the world's largest computer manufacturer and—at time of this writing—about $61.5 billion in revenue during 2011.

A more recent darling of the high-tech world, Mark Zuckerberg, founder of Facebook, was featured in the popular movie *The Social Network* (Brunetti & Fincher, 2010). Among other things, Zuckerberg is renowned as the world's youngest billionaire (with an estimated net worth of $17.5 billion during the writing of this book). Although there is some debate about the accuracy of the movie's depiction of events, there is consensus in the observation that he was not driven to success by money. In the film he resisted commercializing the Facebook site for a long time. As a teenager he developed a computer program called Synapse that sorted music into the listening habits of users. When AOL and Microsoft offered to purchase the program, he turned them down.

Zuckerberg was most excited about the potential of a social network. He was driven by the possibilities of getting more and more people to open up about themselves and network with others online. In 2005, the MTV network wanted to buy Facebook for $75 million. After he turned them down, Yahoo! offered him a billion dollars in 2006. Imagine—a billion dollars! He is among the few people in the world to have ever turned down a billion-dollar offer.

In an interview with the *New Yorker* (Vargas, 2010), Zuckerberg was asked about the deal. To the amazement of Terry Semel, the CEO of Yahoo! at the time, Zuckerberg responded, "It's not about the price. This is my baby, and I want to keep running it, I want to keep growing it" (p. 5).

For something completely different, consider Jerry Seinfeld, who did much to redefine television comedy and wound up with all the tangible evidence of success—multi-million-dollar contracts and a garage full of Porsches. Did he have these things in mind when he was a struggling young man? Perhaps—but they must have seemed awfully remote. Friends have written accounts of Seinfeld's life that describe a down-to-earth personality rooted in solid values. He loved doing comedy and worked hard at it for many years on the stand-up circuit, often in front of blasé or downright hostile audiences. He perfected his routines, carefully studied other performers, and kept a minutely detailed notebook of his experiences and observations (Costanza & Lawrence, 1998). Like Gates, Dell, and Zuckerberg, Seinfeld owes his success to a combination of factors. All four men had a lot of skill and a bit of luck, managed to be in the right place at the right time, and—most important—did what they truly loved to do and knew what they were good at. That's why all of them far exceeded any long-term goals they might have set in the early stages of their careers.

Of course, success in life is measured not just in financial terms, nor is it the purview of men only! Some people are successful in generating change for the betterment of the world. Aung San Suu Kyi is a prodemocracy activist and has dedicated herself to fighting for freedom and democracy in Burma. She has led a peaceful, nonviolent struggle under a military dictatorship to achieve her goals. She leads the National League for Democracy in Burma and has won a number of awards, including the Nobel Peace Prize in 1991. While her struggle continues, she has been recognized internationally for her work. The U2 album *All That You Can't Leave Behind* was banned in Burma because one of the songs ("Walk On") was written about her struggle and how, even when the government threatened her, she "walked on" the other way.

Although Aung San Suu Kyi has not yet won her struggle for freedom for the people in Burma, her perseverance, demeanor, and true grit are having an influence. She was recently elected to serve in her country's governing body. And she has certainly been successful in getting her cause better known worldwide.

Another political activist, Elizabeth Cady Stanton, cofounded the first women's rights organization in the United States and led the campaign for women's suffrage. Cady Stanton grew up in a household with a lawyer father. By age 10, she was already perusing his law books, fascinated with legal issues. Her passion for the law grew into a passion to make it legal for women to vote, an effort she began in 1848 when she organized the first women's rights convention in Seneca Falls, NY. She continued this quest until her death in 1902, still some 18 years before women were granted the right to vote in the United States. Can you imagine the passion and commitment it takes to work for over 50 years to achieve a single goal? Especially when most people in society disagree with you and some are downright hostile?

Finally, let's take a look at Oprah. She's become so famous, we don't even need to give her last name (which is Winfrey, in case you didn't know!). She grew up so poor that she wore dresses made from potato sacks to school. She began working at a radio station at age 14, and by 19 she coanchored the local news. Known for her emotion and the passion with which she tackled tough issues, she vaulted a third tier talk show to the top spot in the Chicago market. Her willingness to address controversial subjects in an open—and not sensationalized—way made her an American icon during the 20th century. But like many who have high self-actualization, Oprah never rested on her laurels, so to speak, and always had another goal on the horizon. Most recently, she began her own television network, the Oprah Winfrey Network (OWN). Many questioned why she would take on such a huge challenge because it would be so difficult to top what she had already achieved. But, like others with high self-actualization, Oprah needs new challenges.

Let Your Internal Light Shine

Self-actualization can combine with emotional self-awareness in that our ability to track our immediate, short-term feelings can help signal something larger in our life. Think of it as an internal light we all carry within us. Some of us are aware of our light and what makes it glow brighter, whereas others ignore their internal light, chasing life goals that have been defined for them by others—whether that is a "good" job, money, or a certain lifestyle. They often work hard enough to accomplish the goal successfully, but end up unhappy, to everyone else's surprise. The story of Ben gives us an example of someone who let his internal light shine.

Ben graduated from the University of Maryland Dental School around 1917. Dentistry was a new profession, one that Ben's parents viewed as a ticket to adult success. But Ben's true passion was playing golf. He had grown up playing golf almost every day after school at the local golf course and worked there as a teenager so he could play for free.

After graduation from dental school, he never practiced a day of dentistry in his life. Instead, he moved back home and went to the local golf club and asked if he could work there as a pro. They said yes, but the job did not pay enough to support his family. So Ben took the job as a pro and found another job to earn more money—mail delivery. Each morning by 4:30 AM he was driving through the Shenandoah

Valley of Virginia, delivering the mail. He finished his route by 12:30 and made it to the golf course by 1:00, where he worked until 5:00 or 6:00 as one of two pros. He spent evenings with his family and was a loving, happy man. One of the authors of this book, Korrel, was lucky enough to be his granddaughter; she remembers riding his mail route with him early in the morning a few times. He spoke of the beauty of the quiet countryside his route covered and watching the sun rise every morning. He loved helping people stay in touch with each other during a time when not everyone had a phone in their homes. And mostly, he loved being a golf pro. He taught Korrel how to play golf when she was five and welcomed her visits to the pro shop.

● Live Life to the Fullest

Setting goals ought to be a lifelong experience. The need doesn't diminish as we age.

Recall the students applying for a prestigious scholarship—Roya, the well-rounded student, and Jason, the very bright young man who loved engineering. Who do you think had the more fulfilling adulthood? Jason spent 60 hours a week at his job and eventually began his own engineering firm. He constantly received work calls at home in the evening and spent weekend hours catching up on email. He had a family and managed to make it to the kids' soccer games, but he was often too busy to spend quality time doing fun things together as a family. He did provide his family with a very comfortable lifestyle, a beautiful home, and many nice things. But as his management and ownership responsibilities grew and his time to practice engineering shrank, he became less and less satisfied because he was moving away from his passion—engineering.

Roya, on the other hand, still lived life to the fullest, working 40 to 50 hours a week leading a non-profit agency that supported foster children. She adopted her own foster child and, along with her partner, began a support group for adoptive parents. She still loved the theatre; she learned to play tennis and often entered doubles tournaments with her partner. She joined a women's book club and met with that group twice a month, once for a "girls' night out" for dinner and once to discuss the book.

● Strike a Balance

Living life to the fullest means, in daily practice, two things. First, self-actualization is the ability to love your work, to really get into whatever it is you do. If you fit this definition, you're very privileged. You're going to perform as well as possible all the time because work is a pleasure, something you'd engage in even if the financial rewards weren't there. As a friend of ours said, "If work isn't fun, you're doing the wrong work."

In our dealings with hockey players and other professional athletes, we've seen young men who are pretty much in it for the money. They tend to be either the sloggers—the ones who work their guts out on the ice without a great deal of success or recognition—and the enforcers—the ones who are sent in to make hard, sometimes vicious, hits on an opponent. Most last a couple of seasons and go back to where they came from. But we've also seen the likes of Wayne Gretzky (the world's most famous hockey player), who earned (and continues to earn) more money than all these other players put together. Why? Because, in addition to his natural ability, Gretzky loves the game of hockey. It is both a constant joy and a constant challenge to his remarkable skills—which is why he transcended it during his playing career. He earned every penny that came his way, but no one ever had to dangle a fat salary in front of him to compel him to go the extra mile.

But work isn't the only game in town. That's why the second key to self-actualization involves the need to be well-rounded, to strike a balance in everything you do. Today's employers are increasingly recognizing this fact. They don't want people who habitually burn the midnight oil in panic mode; they want people who can shut the office door, go home, and pursue meaningful personal interests and hobbies. Remember, then, that self-actualization means being where you want to be, in work and in all the varied aspects of your personal life.

What does self-actualization have to do with your success in life? Quite a lot. The most successful and happy people are those in tune with the things that excite them. They tend to have goals or areas of interest that they pursue with vigor. Identifying what activities you want to spend your time on and who you want to spend time with is the first step. The next step is to work those areas into your busy ongoing life and make them priorities.

Reflection Questions

1. What are the things that most excite you and get you motivated (for example, sports, music, dancing, writing)?

2. Would you want to have a career that includes this activity in some way?

3. What are some career choices that you have been considering?

4. How do these jobs fit with what you are passionate about?

Use *The Student EQ Edge: Student Workbook* to further explore this area.

The Self-Expression Realm

T his realm of emotional intelligence concerns itself with the way we express our emotions and how we come across to others. It includes our ability to state our thoughts, feelings, and beliefs to others in an unambiguous and friendly way. Our ability to act independently by taking initiative and following through also reflects our self-expression.

Figure Part 3 Self-Expression and the EQ Model

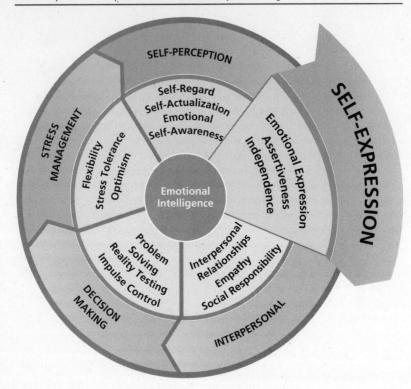

Emotional Expression

CHAPTER 6

Self-expression must pass into communication for its fulfillment.
—Pearl S. Buck

Definition: "Emotional expression is openly expressing one's feelings verbally and nonverbally. Emotional expression extends beyond the simple overt expression of one's feelings, to include the communication of those feelings in a manner that can be understood and experienced by the recipient" (Multi-Health Systems, 2011, p. 4).

Emotions Seep Out (Even If We Try to Hide Them)

Public speaking was a required course at the university. Jose was an excellent student who made the dean's list every semester, but he had delayed taking this course because he did not like talking in front of others. When the first speech was assigned, Jose chose his topic carefully, did lots of research on the topic, and prepared a detailed presentation.

The day of the speech he was nervous, and it showed. Instead of looking at his classmates, he stared at the back wall or at the notes he read. His brow was furrowed as he fought to remain confident. He heard himself say "uh" a lot, and he smiled nervously when he tried to emphasize a point. But his content was fantastic and he knew no one else in the class had done as much research.

When he got the grading rubric, he was shocked to learn he made a C. The professor commented, "While your content was superb, the most important part of a speech is how it is delivered. Excellent content delivered with nervousness, incongruent emotional expression, lack of eye contact with your audience (all of which you did) is not as effective as it could be."

Jose quickly slipped the grading rubric into his notebook. The rest of the class he did not look at the professor, and he sat slumped back in his chair, not taking any notes. When the professor asked him after class what was bothering him, Jose said "Nothing." Jose may have believed he was hiding his emotions from the professor, but the opposite was true.

We often overlook the importance of how we come across to others. In fact, in a series of studies reported by Albert Mehrabian (1971), he concluded that when it comes to the information people take in, 7 percent of what they retain is the words spoken, 38 percent is tone of voice, and 55 percent is body language.

Now this may seem hard to believe, but we can offer an example to drive the point home. You may be familiar with the events surrounding the 1960 election of John Kennedy as president of the United States; maybe your history class has covered this. The campaign between the candidates—John Kennedy and Richard Nixon—was intense, with Republican candidate Nixon slightly ahead before they debated each other. The climax of the election was the first ever televised presidential candidates debate.

The event was widely covered on both radio and television. It drew one of the largest media audiences of all time. During the debate, both candidates spoke about the issues in some detail, at least by television standards. When radio listeners were polled after the debate about who had won, the majority of them thought Nixon had bested Kennedy. But for television viewers it was different; they polled almost two to one in favor of Kennedy as the victor in the debate.

What accounts for this difference? A big part of it has been attributed to the nonverbal aspects of each of the candidates—Nixon looked tired and sweaty, and appeared glowering and angry at times. Kennedy, by contrast, appeared relaxed, vigorous, and fit. Also, whereas Nixon focused on debating Kennedy directly, Kenney spoke directly to the American viewers, smiling when appropriate and providing good eye contact through the camera lens.

How Emotional Expression Plays Out in the Public Eye

In the autumn of 1982, before manufacturers routinely placed a safety seal on the tops of over-the-counter medicine containers, poison was slipped into a number of Tylenol containers, resulting in a number of deaths. Jim Burke, CEO of Johnson & Johnson, went public, and in a television interview he not only decried the tampering with the medicines but also talked emotionally—with tears in his eyes—about the tragedy of the deaths. He then explained that Johnson & Johnson was recalling all Tylenol medications and would see to it that a safety barrier was put over each container.

Burke was quite open about his sadness and pain. His words, his tone, and the tears in his eyes spoke to the authenticity of his emotions. The public—identifying with such genuine feelings and with the steps he was ordering to ensure that it would never happen again—continued to support Tylenol as a trusted medication and did not abandon the company. Although in the aftermath of these deaths Tylenol's market share dropped from 35 percent to 10 percent, it rebounded over the ensuing year, ultimately becoming the most popular pain medication in the United States.

For those watching the interview, it was clear how Jim Burke was aware of and expressed his emotions. The congruity between his behavior and his feelings (both verbal and nonverbal) verified the genuineness of his emotional state. Johnson & Johnson's swift action of recalling all Tylenol medications, and thus putting public safety before corporate profits, was congruent with their CEO's televised message.

Now, consider how Tony Hayward, the CEO of BP, responded to the explosion of the Deepwater Horizon oil rig on April 20, 2010, which resulted in the deaths of eleven people on the rig and the massive leak of up to 100,000 barrels of oil per day from the ocean floor. Although Mr. Hayward initially talked of taking full responsibility for this massive leak, his behavior, of which he seemed completely unaware, showed him instead as a self-absorbed dilettante, unconcerned about the economic, ecological, and human costs of this widespread pollution, and more perturbed by the inconvenience this event caused to his own life.

Consider the quotes attributed to him; do these sound like the words of a contrite, sad person?

"We made a few little mistakes early on" (Webb, May 2010).
"We're sorry for the massive disruption it's caused to their lives," but
then adding: "There's no one who wants this thing over more than
I do . . . I'd like my life back!" (Durando, June 2010).

These comments added to the popular view of Hayward as self-preoccupied and unmoved by the damages caused to others. The fact that he also took time off from overseeing this disaster to attend a yacht race in which a boat he co-owned participated, while the Gulf oil spill continued, only highlighted him as a self-centered elitist, more concerned with his own entertainment and pleasures than about the very real economic and ecological damages caused by the spill on his watch.

In the end, Hayward lost his job as CEO, in part because he was either oblivious to or unconcerned about the image he presented to the public as a business leader more akin to Nero fiddling while Rome burned than to a man with ethics, responsibility, and genuine concern for the welfare of others as exemplified by the spokesperson of Johnson & Johnson.

● Expression of Authentic and Congruent Emotions

The figure of Jim Burke, the former CEO of Johnson & Johnson, talking about and showing his concern and upset over this tragedy had a powerful impact on television viewers, as did his immediate recall of all Tylenol products. This example doesn't just speak to the importance of self-awareness of emotions, but also illustrates the dramatic impact that receiving authentic and congruent emotional messages—his words and his tearfulness—had on the public.

It's important to remember that emotions are expressed verbally (words) and nonverbally (tone of voice, gestures, eye contact, body language). In most cases, in our day-to-day interactions our words and our expressions are in sync. When we are honest about our thinking and feeling, our gestures and expressions are congruent, or all going in the same direction. It is when our communications are out of sync that things tend to go wrong.

● Expression of Noncongruent Emotions

Can you recall a time when you were talking with a friend about something personal and the person was constantly glancing at her cell phone throughout the discussion? What was the impact on you? You probably felt that your friend was treating you as if you and your concerns were unimportant, while simultaneously you felt angry at your friend. Actions speak louder than words, particularly when there's a lack of congruity between them.

The importance of expressing emotions that are in sync with your words is captured in the vignette of the teacher who stated in the first week of class: "From now on, you are all adults and I will treat you as adults. I welcome your opinions and will value your comments. This school is about free exchange of ideas. If you want a good grade in this course, you will learn to discuss your opinions." Sounds great, right? But the teacher delivered these words with folded arms, a slight grimace, and a fixed stare at the wall. Although the words may portray enthusiasm for discussion, the nonverbal cues express something quite different. Which would you pay more attention to?

We often encounter people who are incongruent in their two forms of expression, letting the nonverbal show but not the verbal (for example, slamming the door when you're frustrated at someone but not talking about your feelings) or we may express our feelings verbally but our words (for example, "I'm so glad to see you") are contradicted by our nonverbal expression. A person may say something like, "Oh, it's so nice to see you," yet his face looks like he just sucked on a very sour lemon.

Some people have discomfort with verbally expressing positive ("I love you") or negative ("I'm mad at you") emotions. This, of course, can take a toll on relationships. If you are one of those people, those close to you may never really know where you stand. When that happens, they tend to second guess what you feel and think and look for any nonverbal cue they can find. Although nonverbal cues are typically stronger and more memorable, no one wants to be in a relationship with someone who expresses emotions *only* nonverbally, such as withdrawing when angry or giving a gift to express love. If you can never express your feelings verbally, that person you really wanted to have a romantic relationship with may start to think that you really don't care about him or her. You may assume that your nonverbal cues are enough, but that can be tricky. Your signals don't seem to match your words, which calls into question your commitment or depth of feelings.

Another problem is that we can express negative emotions inappropriately through criticism or contempt of the other person. Dr. John Gottman, a marital therapy researcher, has spent many years studying the ingredients of good and bad marital relationships. He is able to predict the success of a marital relationship after observing a relatively short interaction between partners discussing a contentious issue. He has identified what he calls the "4 Horsemen" that help distinguish the good from the bad. Gottman's research (Gottman, 1994) has shown that divorce or relationship dissolution is best predicted by harmful patterns of verbal or nonverbal emotional expression (criticism, contempt, defensiveness, and stonewalling) rather than the amount of conflict a couple has. In these cases, very strong nonverbal cues—such as rolling one's eyes, loud sighing, or throwing hands up in disgust—undercut the ability to work through problems and challenges. The nonverbal cues are so strong and so harmful that words are no longer processed effectively.

● Do Males Express Their Emotions Enough?

There has been a lot of discussion over whether or not males should express their emotions in public. For example, some claim it is too wimpy or feminine and therefore inappropriate for males to publically emote. In fact, the subject hit the media blogs and airwaves when Bubba Watson won the 2012 Masters Golf tournament. After winning the golf classic, Bubba openly and publicly started sobbing.

Immediately afterward, NBC TV talk-show hosts Kathie Lee Gifford and Hoda Kotb weighed in on the subject of male public weeping.

"You gotta love a man who is that comfortable with his emotions," said Kathie Lee Gifford.

But then she qualified the statement, suggesting that it's okay to break down in front of a lot of people only if you've just won a huge golf tournament or lost someone close to you. Hoda responded that she thought it weird when men cry a lot during movies, and Gifford agreed that guys who blubber all the time should "go home to Mommy and get a shrink." Well, there are no set rules on males expressing their emotions, but clearly, being seen as overemotional or showing too much emotion can lead to criticism from some people.

Two other cases of public crying by male athletes are also notable. Wayne Gretzky, the hockey legend, cried at a press conference when he announced his trade to the Los Angeles Kings from the Edmonton Oilers. Champion tennis player Roger Federer cried after losing the Australian Open in 2009.

Evolutionary biologists make the case that crying is a highly evolved behavior that emotionally bonds people to you. After all, that's what infants use to call others to help them in times of need. Bubba, after his crying spell, was hugged first by his caddy and then by his mother. And he likely received symbolic hugs from the millions of television viewers who had witnessed the event. In Bubba's case, not letting his tears flow would be like bottling up emotional toxins.

● A Note About Anger

Anger is a tricky emotion. Many times we may think we're angry when we're actually experiencing a completely different feeling. Consider the following examples of anger:

○ Kristie is a star on the basketball team. In a game against the rival school, she made a bad play, and the coach started yelling at her from the sidelines. During the time-out, the coach got very close and continued to yell. Her team won the game, but Kristie was fuming mad. She spent the rest of the evening venting about the coach to her friends.

○ Then there's Shawn, who loves to go fishing with his dad. A lake in their hometown had just been stocked with fish, and Shawn and his dad made plans to go fishing Friday night at dusk. Around 7 PM, Shawn's dad called him to report that there was a big project at work he wanted to get done before he left so that he wouldn't think about it all weekend. "We can go fishing tomorrow morning," his dad said.

"No, we can't. I have to take the SAT then," Shawn replied.

"Oh. Well, how about tomorrow night?"

And so it went. Shawn's weekend was full, and his dad could have done that project later.

"Just forget it, Dad," Shawn said with irritation.

○ Now consider the story of twins Elise and Eleanor. They've always been good at doing things separately with other friends and not feeling like they always had to be together. So when Elise received an invitation to go with her best friend Katrina, to her family's beach home with four other girls for a week, she accepted. But when she told Eleanor about the planned beach trip, Eleanor yelled at Elise, "Why didn't you ask if I could go? I'm friends with Katrina too. And you know how much I love the beach!"

On the surface, each of these people seems to be angry. But there's probably another emotion driving their responses. Reread the scenarios and see if you can identify it.

Kristie, our basketball star, could have been experiencing fear or anxiety. Having a really angry person get close to us and scream certainly induces fear in most of us. Even if Kristie knew the coach would not touch her, she could have also been anxious about making such a big mistake and getting taken out of such an important game. And she's probably embarrassed too.

What was Shawn feeling? Most likely, he felt disappointment or sadness. He looked forward to these times with his dad, and it seemed that all too often, his dad's work came before time with Shawn.

And what about Eleanor? Put yourself in her place. Would you be hurt that your sister hadn't looked out for you? Embarrassed at not receiving your own invitation? Possibly even scared that your twin would develop relationships more important than the one the two of you shared?

Many of us find it okay to express anger but have a harder time with anxiety, hurt, disappointment, or embarrassment. For some reason, these emotions make some of us feel a lot more vulnerable. Rather than focusing on our true feelings and what triggered them, it's easier to get angry at the other person. So, part of authentic and healthy emotional expression involves first understanding all the different emotions that have been triggered.

Keep a log for a few days or weeks. Every time you get angry, question yourself about what other emotion may be lurking just beneath the surface. Try to address that emotion first; when you do, typically the anger will dissipate pretty quickly.

Bottling up your feelings doesn't make them go away. Learning how to constructively and congruently express feelings—whether at home, school, or work—will add richness to your life.

Reflection Questions

If you want to be effective at emotional expression, ask yourself these three questions:

1. Do my words and behaviors match?
2. Am I comfortable expressing my emotions with words?
3. Do I effectively express my emotions nonverbally?

If you can answer yes to all three questions, you're on the way to more successful relationships.

Consult *The Student EQ Edge: Student Workbook* to find exercises that will help you understand and develop your emotional expression skills.

CHAPTER 7

Independence

Few is the number who think with their own
minds and feel with their own hearts.
　—Albert Einstein
Your child will be better prepared to tackle the bumps on the road
of life if he has been given the gift of guided independence.
　—Jacqueline McTaggert

Definition: "Independence is the ability to be self-directed and free from emotional dependency on others. Decision making, planning, and daily tasks are completed autonomously. Independent people are self-reliant in planning and making important decisions; however, highly independent individuals may seek and consider the opinions of others before making the best decision. Seeking consultation or advice and gathering information are not signs of dependency. Independence is the ability to function autonomously without protection and support: independent people avoid clinging to others to satisfy their emotional needs" (Multi-Health Systems, 2011, p. 5).

● Can You Help Me?

Sam was a friendly enough person. He was in his second year of college and had a large circle of acquaintances. He missed classes and constantly relied on others for their notes, but he managed to scrape by. He would become a close enough friend with someone for as long as he could use him or her to help him get through whatever course they were in together. He couldn't even study alone. Somehow, he was able to manipulate others well enough to get their notes and receive their help with assignments and essays. He even had people walk him through material he had to learn for tests and exams.

Sam is a perfect example of a leech or mooch. He was completely dependent on others to get him through his academics. When he was in high school, his parents, along with an endless string of tutors, got him through his assignments. No one had ever taught Sam study skills or had ever allowed him to be responsible for his own performance. Now he was terrified of being left on his own for even the simplest assignment.

How will Sam survive in the real world of work—should he ever be responsible enough to get his own job? What can be done to help Sam become more independent, more responsible for his own behavior? It will be difficult for someone like Sam to change until his back is up against the wall.

● The Buck Stops with You

Let's redefine independence as the ability to stand on your own two feet (which is why it's tied to assertiveness) and to acknowledge that the buck stops with you. It means taking charge of your own life, being your own person, and seeking your own direction. People who crave acceptance at any cost and are scared stiff of giving the slightest offense have grave difficulty exercising independence. You must be prepared to adopt a course of action, having first justified it in your own mind, and then to deal with the possibility that other people will disagree with you. So be it. You must also respect their need for independence and give them the same amount of rope.

Obviously, independent action involves a degree of risk, and sometimes you'll do or say the wrong thing. Learn from these situations, forgive yourself for them, and don't let them hinder you in the future. Usually, although you may not believe it at the time, you really don't have all that much to lose. Weigh the alternatives carefully, looking at the benefits of each possible response. Then consider the downside—the very worst that could happen if you follow through with each of your choices. To your surprise, you may find that only in relatively few cases will the world come crashing to a halt if you aren't 100-percent correct.

That's the point—no one is right 100 percent of the time. If a baseball player hits three balls out of 10, he's a hero. Some of history's most successful and honored men and women made huge, seemingly irreparable mistakes somewhere along the line, or went up countless blind alleys in pursuit of a goal. Thomas Edison once confessed that he'd devised 3,000 different conceptual models in connection with the electric light. Only one panned out, but it made up for all the rest of them. Think of the world leaders and prominent personalities who've rebounded from apparent failure (and in some cases downright disgrace) to achieve great things. Making mistakes is profoundly human, as everyone knows. Very few people will remember your missteps along the way. Instead, they'll applaud your achievements.

● Be Decisive

Jing-Wei sailed through high school and college, gaining high marks in every subject. Still, she always seemed to be in need of reassurance, and she never expressed confidence in her abilities. She socialized with only a small circle of friends. She was attractive and fashionable, but on close inspection her style was always a matter of following the crowd, rather than making a statement of her own taste.

With her undergraduate degree in hand, Jing-Wei applied to and was accepted at a prestigious law school. But before she began, she found herself growing increasingly disenchanted with law school. She therefore decided to first work for a year, hoping this would help her determine a direction in life. Having put her finances in order, she could then decide whether to pursue law or find a new career. She got a job as a customer service representative with a mail-order company.

Two months later, Jing-Wei knew more about the firm's products than some of her coworkers who'd been there for years. She had an easy manner and was well equipped to deal with customers' questions and complaints. But Jing-Wei also had a problem. She was terminally unsure of herself. She was entirely aware of the firm's policies regarding returns and warranty service, but after obtaining all the facts she needed, she was unable to move on a complaint until she had checked with someone else. Often she checked with everyone in sight, which created tension throughout the office. Her coworkers felt that she didn't trust their viewpoints, and they responded by gradually becoming less willing to help her out.

Part of this sorry state of affairs was Jing-Wei's lack of confidence. Another part was her need to protect herself from blame, in case she made the wrong decision. As a result, she wound up with a long list of impatient customers who complained to her supervisor, who then had to investigate each claim. Whenever her superior confronted her, Jing-Wei would instantly go on the defensive. Privately, she confided to her friends that the job was beneath her. Her refrain was constant: she'd been accepted by a prestigious law school, and all her coworkers were glorified clerks who had no right to criticize or question her.

Jing-Wei's behavior is an example of how high IQ can backfire if EQ isn't up to par. The ability to be independent is a skill that affects both our personal life and our value to an employer. The less supervision an employee requires, the more productive he or she can be.

The Many Facets of Independence

In her senior year, 18-year-old Sophie convinced her parents to let her go with friends on a spring break trip without a chaperone. She promised they would not party. A week before the trip, Sophie asked her parents how much money they planned to give her for the trip. They told her that she would need to pay for the trip by herself. Sophie was furious. Her parents knew how much she was looking forward to this trip. How could they not pay for it?

Her parents explained if she was old enough to go by herself, she should also assume responsibility for paying for it. And Sophie had not asked for money when she presented the trip idea to her parents. Sophie had enough money for only her share of the room. The day of the trip, she raided her parents' pantry at home for food and packed a cooler full of things from the fridge.

But her friends wanted to go out to eat, so she constantly borrowed money from them with a promise to pay it back. By mid-week her friends were running out of money, so Sophie called her parents and begged them to add some money to her bank account. She promised to pay it back.

A day later, Sophie began running a fever. She felt nauseous and threw up a couple of times. One of her friends had gotten a stomach virus the previous week, and she told Sophie it would last only a day. Sophie was miserable lying around in the room while her friends went to the beach, so she called her mom. Sophie wanted her mom to talk with her the whole time her friends were at the beach, but her mom was at work so she could talk for only 10 minutes. After her mother hung up, Sophie spent the rest of the day talking on the phone to one friend after another until her friends returned from the beach three hours later.

Was Sophie right in depending on her parents to fund her trip? Or was she ready at this stage of her life to be responsible for financing her leisure expenses? How financially independent of your parents are you?

What about Sophie's dependence on talking to others to keep her entertained while her friends were at the beach? Some people are uncomfortable with alone time. They seem to be dependent on others and don't know how to manage their own time.

As you can see in these examples, independence can happen at different levels. You can be independent or dependent financially, emotionally, socially, or academically. How do you see yourself in each of these areas? Are you more independent in one or more areas than in others? Or do you think some people are just more independent overall? Think of things you can do to be more independent in your dependent areas.

● Pursue New Interests

Independence is also linked to self-regard—when you feel better about yourself, you are probably more willing to do things alone, and others respect you more. Making decisions and acting on them, then following through to deal with the consequences, is a sequence of skills that is important to success. The more you practice, the better you become, and the more your confidence will rise.

Keandra, an attractive and somewhat shy 20-year-old, had many acquaintances but few close friends, and she attended a college that— like so many others—was awash in cliques. Keandra floated around between groups. Her social life, to be frank, was going nowhere. No one really disliked her, but no one felt warmly enough toward her to invite her into their particular set. As well, just like Jing-Wei the service rep, Keandra hated to make decisions. By Thursday night, she'd be in a state of high anxiety about her weekend plans. She wasn't on anyone's party list and didn't know how to get herself included. And she certainly never took the lead to plan things.

Although Keandra might be considered shy or introverted, all she needed was an emotional kick start. She had no difficulty carrying on a conversation once it got under way. She had a good sense of humor, and she showed real concern for her friends. But she seemed to always be a follower, never taking the initiative. Even her friends recognized this. There was a pleading, almost desperate quality to her phone calls, which is why all the plan making frequently came to nothing. She'd wind up home alone because she was reluctant to go anywhere without someone to hold her hand.

One weekend when she was home visiting her family, her mother gently but persistently began to confront her on the issue. She urged

Keandra to stop waiting for her cell phone to ring and to stop insisting that one of her friends accompany her wherever she went. Instead, her mother said, she ought to do things on her own—at first, little things and without telling anyone—so as to lessen her anxiety. So Keandra started off, simply enough, with a solo trip to the shopping mall. She found it strangely liberating to be lost in the crowd, with no need to pay attention to what her friends might think. After a couple of visits, she realized that she was starting to notice things—new fashions, interesting people—that she overlooked when she went to the mall with her friends. These were duly reported to her friends, who began to wonder what they were missing.

From this promising beginning, Keandra followed a series of gradual steps, going to club meetings, farmers' markets, the local Starbucks, and used-clothing stores. To Keandra's surprise, her new activities were of interest to her friends, who started hanging around her more often. They wanted to know where she was going and what she was doing. She'd tell them, and ask if they'd like to come along. Were they interested? Of course they were; step by step she was becoming a more independent and therefore a more interesting person.

Remember, though, that true independence doesn't mean ignoring everyone else and charging off in your own direction. Never turning to others for help is just as bad as always doing so. If you have to prove your independence by making it a point of pride to reject sensible advice, you're in trouble. The idea is to be smart enough to consult a wide variety of sources, and selective enough to weigh the results and reach a decision that you find satisfactory.

● Making Your Decisions Your Own

As an editor for the school newspaper, Alex seemed to have a strong capacity for solving problems independently. He understood the difficulties and could develop and implement solutions and keep track of the outcomes. He had a very strong and close working relationship with Dhara, the senior editor to whom he reported, and, after two

years in this position, he knew how Dhara wanted problems identified and solved and the solutions implemented. Although he turned
to Dhara frequently for direction during his first two years, by his
third year Alex seemed to be functioning quite independently.

When Dhara graduated from college, Alex was a shoo-in for the
vacated senior editor role. And he acquired it easily. However, once
in this position, he seemed quite uncertain about decision making—
especially when it came to roadblocks and obstacles to the paper's
goals. He waffled. He could not take a stand or be decisive. He turned
to others, seemingly for input, yet on closer examination it seemed
that what he really wanted was for others to make decisions for him.
Despite mentoring on how to prioritize problems and a course on problem solving, Alex became increasingly uncertain and self-doubting.
Ultimately, he resigned.

What had happened? Alex did not function well independently. It
had taken him two years to become comfortable in his editor role, and
before he stopped turning to Dhara for direction, even during his third
year on the job, he was still highly dependent on Dhara, both implicitly
and covertly. That is, he was good at his job not because he was truly
independent—although he seemed so on the surface—but because he
had memorized Dhara's way of problem solving for his particular role.
The steps of brainstorming, solution seeking, and implementation were
not authentically his, but Dhara's. He mimicked her approach step by
step. It was not truly his own. It was not based on pondering the issues,
selecting what he thought was the best solution, or flexibly implementing it. It was simply a memorized template that he inflexibly followed.

In his new position of senior editor, with its new challenges,
different obstacles, unfamiliar solutions, and increased routes of
implementation—and without Dhara to give him a template—Alex's
underlying dependency emerged in full force. Unable to stand on his
own two feet, worried about making errors, insecure about his own
abilities, Alex became increasingly anxious and paralyzed. The mentoring courses he was offered missed the point: they did not acknowledge or help him deal with his underlying dependency.

This vignette illustrates how some people appear to be independent, as long as they have someone on the sidelines who allows them to feel secure, but once they are really on their own, knowing that the buck stops with them and that it is up to them to make the final decision, these individuals' true colors—their underlying and powerful dependency—emerge. This vignette also speaks to the importance of leaders paying attention to and scanning for clues as to whether an individual is truly independent or only looks that way under special situations. If Alex's superiors had paid more attention to the amount of time it took him to settle into his previous editor position, had noticed the very close working relationship he had with Dhara, and had explored whether his seemingly independent style was more a reflection of his memorizing and inflexibly applying Dhara's ways of doing things, they might not have been so quick to promote Alex to a position that called for the independence he did not truly have.

Making your own decisions is especially valuable in resisting peer pressure. Are you independent enough to say no to unwise or illegal behavior? Are you willing to call a taxi rather than ride with someone who has had too much to drink? Can you resist the pressure to take that weekend trip with your friends when you really don't want to go? Although we all succumb to some level of pressure from others, can we, when it really counts, stand by ourselves if need be?

● Can You Be Too Independent?

It's worth pointing out that research with college students has found that high independence can be negatively related to student success in college (Mann and Kanoy, 2010). That's because those students did not ask for help even when they needed it, did not use available resources on campus, and tried to navigate all of the challenges of college relying too much on just themselves. So one key to successful independence is knowing when to ask for help because you genuinely need it and when to be comfortable operating free of others' approval or reassurance.

The capacity to be independent—to be self-directed in your thinking and actions—is another vital component of success. At its core, independence reflects a pervasive sense of autonomy: the ability to pursue your own thinking and go after your own self-determined goals. If you cannot define what you want, cannot figure out how to get there, or cannot be definitive, you will be hampered in your pursuit of success. People who lack independence tend to be clingy and needy. They chronically seek protection and support from others, which undermines their ability to determine what they want and to be confident enough to pursue it.

Reflection Questions

1. Do you consider yourself an independent person? In what areas of your life are you the most independent—academic, emotional, social, or financial?

2. Who do you lean on when you need advice about school? career? life?

3. Describe a time when you did not follow advice. How did you feel striking out on your own?

4. Do you think of yourself as a leader or a follower?

Consult *The Student EQ Edge: Student Workbook* for more exercises that will help you develop independence.

Assertiveness

CHAPTER 8

No person is your friend who demands your
silence, or denies your right to grow.
—Alice Walker

Don't tell me what you're not, or what you're against! Tell me who
you are and what you stand for.
—Mario Cortes

Definition: "Assertiveness involves communicating feelings, beliefs, and thoughts openly, and defending personal rights and values in a socially acceptable, non-offensive, and non-destructive manner. Assertiveness is a complex and essential component of emotional intelligence that transcends one's ability to express emotion. Assertiveness includes the expression of feelings, but further encompasses one's ability to openly express thoughts, beliefs, and ideas, even in the face of adversity, and to defend and stand up for one's personal rights" (Multi-Health Systems, 2011, p. 4).

● Speak Up or Get Passed Over

Kristen was a brilliant young marketing assistant at a large advertising agency. She had excelled in all her subjects throughout high school and college, always placing in the top 10 percent of her class. One of her pet peeves, however, was that class participation contributed to the grade in some of her courses. She tended to take courses that relied on tests, essays, exams, and various assignments that excluded presentations or class participation.

She had a quick wit and a keen eye for details. She was devastated, however, when after her first year at a prominent New York City ad agency she was not among the few who were fast-tracked for promotions. Although she worked hard and her work was of high quality, others always saw her as being behind the scenes.

In meetings, she listened carefully but did not actively contribute to discussions. Even when great ideas came to her, she withheld them for later, when she could quietly think them through and then enter them into her computer. But she noticed that the people who did speak up at these meetings, whether their comments and ideas were well grounded or not, were the ones who were quickly moving up in the company. Finally, when she realized that her unwillingness to speak up was holding her back, Kristen decided to enroll in an assertiveness-training seminar.

Kristen learned to rehearse the assertiveness skills she needed to present her views to a group. The first issue was her anxiety. She learned to take several slow breaths, which allowed her to focus. She visualized scenarios, so she could practice entering into conversations. She rehearsed different approaches, and prepared, as much as possible, ways to deal with any opposition to her views.

A few weeks after the seminar finished, Kristen sat in on a strategy meeting to decide whether a TV commercial script under review for one of their largest clients was suitably focused on the client's key message to consumers. Kristen knew right away that the message wasn't geared to the young audience the client was aiming at.

Waiting for an appropriate break in the discussion, Kristen intervened: "Can we just step back a bit? If you don't mind, I just want to mention something that the client stressed at our first development meeting. They wanted a campaign that spoke directly to youth. This piece goes over the heads of our key audience."

She went on to offer two specific examples of how they were missing their objective. There were some people with objections to her perspective, but taking their criticisms into account, and presenting her well-thought-out case with just the right combination of reason and emotion, she convinced the team she was right. She then went on to spell out what elements the new campaign should have to meet the client's needs.

Speaking out in a work-group setting was not easy for Kristen. Not doing so before had hindered her ability to be recognized for her work. Now, after a year and a half at her job, she was finally being noticed. She started getting the recognition she deserved, and she soon got the promotion she desired. Her new assertiveness played a big role in Kristen's increased success at her job. Moreover, she was better able to deal with group situations in other areas of her life.

● What Is Meant by Assertiveness?

Assertiveness is much misunderstood. That's ironic because assertiveness involves the ability to communicate clearly, specifically, and unambiguously, while at the same time being sensitive to the needs of others and their responses in a particular encounter. So assertiveness is all about "being understood."

One very interesting study we released back in 1999 garnered a fair degree of media attention. We'd found, based on the administration of the EQ-i to 4,000 people, that Americans scored significantly higher in emotional intelligence than did Canadians in several areas, notably reality testing, happiness, optimism, and assertiveness. The lower Canadian scores on this last scale reflected the fact that the Canadians surveyed were more reticent, more apt to take the overly polite way out, less able to express what they wanted and why. But the commentary was startling. When one of us (Steven) was interviewed on radio and TV talk shows, many of the hosts and most of the callers took us to task for suggesting that Canadians ought to be "more like" our neighbors to the south. The last thing in the world they wanted, they said (at considerable length), was to be as "loud" and "pushy" as they perceived Americans to be (Stein, 1999a).

Well, that's not what we mean by assertiveness. According to our original findings, Canadians do tend to be more passive and—a key word—*indirect* in their dealings with others. Americans are more to the point, more no-nonsense. But the distinction was one of degree, not kind. In fact, there's no single way of being assertive. Within the definition of assertiveness, there is latitude for interpretation. Each of us has our own style. We can be humorous or serious, concise or eloquent. We aren't all the same, and the idea isn't to use the concept of emotional intelligence as a whole to turn Americans and Canadians or anybody else into clones.

The ability to act with a proper degree of assertiveness breaks down three ways. First, you must have sufficient self-awareness to be able to recognize feelings before you express them. Second, you must have sufficient impulse control and emotional expression to express disapproval and even anger (if a degree of anger is called for) without letting it escalate into fury, and to express a range of desires in the appropriate way, with the appropriate intensity. Finally, you must stand up for your own rights, your own causes and deeply held beliefs. This means being able to disagree with others without resorting to emotional sabotage or subterfuge, and being able to walk a fine line, defending your wishes while at the same time respecting others' points of view and being sensitive to others' needs.

This often results in a constructive compromise—what's known as a "win-win" situation. Because the bonds of a relationship are strengthened when both parties show consideration, both are far more likely to walk away from the encounter with their needs at least partially fulfilled.

By the way, as part of our work on the EQ-i 2.0 we reexamined the differences in emotional intelligence between Americans and Canadians. This time, based on testing over 6,000 people in 2010, we found there have been changes since our original data collection in 1997. Canadians are now pretty much equivalent to their American neighbors. There were a few minor distinctions. Americans have slightly higher impulse control than Canadians, but Canadians are a bit more flexible. Canadians also seem to be a tad higher in stress management (Stein, 2010).

● Assertiveness Is Not Aggression

A very common mistake is to confuse assertive behavior with aggressive conduct. Indeed, this is why some people shy away from the very idea of assertiveness. To them, it equals aggression; they fear that they'll hurt others, or that they won't seem likeable. This is not true. Assertiveness is characterized by a clear statement of one's beliefs and/or feelings, accompanied by a consideration of the thoughts and feelings of others. Without this consideration, certainly, assertiveness becomes aggression, as can be seen in some of the following examples. Let's take a look at an appropriate level of assertiveness first.

Sergio and Mark were assigned to be roommates at college. Sergio is becoming frustrated by the fact that Mark is staying up late to play computer games and is interfering with his sleep.

Sergio: Hey Mark, I know you really like playing your video games, but the noise is keeping me awake, and I have an 8 o'clock class.

Mark: But I need to play the games to get me relaxed before bed.

Sergio: I know, but I don't think it's fair for you to keep me awake for two hours after I go to bed. Maybe you could play the games earlier or find another way to relax.

Mark: I don't know anything else I could do.

Sergio: What if you use my iPad? You could use my headphones, or surf the net or play games that don't make noise.

Mark: Okay, I'll give it a try.

This simple example provides an excellent illustration of assertiveness. Sergio is clear about his wishes: to have Mark make less noise when Sergio wants to sleep. He explains that he has to wake up early for a class. He recognizes that Mark needs time to relax before going to bed. He considerately addresses his concern by offering him an alternative—use his iPad so he can continue to play games, but more quietly.

But let's rewind this scenario to see what would happen if Sergio behaved aggressively rather than assertively. Although assertive people clearly articulate and defend their wishes or thoughts, they are also considerate of the other person's position and sensitive to the other person's feelings. The latter point distinguishes assertiveness from aggression. Aggressive people do not respect anyone else's viewpoint, nor are they considerate of the other person's needs or feelings, and their actions are intended to harm. They force their views or desires to be accepted through bullying, intimidation, and manipulation. Aggression leaves no room for compromise. Rather, it is one-sided: an unremitting expression of what the aggressive person wants and a simultaneous attempt to force others to acquiesce.

Sometimes aggression is easy to spot—the perpetrator just bulldozes ahead. But other times aggressors are strangely indirect in expressing their wishes, as if they need to get the lay of the land before coming out and saying what they mean. Often this leaves the other person feeling that aggressors have a hidden agenda. We know they're being rude, uncooperative, and domineering, but we aren't sure exactly what they're after. We sometimes refer to this as being *passive-aggressive*.

In either case, aggressive people offer little or nothing in return for the satisfaction of their agenda, hidden or otherwise. Over time, others react to them with mistrust and anger. They seek to retaliate by undermining the aggressor or by looking for ways to pay him or her back. Or, more commonly, they simply tune out and avoid any further interactions. As a result, aggressive people end up feeling isolated and alienated, without anyone in their corner and devoid of meaningful social support—all of which fuels their aggression or drives them toward even more aberrant behavior. So although aggression is *destructive* in both intent and action, assertiveness is *constructive* in both intent and action.

If Sergio were to behave aggressively, the interchange with Mark might unfold very differently:

Sergio: Hey Mark, how was class?
Mark: OK, but I'm pretty tired from taking that test.

Sergio: Yeah, I'm tired too because you keep me up so late at night playing those stupid video games.

Mark: Hey, that helps me relax.

Sergio: But what about my sleep?

Mark: Well, you should have told me that bothered you.

Sergio: I'm telling you now, and you don't seem to care. If you don't cut it out, I'm going to ask to switch rooms.

Mark: Go ahead, I don't care.

Sergio: OK, I'll also take all my computer stuff and sound system.

Even if Sergio eventually got his way through threats and bullying, he would have done so with a complete disregard for Mark's feelings. He started out in a friendly mode, likely catching Mark off guard. So by starting off friendly and seeming concerned about Mark's day, he felt he was being a caring and respectful roommate. Of course, that was just a ploy to soften Mark up for the hammer that was about to follow. Although Sergio won the battle, he will probably lose the war because his ongoing, relentless bullying and dismissal of Mark's needs will ultimately demoralize and alienate Mark and weaken any sense of collaboration or goodwill in their relationship.

● Using Assertiveness at School

Aggression is a very common and corrosive dynamic at school. Consider the following interaction between a student, Daniel, and his professor.

Daniel: Professor Ray, I don't understand how I could have made a C on that paper.

Professor: I expect papers to include a comprehensive literature review, your own critiques of the research, and your opinion about the topic as well as future directions for research. Additionally, to get a high mark the paper has to be submitted on time and the grammar has to be correct.

Daniel: But I didn't know that you were going to take off points for grammar, since this isn't an English class. You're not being fair.

Professor: Yes, grammar is important, even in a psychology class. It's part of good writing.

Daniel: Well, I just wish you had made clear that we could *lose* points for things like grammar. You never mentioned it, so how could I know.

Professor: The grading rubric was posted online with the other course materials.

Daniel: You should remind us to look there. I forgot about it.

Daniel had to accept his fate—and his grade. Daniel's aggressive behavior lost him any extra support or sympathy his professor might have for him in the future.

Let's see how this scenario might have played out had Daniel been assertive instead of aggressive:

Daniel: Professor Ray, I'd like to better understand my grade so I can do better on the next paper.

Professor: Well Daniel, it looks like you did a good job reviewing the literature and critiquing it. You also gave some interesting opinions on your topic. However, you handed your paper in late, and you made a number of grammatical mistakes, which, unfortunately, cost you some points.

Daniel: I didn't realize grammar mistakes counted.

Professor: The grading rubric was posted online. It clearly lists writing mechanics as part of the grade.

Daniel: I forgot that the rubrics were posted. I still don't like my grade, but at least I understand it better. Would you be willing to show me how to fix some of these errors I made?

Professor: Sure.

In this scenario Daniel still stands his ground, but he is less challenging and confrontational with his professor. He asks for and receives feedback on his performance, and he behaves less defensively about his grade. Although he may not be happy with the answer he gets, his relationship with his professor is still intact, and he has maintained positive feelings. He is more likely to get extra support from his professor in the future than if he had been aggressive.

This interchange left Daniel feeling quite positive, even though he still ended up with an undesirable grade on his paper. He feels good because he was clear about his concern and he feels he was listened to. He was not intimidating or demanding; rather, he invited his professor to be part of the solution—and not once did he use confrontation to intimidate him.

Overcoming Passiveness and Passive-Aggressive Behavior

Assertiveness is often characterized as a midpoint along a line drawn between passiveness and aggression. But that's not accurate. Passive people have difficulty expressing themselves to others. They bottle things up and avoid dealing with uncomfortable situations; they wait for others to come to them, for things to be handed to them on a platter. But because they don't or can't communicate what they want, others aren't likely to provide it or aid them in obtaining it. That is why they frequently miss out on many of life's opportunities, and why others may take advantage of them. Passive people often feel like the proverbial doormat, always being stepped on. Some just lie back and take it; others resent being taken advantage of but don't feel capable of changing their situation.

Others, though, are what's known as *passive-aggressive*. Instead of speaking out or confronting the issue in an honest way, they repress that anger. But only for a while. Then, usually when it's least called for, they lash out, at times subconsciously.

Passive aggression can manifest in a variety of ways. Sometimes it's as simple as not responding to requests or expectations, like the teenager who agrees, in his best Darth Vader voice, to take out the garbage "after the next commercial." Of course, the garbage trucks come and go and the teen remains on inactive duty in front of the TV, having "gotten back" at his mother for her constant "nagging."

Other times it can be more complicated, like getting back at a roommate for what is seen as a long history of injustices. Perhaps your roommate has been too strict about rules around your dorm room—like how messy your side of the room always is. Instead of reacting directly to her behavior, you choose instead to leave litter on the floor. When she starts seeing your messes, you know that will get her angry—and what better way to "get back" at her? This kind of thinking, however, is short-sighted. By leaving more of a mess, you only escalate the conflict and get more consumed with being right. Then your friends tend to get drawn into it and it takes on a life of its own, consuming way more of your time than it's worth.

What's really important here is feeling comfortable with expressing your needs or anger appropriately. Although not all people are easy to deal with, you'll need strategies to get their attention in a more positive way.

Passiveness and passive aggression are clearly long-standing patterns of behavior, and they're hard to break. In hopes of doing so, back in the mid-1950s, Dr. Albert Ellis developed his rational emotive behavior therapy (REBT) (Ellis, 1955), as described in Chapter 2. Several years before writing this book, one of us (Steven) had the opportunity to participate in the Associate Fellowship Program that Ellis runs at his New York Institute. One of the assignments included an exercise designed to help people overcome the passive or passive-aggressive form of assertiveness deficiency.

Each participant was asked to describe something that he or she was afraid to do in public—the only conditions being that the activity couldn't be illegal or unethical or lead to any real harm or danger. In fact, most of the activities involved baseless fears—the idea that, if the participant were to do the feared thing, other people would think the participant silly. The exercise demanded that each person carry out this very activity. One woman dreaded the idea of riding the subway and having people watch her. Her assignment was to not only board a train but also to shout out the name of each station as the train pulled in. At the end of the day she could easily have been hired as a conductor.

Another participant was a young man (we'll call him Stewart) who must have weighed at least 300 pounds and stood six foot five. He was a successful psychologist, but he too had a secret fear. To be precise, when he received food in a restaurant that was improperly cooked, he was incapable of reporting the problem to his waiter; he'd rather eat something raw or broiled past all recognition than ask to have it taken back. You can easily guess what his assignment was.

On Sunday afternoon, several of us accompanied Stewart to a nearby Chinese restaurant. The waiter stood about five feet tall, and weighed perhaps 125 pounds, but Stewart could scarcely bear to look at him. When the soup arrived, Stewart started wolfing it down, in the hope that he'd finish before the waiter returned. No such luck. Stewart was in obvious distress; his face was flushed and his hands were shaking. His anxiety, which we'd been on the verge of making fun of, was very real. At last, summoning up every ounce of courage he could muster, he asked in a voice barely louder than a whisper that the "too cold" hot and sour soup be returned. Of course, the waiter politely whisked the bowl away, and Stewart's body instantly relaxed. He looked as if a tremendous weight had been lifted from his shoulders—and he admitted that he felt that way too.

Stewart's experience demonstrates that it doesn't matter how big you are physically, or how much power you may wield in a given social interaction. The ability to assert yourself is a state of mind, as well as a skill that can be fine-tuned with practice.

● Indirect Assertiveness

At times, the impact that speaking up might have on others who are present at the interaction requires that we mute our assertiveness. Victoria had been invited to a party at a fraternity house. While the guys who were members talked about the benefits of their fraternity over many of the others, Victoria listened silently. They went on about how they attracted the best students as members, the lavishness of their parties, and how members supported each other, even in tough times.

Victoria had been concerned for some time about the restrictiveness of their membership, especially since there were no sororities on campus. After all, it was the 21st century, and times had changed significantly since the founding of the fraternity. Back then women hadn't been allowed to vote yet, nor had they been admitted to that university. So when there was a lull in the conversation, she gently asked, "What about your membership policies?"

"What about them?" Will asked, a bit puzzled.

"Well, how many female members do you have?" Victoria asked pleasantly.

"Sorry. We're not that advanced yet," Will replied with a frown.

Victoria had considered keeping silent about the issue. But it did bother her. She didn't expect to make any major changes; she just felt she had to be heard. She also didn't want to make any major waves or ruffle feathers, as she valued their friendship. She decided to voice her concerns, but in a manner that would get her point across without causing unnecessary embarrassment or tension at the party.

The party continued, and Victoria felt good about the stance she had taken. She knew she would have reproached herself later if she hadn't spoken out, and she was satisfied at having found a position midway between passive silence and more forceful assertiveness, which might have offended her friends.

Much has been made lately of the virtues of standing your ground, of gaining self-respect by refusing to let others trample on your legitimate feelings. Fair enough—but often the way we express this new confidence kicks off another set of difficulties in our relationships. Making your own views known or getting what you personally want forms only half of the picture. Focusing on that component alone can be aggressive. Bearing in mind the wishes of others while attempting to get your own wants met by legitimate means is assertive.

● The Benefits of Assertiveness

There's very little to be gained from being passive. Passive people fail to voice their wishes at all—or, if they try, they take refuge in an unclear and ambiguous manner. They tend to back down, cave in, and acquiesce to someone else's position. As a result, they feel constantly unhappy and defeated.

Passive-aggressive behavior does its perpetrator no good, either. It's like the stack of oily rags in the furnace room that sooner or later flares up in seemingly spontaneous combustion. People who behave in this way may seem to be pushovers, but they're prone to brooding and tend to nurture long-delayed revenge. Then they suddenly explode in ways that—because they've been bottling up their unhappiness for so long—are way out of proportion and unrelated to the events at hand.

Aggression dead-ends; it never succeeds for long. For one thing, the aggressive and anger-driven personality is under nonstop self-inflicted stress. This is a very unpleasant state of mind and body; it's terribly draining to be forever argumentative and looking for a fight. As well, you never know when someone bigger, louder, and pushier than you will come on the scene. Worse yet, you never know when your aggressive ways will catch up with you in deadly earnest. Several recent reviews have confirmed the significant role that hostility, anger, and aggressiveness play in predicting coronary heart disease (heart attacks) even when compared with stress, cholesterol level, nutrition, exercise, and other factors (Sirois & Burg, 2003; Smith, Glazer, Ruiz, & Gallo, 2004).

Assertiveness, however, delivers many benefits. It's really quite liberating, as many formerly passive personalities have found. It opens up many new possibilities and does indeed "win friends and influence people," bringing you into closer and more honest contact with those you meet. This is one of the key distinctions between assertiveness and aggression. When you're assertive, even in an unpleasant or uneasy situation, the other person feels respected and accepted, not put down. Behave aggressively, and he or she reacts defensively and angrily, tries to make an end run around you by achieving some unrelated effect, or walks away laden with unpleasant thoughts and feelings directed toward you. Being assertive means that you must constantly bear other people and their reactions in mind. Eye contact, body language, tone of voice, and choice of words are all important, along with a degree of tact that, if mastered, could get you into public relations in no time flat.

● Success: Achieving Your Goals

Success means achieving what you set out to attain. Assertive people are positioned to achieve their goals in part because they tell others what they want, what they believe in, or how they feel in a clear, unambiguous way, while considering and respecting other positions. And they stand their ground when others offer resistance. This combination of clearly articulating what they want and where they stand while being respectful of the needs of others increases the probability that they will obtain their wishes.

Success eludes passive people because they are often not clear in their own minds about what they want, and they certainly have difficulty expressing their wishes or needs clearly and unambiguously to others. So how can others give them what they want or aid them in obtaining it? Passive people also cave in, change their minds, or withdraw their requests at the slightest sign of resistance.

Aggressive people have trouble achieving their goals because although they might be clear about what they want or where they stand, they present their wishes and beliefs in ways that are disrespectful, inconsiderate, or belittling of others. As a result, those around aggressive people perceive them as destructive, self-centered, self-serving, or angry, so they either avoid them or agree to go along with them under pressure but ultimately withdraw support or sabotage them.

In contrast, if you can learn to recognize what you want, what you believe in, or how you feel, and you put this forth without beating around the bush (in other words, by being assertive), typically there is no reason why others will not give you what you want—or help you obtain it.

Reflection Questions

Think of a time when you were

1. Passive
2. Assertive
3. Aggressive
4. Passive-aggressive

Write down a brief description of each situation and how you behaved. Then analyze the various situations. Which situation turned out the best? Explain your reasoning.

For more practice building your assertiveness skills, consult *The Student EQ Edge: Student Workbook.*

The Interpersonal Realm

This realm of emotional intelligence concerns what are known as people skills. Those who function well in this area tend to be responsible and dependable. They understand, interact with, and relate well to others in a variety of situations. They inspire trust, and they function well as part of a team.

Figure Part 4 Interpersonal Skills and Emotional Intelligence

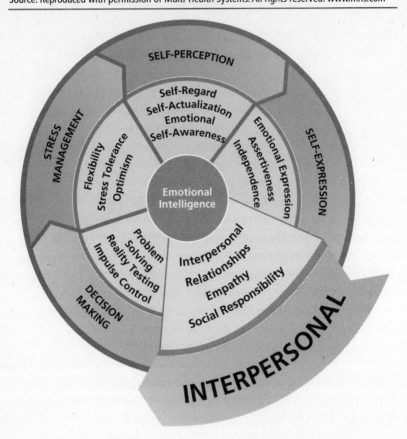

Interpersonal Relationships

CHAPTER 9

Consider the following. We humans are social beings. We come into the world as the result of others' actions. We survive here in dependence on others. Whether we like it or not, there is hardly a moment of our lives when we do not benefit from others' activities. For this reason it is hardly surprising that most of our happiness arises in the context of our relationships with others.
—Tenzin Gyatso, 14th Dalai Lama

Definition: "Interpersonal Relationships refers to the skill of developing and maintaining mutually satisfying relationships that are characterized by trust and compassion. Mutually satisfying relationships include social interchanges that are potentially meaningful, rewarding, and enjoyable. Among positive interpersonal relationship skills are the ability to connect with others by remaining open and by a willingness to both give and receive affection and intimacy; and the ability to remain at ease and comfortable in social situations. This emotional skill requires sensitivity toward others, the desire to establish meaningful relationships, and the ability to feel satisfied with relationships" (Multi-Health Systems, 2011, p. 5).

● Too Much Fun or Too Serious?

Jose and Julio met as young men during their first week of dental school. Jose's two passions in life were getting to know others and having fun. He did reasonably well in his studies, but when it came time to graduate, he was bouncing around in the bottom half of the class. He didn't care because he had formed wonderful relationships and had learned enough to be a good dentist; he just didn't drive himself crazy with studying. One year he'd been elected class president, which had pleased him hugely. He was now, at age 45, overweight and quite bald, but he loved people, and they loved him in return.

Julio, on the other hand, was slim and fit, an absolute perfectionist who studied long and hard. This seemed to pay off; his grades were spectacular. In contrast to the gregarious Jose, he confined himself to a small group of like-minded peers. When other students needed help in their courses, he was considered the person most likely to know the answer to a difficult question. He was also considered the person most likely to succeed.

Both men completed their programs, married, and began to raise families. But their approaches to their work were as different as their personalities. Jose delighted in attending all sorts of dental profession functions and talking to fellow practitioners—just as he enjoyed talking to everyone who crossed his path. He therefore built up an enormously useful network of referral sources. As a result of this, his practice thrived from the very first day he opened his office door. Because his patients thought he was the best dentist they'd ever met, they were keen to recommend his services. Eventually Jose was elected president of a major dental association. He enjoyed his life and his work.

Not so for Julio, who struggled to get his practice off the ground. He didn't believe in marketing himself—indeed, he said the word with a contemptuous sneer. He avoided professional gatherings and did not socialize with other dentists. He knew that his work was of the highest quality, but he couldn't bring himself to advertise the fact. He sent lengthy and detailed reports to dentists who referred patients to him—reports that stopped just short of criticizing their work. What he thought of as "small talk" evaded him; he had, in short, no chair-side manner. Nor, unlike Jose, could he initiate and cultivate a relationship.

As far as Jose was concerned, people were great. He was genuinely keen to learn more about them, and he remembered the minutest details of their lives. His enjoyment and interest were evident and infectious; people felt good around him. These factors marked the difference between his success and Julio's failure to fill his appointment ledger.

Jose's ability to build robust personal relationships with others, intertwined with his capacity to show interest in them and their concerns, was far more important in driving his success than his technical skills. In contrast, Julio's aloof and critical style alienated prospective referrers as well as patients, despite his Harvard post-graduate training and his impeccable technical skills. Jose never mastered how to form relationships, and thus his business and his personal life suffered.

● Key Skills for Better Relationships

In many occupations, good relationships with a wide range of other people are necessary and expected. They come with the territory; they're part of the job description. It's difficult to imagine a salesperson, a politician, a member of the clergy, a social worker, or a teacher who has poor interpersonal skills—but our research has shown that these skills are also advantageous in fields that don't immediately spring to mind as "people professions." Such seemingly unlikely groups as computer programmers, engineers, mechanics, accountants, scientists, and plumbers all achieved a higher rate of success if they had high EQs. The reason is simple: if large numbers of people in a given field are all more or less on par in terms of their professional competence, what could enable some of them to move ahead of the pack? Having read this far, you know that the answer is emotional intelligence.

Even for a student, interpersonal skills have their rewards. Think about having to connect with teammates on class projects or on sports teams. Or meeting new people, creating relationships, and finding people to hang out with; high school and college are a time of relationships. We meet people in school whom we may keep in touch with for a lifetime.

However, one of the downsides for some students has been an excess of interpersonal skills. These are students who spend so much of their time in social activities they barely have time for assignments, preparing for tests, and in more extreme cases, even showing up in class. There are many examples of students who fail to graduate because they treated their education more like a vacation—developing social relationships, having fun, and attending parties.

What are the secrets to initiating and maintaining good interpersonal relationships? As with every component of emotional intelligence, there are specific skills involved—and once again, the good news is that they can be learned, as proven by the noted psychologists Samuel Turner and Deborah Beidel, who've developed a program known as Social Effectiveness Training, designed to assist people who suffer to some degree from social anxiety (Beidel, Turner, & Morris, 2003). By understanding how some of us perform exceptionally well in social situations and by studying others who are experiencing social problems, they've uncovered several key skills that will, with practice, make a difference.

These skills may strike you as quite basic, verging on simplistic. But we've found that even the most mature and otherwise successful individuals are often unaware of these principles. When we sit down with them and work our way through a particular interaction that in some way proved detrimental to them, they're constantly surprised.

Basically, the Turner-Beidel program is divided into three parts. The first involves becoming aware of your social environment; it teaches you when, where, and why to begin and end a variety of interactions. The second part, interpersonal skills enhancement, covers verbal and nonverbal aspects of these interactions—how to be a good listener, how to switch topics, and so on. These parts can also be broken down to meeting a stranger, getting to know an acquaintance better, and becoming closer to someone you are already connected with.

The third part centers on presentation skills. If you're comfortable talking to a group of people, you have a far better chance to develop useful networks and cultivate long-lasting, meaningful relationships. The skills here involve learning how to build a speech, which usually has three parts—introduction, body, and closing. Basically, you tell them what you are going to tell them, then tell them, and then tell them what you told them.

Let's look more closely at some of these skills. If you want to initiate conversations with ease, you must pay attention to the social environment. Perhaps you want to introduce yourself to a stranger you happen to see at the bus stop every day, or be ready to respond when you bump into someone in one of your classes in a different setting (say, in a mall or at a theater). Perhaps the environment is more or less purposeful and structured—in a school club meeting, at the gym, or on Facebook—or a "forced confinement" situation such as riding in an elevator or standing in line.

How do you approach people in these diverse settings? First, you want to make sure you have their attention. Are they busy with an activity, or do they acknowledge your presence and smile?

If the situation matches the latter description, the easiest icebreaker with a stranger is simply to smile back and introduce yourself. You might want to comment on something you have in common (say, the upcoming big game with a rival school or classes you have in common).

Selecting a topic for conversation is more important. Three general areas can be regarded as "safe" to discuss: current events (but avoid politics or religion!), school, and shared interests. Most of us, if we're inclined to talk at all, have something to say about what's happening in the world or at school, or we can describe our hobbies.

Keeping the conversational ball rolling is easier if you start with tangibles—a person's car, or his or her choice in dorm room posters.

With strangers, the idea is to draw them out by asking questions that begin with specifics (how long have they been coming to wherever you happen to be) and move to more open-ended queries (what other places they have been to and which were their favorites).

Here's a typical situation that you can easily play out in your mind. You're waiting in line at a local store, and you notice that the person in front of you is someone you've seen before at school. He notices you and smiles—a cue that he's open to conversation. How will your conversation unfold? Imagine what you'd say about a number of topics, and how you'd shift gears if things started to go a bit flat. See how long you can keep this imaginary dialogue going and look toward ending it on a graceful note.

While you're doing this, be aware that a conversation flows more freely if you pay attention to the other person, remembering clearly what he or she has said. Sometimes when we meet someone, we're so concerned about our own issues—how we look, what sort of first impression we'll create, whether or not we'll say the right things— that the conversation dwindles into separate monologues, instead of establishing or increasing the bond between the two parties.

But you can practice paying attention to others, just as you can practice all the other components of emotional intelligence. In fact, this skill is closely tied to empathy (see Chapter 10). Think back now to several people you've recently met. What stands out most in your mind? Would you find it useful to keep brief notes about them and others you meet, so you'll be able to recall important details? You'd be surprised to know how much it means to people in this busy and impersonal world if you remember things about them, demonstrating that you value them and brought something away from your previous meetings.

Another important conversational skill is the ability to change topics smoothly and appropriately. Once again, be alert to cues that indicate that it's time to do so. Simple transitional phrases such as "come to think of it," or "that reminds me" may do the job. Be careful, though, to stick with a particular topic as long as it's mutually worthwhile. People who seem to jump around all over the conversational map are sometimes thought of as shallow or superficial.

Give and take is the key to building successful relationships. Individuals who only give are often experienced by others as lacking self-regard and as being too compliant. Such people may have difficulty being assertive, which fuels their "overgiving." On the other hand, individuals who only take from a relationship are ultimately experienced by others as selfish or bullying. They, too, have difficulties with assertiveness, confusing it with aggression (as explained in detail in Chapter 8). And both types of individuals—those who give too much and those who take too much—are generally unsuccessful in building solid relationships.

Students and working people—from all walks of life—intuitively know that relationships are built on reciprocity of give and take. They know one other crucial factor in building firm and resilient relationships: they listen more than they speak, and they listen deeply and intently to the other person. Of these people, others say, "She really took me seriously . . . I felt as if I were the only person in the whole room in whom she was truly interested . . . for those five minutes I felt valued, appreciated, taken seriously, and the center of her attention."

Why such responses? Authentic, active, deep listening forges strong relationships; when listened to in this manner, the speaker feels valued, attended to, and interesting. Too often we think that developing a relationship means that we have to talk a lot, impress others with our achievements, let the world know of our past accomplishments and future dreams. Not so. That behavior puts us at risk of being experienced as braggarts, interested only in ourselves. There's a familiar saying: "We are given two ears and one mouth as a message to listen at least twice as much as we talk!"

● Making and Keeping Friends

Good, supportive friends are among life's greatest rewards. They're the people we turn to in times of happiness and distress or simply to talk about life's daily grind. The give-and-take of these vital relationships pays off in small, almost imperceptible ways in the short term, but pays big dividends over time.

Where can you meet new friends? How can you establish new and interesting relationships? Well, there's no shortage of places to meet people—the library, a party, places of worship, and classes are great places to start. Fitness is good for both body and soul, and going to the gym to work out or to sports events such as football or basketball games attracts a wide cross-section of other students. You might enjoy looking into one of the many clubs or organizations at school or working with a political party. Or think about extracurricular activities like band, drama, or photography, or joining a fraternity or sorority.

But knowing where to meet people is only a first step. Next, you have to initiate contact, by recognizing the cues that suggest another person is interested in pursuing matters. Conversation leads to invitation, starting with smaller, noncommittal activities (sharing coffee precedes meeting for lunch; a successful lunch comes before an evening out together). Present the invitation in a way that will allow you to gauge the other person's interest, perhaps by suggesting that you might do something "sometime." A positive response means go; a neutral one means try again some other day.

Once you've established a relationship with someone, the next phase involves continued contact in person or by phone, text, or e-mail. This is important so that both parties know the other hasn't lost interest; by staying in touch, you give the new friendship the attention it needs to develop and grow.

There are very few, if any, successful hermits. Part of success is the ability to cultivate and develop meaningful relationships with others. Close interpersonal relationships add to the richness of life and provide valuable support in times of need. For example, social support has been found to be a significant variable in helping people cope with serious illnesses.

Taking an interest in others means asking them personal questions. Many people shy away from this because they think it may be seen as intrusive, but wrongly so—people love to talk about themselves. Most of the time, others feel wonderful when they sense that you take an active interest in what they are saying. Listen deeply and ask questions that facilitate their telling you even more.

Reflection Questions

1. What would others say about your skill in forming relationships with others?

2. What tips have you learned in this chapter that will help you form relationships with others?

3. Some of us keep others at a distance; others share too much too soon with others. Which style is generally more true of you? What can you do to make sure that you connect with others without scaring them away?

For some practical suggestions and exercises in this area, consult *The Student EQ Edge: Student Workbook.*

CHAPTER 10

Empathy

Seeing with the eyes of another, listening with the ears of another, and feeling with the heart of another.
  —Alfred Adler (1870–1937)

Definition: "Empathy is recognizing, understanding, and appreciating how other people feel. Empathy involves being able to articulate your understanding of another's perspective and behaving in a way that respects others' feelings. At the core of empathic behavior is being able to perceive and appreciate what, how, and why people feel the way they do—being able to emotionally 'read' other people—while demonstrating an interest in and concern for others" (Multi-Health Systems, 2011, p. 5).

● I'm Sorry, Coach

It was the day of a big game, and Casey, the captain of the team, was late getting to the locker room because his girlfriend's car had broken down, he'd unexpectedly had to pick her up, and then they'd gotten stuck in traffic behind an accident. When he rushed into the locker room, the coach yelled at him for setting a bad example as a captain and not caring enough about the big game. Here's how the encounter continued:

Casey: "Sorry, Coach. I know how important this game is to you and the team. It's important to me too, and I know it looks bad when I'm late."

Coach: "You're never late. Is everything okay?"

Casey: "Yeah, everything's fine. My girlfriend's car broke down on the way home from work, and she was stranded. I thought I had time to go get her and be here on time, but the traffic was horrible because of an accident."

Coach: "Okay, glad nothing's wrong. I'll let the team know why you were late."

Casey's empathic response—showing concern about his lateness and its effect on the team—helped to calm down the coach, and it shifted the adversarial tone of the coach's first response to a much more collaborative one. With this new collaborative tone, the coach was now willing to hear Casey's reason for being late, without perceiving it as an excuse. When he heard that Casey's girlfriend had needed help, his anger dissipated (well, mostly), and Casey was no longer in trouble.

What Empathy Is and What It Is Not

Empathy is essentially the ability to see the world from another person's perspective, the capacity to tune into what someone else may be thinking and feeling about a situation—regardless of how that view may differ from your own perception. It is an extremely powerful interpersonal tool. When you make an empathic statement, even in the midst of an otherwise tense or antagonistic encounter, you shift the balance. A contentious and uneasy interchange becomes a more collaborative alliance.

When a relationship is an effective collaboration, you maximize your ability to get what you want or need from the other party. After all, others are not going to give you what you desire if they feel misunderstood or attacked. In that case, you'd be viewed with mistrust or anger. But when others feel that you're in tune with them, they feel validated. The emotional bond between you strengthens, and the other person is more apt to work with, not against you.

For such a powerful tool, empathy is underused. There are three main misconceptions about empathy that prohibit many people from turning it to their advantage.

First, people sometimes confuse empathy with "being nice"—that is, making generally polite and pleasant statements. This is not what empathy means. For example, in the overenrolled class scenario described in Chapter 2, John started by telling the professor he knew that he must get a lot of student requests to overenroll in his class—acknowledging that this must be an annoying request for the professor. John was very accurately putting into words his perceptions of the professor's thoughts and feelings, but this is different from being nice. The professor didn't know—and didn't need to know—whether John was nice to everyone he met. He may well have been, and chances are he was, but it wasn't important to their interchange. As a result of John's empathic comments, the professor felt a sense of connection with him, and he became more interested in John's situation. Later, during class, when no one else spoke up, John again displayed empathy by answering the question the professor posed. He understood the professor's desire for student discussion and acted on that by speaking up.

Second, many people confuse empathy with sympathy, but the two are actually quite different. Basically, sympathy puts the speaker first, by putting into words our reactions to and feelings about another person's situation. In the overenrolled class scenario, John eventually expressed sympathy, apologizing for taking up the professor's time. But to have begun their conversation with that remark would have been a mistake on his part. Instead, he wisely made the professor's thoughts and feelings his paramount consideration. Empathic statements usually begin with the word "you"—as in, "You must be feeling or thinking [a certain way]." Sympathetic statements begin with "I" or "my," and reflect the speaker's perspective. For example, you might attempt to comfort a friend who was broken up with by a partner by saying, "I'm sorry he dumped you" or "I hate it that he didn't care more about you"—these are expressions of sympathy. They are welcome sentiments and wholly appropriate to certain situations. But they're not empathic, and they don't have the power to change relationships. Empathy—viewing the world from another's perspective—would sound more like, "You don't deserve to be treated this way. Sending you a text to break up with you is a lousy thing to do."

Third, some people believe that, by making an empathic statement, they'll seem to be agreeing with or approving of the other person's position, when in fact they may be opposed to it. Not so. Empathy is simply an acknowledgment that the other party holds that viewpoint. By expressing empathy, you recognize its existence without passing judgment on its validity.

Unfortunately, empathy often falls by the wayside because when we need it most, we're least open to using it—that is, when we're under stress, misunderstood, irritated, or defensive. At times like these, our comments automatically reflect our perspective. We're quick to argue our position, defend our behavior, and attack the other person's stance.

The other person, in turn, tends to react in exactly the same way. The result is a lockstep escalation of emotional push and counterpush, which of course ends up being counterproductive for all concerned.

● Put Emotions on Hold

Empathy requires that we sometimes control our initial reaction long enough to consider the other person's perspective. If you are prone to be short-tempered—as all of us are at one time or another—why not learn to take your emotional temperature before it climbs into the red? That reading can serve as a kind of radar or early-warning system that guides you through your interactions with others by offering signals that allow you to interact more effectively.

Let's imagine, for example, that your roommate comes back to the dorm late at night from a basketball game. He and his team just lost. He yells at you for having the window open and the room being too cold. Your first inclination is to respond in kind, snapping back at him. After all, it's not your fault they lost the game, and he shouldn't take it out on you. If you respond with something like, "Hey, don't yell at me. I didn't lose the game for you," this ups the ante, and he will explode in earnest.

Saying, instead, something like "You must be ticked off about losing the game" opens the door for a better interaction. Here you are empathically commenting on what you think might be his inner experience—one of being upset. Empathic comments such as this one allow the recipient to feel understood, and that feeling strengthens the sense of being on the same side.

Empathic comments also allow the recipient a chance to talk more about what is truly bothering him or her. In this example the roommate replies: "Of course I'm upset! We just lost the semi-finals." Another empathic comment, such as "That's terrible—you guys worked so hard," would further calm him down.

Instead of being reactive, slow down. Stop and think for a second. Your roommate's purpose in behaving this way isn't to get you upset. The wise approach on your part is to turn on your radar. Your anger serves as a warning to you. Something is bothering him, and it's important for you to hold back until you realize what's going on. You detect that he's upset not at you, but at himself and his team for losing. He's angry not at you, but at the other team for winning, and at himself and his team for not playing well. Now is the time for you to be understanding, to defuse the confrontation rather than give into your own anger and allow it to escalate.

There's a twin challenge here: (1) to use self-awareness to gauge our mounting irritation, contain our impulses and act sensibly in the face of provocation; and (2) to call on our empathic side in order to grasp the other person's position.

Returning to John and Brett, the students both trying to get in the overenrolled class: John succeeded in being empathic while trying to sign up for an overenrolled class, whereas Brett, his hostile fellow student, failed. Brett spoke exclusively from his own selfish point of view—railing on about his importance, his inconvenience, his threatened retaliation if the professor did not let him in the class. John, in contrast, put his reactions on hold and put into words how he believed the professor must have felt. The professor in turn felt relieved, validated, and understood, with the result that John was successful in getting into the class and Brett was locked out and his graduation delayed.

● Ask Excavating Questions

Of course, empathy (or any other component of emotional intelligence) isn't a magic wand. An encounter may not immediately take a turn for the better just because one party expresses empathy. In fact, the other person's anger may momentarily increase. Knowing that someone sees her point of view, she may feel more comfortable about freely venting displeasure or hurt feelings. As well, a long-standing relationship between two people may serve to muddy or complicate what kind of statements can productively be offered in an empathic way. If there's an atmosphere of distrust or competition, especially in the classroom, it can be even harder to call on your empathic abilities. For example, Charlie may tell Amaya that he understands how disappointing it must be for her to have gotten a C after studying so long and hard for their recent exam. Knowing that Charlie got an A with little effort may make his empathic response sound a bit disingenuous.

It's tempting to believe that if we know a person reasonably well and can recall his thoughts and feelings, as expressed in previous and vaguely similar encounters, we can make a fairly accurate guess as to what his feelings are likely to be in the present. But it's a mistake to assume too much about anyone, whether a stranger or a friend. That's why what we call *excavating questions* are an important prelude to expressions of empathy.

Excavating questions help you dig for the truth of the matter. They uncover another person's innermost emotions and thoughts by requiring that person to provide more information about herself— information that will enable you to formulate an empathic response. These questions can't be answered with a simple yes or no. They're personal and open-ended, though often outwardly nonspecific and general: "How did you feel (or what did you think) about this or that?" or

"What did you wish might happen?" And "What's upsetting you?" or an invitation to "Tell me more" are both empathetic as well.

To express empathy, you first need to be aware of the need to cue into what someone else is expressing. Then, you need to pay attention to what they express—thoughts, feelings, desires and expectations.

Consider this exchange between Greg—a 16-year-old with a problem on his mind—and his father, Warren.

Greg: I can't believe it's Monday, and the exam's tomorrow. I figured I could get in three hours of studying a night, but no way. I wish I was ready for it.

Warren: Well, if you'd organized your time and watched less TV, you wouldn't be in this mess.

Greg: Yeah, that's right. Climb all over me the day before the exam. That's just what I want to hear. And how do you know how much TV I watch? You're not around here often enough to know.

How do you think Greg felt in this instance—understood and soothed? What about the relationship between him and his father—is it one of alliance or contention? Clearly, Warren spoke from his own perspective in an entirely critical way, spurring Greg's angry and petulant response.

Now let's alter the dialogue slightly and see where it leads.

Greg: Here it is Monday, and I'm not ready for the exam tomorrow. I tried to get in three hours of study a night, but there was no way.

Warren: It won't do any good to worry now. It's too late; there's nothing you can do.

In this case, do you think Greg felt reassured or coldly dismissed? Does he think his father knows or cares about what he's going through? Do you predict a bright future for their relationship?

Now let's shift the dialogue again. This time, after Greg confesses his unease, Warren connects with his son's feelings and emotions and calls on his empathic skills.

Greg: Here it is Monday, and I'm not ready for the exam tomorrow. I tried to get in three hours of study a night, but there was no way.

Warren: Gee, that's too bad. Sounds like you're pretty worried about it. What do you think will happen?

Greg: I don't know. I'm not sure I'll pass if I bomb the exam. I thought I had allowed enough study time.

Warren: Is there anything I can do—anything you want to bounce off me between now and tomorrow?

Greg: Yeah, I need to go over those Spanish vocabulary words again. Would you call them out to me?

This time, Warren showed concern and a degree of empathic understanding of his son's situation ("Sounds like you're pretty worried about it"). That's exactly how Greg felt. Feeling that his father grasped and acknowledged his perspective, Greg was more open and willing to listen. Warren followed up by waiting for his son's response, and then he suggested—but didn't impose—a possible solution. Even if the last-minute cramming session doesn't work, the relationship is in far better shape.

● Focus on the Other's Subjective Perspective

What makes some people naturally empathic and others less so? One factor, as noted, is the ability to ask questions that take the interchange away from superficial concerns to focus on understanding more about the other's perspective, especially if it is different from your own view. As Stephen R. Covey (2004) explains in his book *The Seven Habits of Highly Effective People*, listening gives us information to work with. By listening, we can tune in to the other person rather than interpreting things through our own experiences or motivations.

This can be particularly difficult in a complex and long-standing relationship, as shown in the following conversation between Eric and his girlfriend Emma:

Eric: I didn't make the varsity hockey team.
Emma: Gosh, that's too bad.
Eric: [after a moment's sullen silence] You don't know what that's like.
Emma: It must feel awful. I know you had your heart set on it.
Eric: What do you know? You told me you couldn't care less about hockey.
Emma: Okay—but I've had lots of letdowns.
Eric: I'm not talking letdowns—I'm talking hockey.
Emma: Yes, I know, but—
Eric: No, you don't. You don't know, and you don't understand.

How is Emma doing here? At first glance, she's trying to do all the right stuff. She talks about how disappointed Eric must be, which seems to her an empathic comment. In fact, it is, but it doesn't go far enough. Eric's response shows that his girlfriend isn't homing in on what he's thinking and feeling.

Then Emma compounds her error by talking about herself and other unspecified disappointments in life, which in Eric's mind pale beside hockey. By doing so, she moves further away from seeing matters from her boyfriend's perspective.

Let's continue the dialogue and aim for a more satisfying conclusion. Now Emma tries to stifle her defensiveness and experience the moment from Eric's standpoint. She gets part of the way there and gets at least an inkling of what it might be like for an athletic guy who lives and breathes hockey to even think about discussing his woes with a girlfriend who wouldn't know the difference between the third period and the sixth inning.

Emma: I guess it's hard talking to me about hockey. You figure I don't know anything about it, and it means so much to you.

Eric: Yeah, well . . .

Emma: Maybe it doesn't get any easier when the other guys have girlfriends who do know about hockey and come to games to cheer them on.

Eric: Well, you show up once in a while, and you cheer, but we're not really together about it, are we? And we don't talk about it. And I don't think you understand how important it is.

At about this point, Emma might begin, again, to get a bit defensive. She knows perfectly well that Eric is out playing hockey five times a week, taking away from time they could be together. She also knows that she's paid for some of his equipment as birthday and holiday gifts. These are objective truths, but they're not the point of the conversation. On this score, if she raised these issues Emma would get low marks for empathy because empathy has relatively little to do with objective truth. Rather, it hinges on grasping the other's subjective truth—in this case, Emma's being able to tap into what Eric feels about his failure to make the team, and about her failure to grasp the significance of that event. The point isn't what Emma sees from her self-sacrificing perspective. The point is how an 18-year-old experiences his girlfriend and whether or not his girlfriend knows how vital hockey is to him. This is what Emma must focus on, so she changes tack.

Emma: Okay, maybe I don't know how important hockey is for you. What can I do now that would help?

Eric: Well, just talking like this helps.

Emma: I guess it's not much, but I can promise you I'll be at your school games. And maybe you and I could go and watch the Leafs play sometime. We've never done that, but I'd like it. How does that sound?

Eric: Sure. That would be okay.

Perhaps you're wondering what might have happened if Emma had made this offer earlier in the conversation, when Eric was really upset. Most likely it wouldn't have worked; Eric would have smelled an attempt to placate him and buy him off. He had to first feel understood, to know that his girlfriend could at least partially see the world from his perspective. That's why Emma's empathic comments were vital. She had to solidify a ruptured bond before Eric would value any sort of peace offering.

The power of empathy is that if you can grasp what another person is thinking and feeling—even if it differs wildly from your own perspective—and put your comprehension into words, the other person feels understood. This offsets any degree of tension that exists between the two of you and forges a strong bond of collaboration that helps you get what you want: to solve problems and create successful interpersonal relationships.

Do you take the time to listen to what others are telling you? Do you accurately understand what they're saying before you respond to them? Remember, in the early stages of a conversation, it's important to be a sort of neutral recording device. This is not the time to superimpose your own version of what they're telling you or to jump in with statements of your own feelings, thoughts, and opinions. Instead, keep asking excavating questions until you fully understand that other person's thoughts and feelings. Once that person knows you understand, the rest of the conversation will go much better.

Reflection Questions

1. How closely do you listen to what other people are saying?
2. Do you just listen to the words, or do you pay attention to their tone of voice, facial expression, and body language?
3. Next time you disagree with something someone has said, instead of arguing with them, think of some questions you could ask them about the issue. For example, "Why do you feel that way?" or "How strongly do you believe that?"

For some practice in developing empathy, consult *The Student EQ Edge: Student Workbook.*

CHAPTER 11

Social Responsibility

If a free society cannot help the many who are poor, it cannot save the few who are rich.
—President John F. Kennedy, 1961

Definition: "Social Responsibility is willingly contributing to society, to one's social groups, and generally to the welfare of others. Social Responsibility involves acting responsibly, having social consciousness, and showing concern for the greater community" (Multi-Health Systems, 2011, p. 5).

● Social Responsibility Is Caring and "Moral"

Following one of our presentations on emotional intelligence at an event sponsored by a major social service agency, we were approached by a local rabbi. His reaction was unusual; we'd never encountered it before. He began by talking about EQ's intrinsic morality. We asked him to explain what he meant.

"Cognitive intelligence is amoral," he said. "Anyone can have a high IQ—it's a matter of luck. Murderers, criminals, and Nazis could have all had high IQs. But by their deeds, they could not have had high EQs. Thus, EQ involves morality. I like that."

We do too. By definition, EQ includes social responsibility— a concern for the welfare of others, the ability to integrate yourself into the community at large, and a desire to further the betterment of your time and place. At a time when much of the so-called personal growth movement that started so promisingly can appear almost Machiavellian (designed primarily to achieve a particular, often self-absorbed and inward-looking end), it's refreshing to note that emotional intelligence refers to—indeed, it demands—a well-rounded and outward or other-looking approach to life.

The Queen of Hearts

Diana, Princess of Wales, fascinates the world even long after her death. What was it about her that spurred such a global outpouring of grief? Why did people feel a personal loss at her passing and feel so drawn to her while she lived? What did she do to transcend the bounds of mere celebrity?

The Diana phenomenon cannot be explained by her royal status. Barring the late Queen Mother, whom everyone liked, and perhaps Diana's son Prince William, few people really care deeply about the rest of the House of Windsor. Diana's beauty certainly played a part. Had she been plain—a latter-day Eleanor Roosevelt—we might not have followed her doings quite so ardently. But many other equally beautiful women and handsome men fail to command the same reaction.

Nor did Diana's riches account for her popularity. Other fabulously wealthy people go about their business almost unnoticed. Nor was Diana's appeal based wholly on social responsibility, as some have claimed. Yes, she engaged in tireless volunteer work—but so did Mother Teresa, who died at about the same time. The world mourned her passing as well, but not quite so intensely, considering that Mother Teresa in fact gave more of herself to her chosen causes than any other public figure of our time, devoting her entire life to the world's most downtrodden.

What was unique about Diana? We believe it was the powerful combination of social responsibility and empathy. She embraced causes that were dear to her heart, going far beyond what was expected of her or what her advisors considered prudent. It was apparent, in the way she talked to people and in the way that she promoted her chosen causes, that she genuinely cared about those on whose behalf she worked. That commitment is rare, particularly in the rich and famous. Diana could have made obligatory appearances, lending her name to various charities. Good would have come of this; the media would have paid attention. But she went beyond that, bringing emotion and real feeling wherever she went.

This sort of thing cannot be faked for long. Diana was no stranger to galas, but when she attended she made sure the spotlight shone on those in need. People whom she touched directly responded to her, even loved her. Those who witnessed her touching others loved her for doing so. She could empathize with the elderly, children, and the sick, particularly those in the terminal stages of AIDS. She had no fear of approaching them, or comforting those who had lost limbs to land mines. She would look into their eyes, listen to them, and speak to their concerns. She also showed her own vulnerability, something everyone could relate to. Despite her exalted position, she suffered through an unhappy marriage, anorexia nervosa, and the suffocating attentions of the British press. Her emotional sincerity, coupled with her social conscience, made her, as she wished, the Queen of Hearts.

Much of her goodwill seems to have been picked up by her son Prince William. Even before he turned 30, the prince was involved in numerous charities, including helping children in East Africa deal with malnourishment and hunger, doing community work in Chile, and supporting charities for disadvantaged youth.

On a visit to Canada he stopped over in Quebec, clearly the least popular place for any member of the British royal family to stay. French Canadians have long advocated doing away with the monarchy in Canada, which they see as a holdover from the days of British influence and rule. As well, the royal family has been perceived as aloof and out of touch with the modern realities of life.

While in Quebec, he toured a center for street kids in Quebec City. Together with his then new wife, Kate, the Duchess of Cambridge, they spent some time interacting with the youth and then joining some of them to play foosball. The troubled adolescents seemed impressed by the royals' ability to connect with them. This episode was captured by the media and not lost on the skeptical Quebecers. Following William's interaction with these youth, the reaction to the royal couple changed dramatically. Once-skeptical teenagers throughout Quebec suddenly became excited and enthusiastic fans of the prince and his bride.

Of course, William's mother, Diana, was not alone in her espousal of good works. Renowned film stars and rock musicians such as Angelina Jolie, Brad Pitt, Sandra Bullock, Bono, Celine Dion, and before them, Elizabeth Taylor, Jane Fonda, and Barbra Streisand have used their privileged positions to give something back. So do the many business people, including Bill Gates, who establish foundations, endow scholarships, and so forth. More good works are done behind the scenes than we know about, and more are always needed.

People are often aghast at the extraordinary salaries that professional athletes pull in—especially when compared to neurosurgeons, cancer specialists, firefighters, homicide investigators, and various high-risk professional groups. Some athletes, however, give back to worthy causes and use their celebrity to help others less fortunate. For example, tennis player Andre Agassi has contributed to numerous worthy causes aiding disadvantaged youth in Los Angeles. He has also supported Child Haven, a six-room classroom (renamed the Agassi Center for Education), the Andre Agassi Cottage for Medically Fragile Children (for children with serious illnesses), and the Andre Agassi Preparatory Academy in Las Vegas for at-risk youth, among other causes. Together with Mohammed Ali, Lance Armstrong, and other well-known athletes, Agassi helped found Athletes for Hope—a charitable organization that helps professional athletes get involved in charitable causes.

● Corporate Social Responsibility

Until quite recently, social responsibility had no place in the corporate boardrooms of the nation. Today, however, we see pulp and paper conglomerates pledging to preserve our forests. Oil companies tout the necessity of pristine oceans and reducing dependency on fossil fuels; brewers urge moderation and exhort us to intervene if our friends intend to drink and drive.

Social responsibility has always made good sense, but only recently has it begun to make good business sense as well—witness the courses in corporate ethics now prevalent at every major business school. Our research identified a watershed event in this evolution: the creation, in Britain, of a chain of cosmetic stores called the Body Shop. Its founding president, the late Anita Roddick, launched her products by advertising the fact that none was laboratory-tested on animals and announced that her business was dedicated to the pursuit of social and environmental change. At the time, most people didn't know about animal testing of such products. But the campaign proved a success—and since then, many firms from different industries have followed suit.

Examples of this new mind-set abound. For example, Christine Magee, owner-operator of the bedding chain Sleep Country Canada, donates customers' old but salvageable mattresses to suitable charities; the firm picks these up and delivers them at no cost. Jeffrey Swartz, a well-known speaker and CEO, often talks about his experience at Timberland, the boot, shoe, and outdoor clothing manufacturer. His presentation narrative describes the metamorphosis of his ascension to CEO of the family business. Starting out as a "spoiled rich kid," he was transformed through an experience of donating shoes to homeless people in Boston. As a result, he refocused the company's mission, with social responsibility as one of the pinnacles.

Swartz's company was singled out in *Business Ethics* magazine (Raths, 2006) as one of the top 100 American corporate citizens in 2006. Timberland jumped from number 74 to number 6 in just one year, fueled by one of the strongest employee volunteer programs in the country. Timberland encourages service by giving employees 40 hours of paid time annually to contribute to their communities during working hours. That same year Timberland also introduced the equivalent of a "nutritional label" on their shoebox, letting consumers know where the shoe was made, what environmental impact it incurred, and how communities were affected by Timberland's production practices.

You may not know that retaining current employees can save employers significant money—even in the millions for large employers. After Timberland became a caring, socially responsible company, staff retention went up significantly. People there now think of themselves as being part of an organization that makes the world a better place as opposed to just working at a shoe manufacturing company.

Women point out, correctly, that the glass ceiling still exists; that they may have come a long way, but there's still a long way to go. Although women make up only 2 percent of the bosses of America's largest corporations, at the time of this writing there are 15 women CEOs of Fortune 500 companies. These include Brenda Barnes (Sara Lee), Carol Bartz (Yahoo), Angela Braly (Wellpoint), Ursula Burns (Xerox), Lynn Eisenhans (Sunoco), Christina Gold (Western Union), Susan Ivey (Reynolds Aluminum), Ellen Kullman (DuPont), Irene Rosenfeld (Kraft Foods), and Indra Nooyi (PepsiCo). These women earned their positions in direct competition with the best and brightest men—but we believe that they were aided in their success equation by their empathy and social responsibility skills, two emotional intelligence areas in which women tend to score higher than men.

● Helping Others Helps Yourself

Empathy and social responsibility skills are part of a balanced package that's increasingly being recognized as desirable in today's business climate and in everyday life. More schools are requiring service learning or community service as part of the learning experience, and students are becoming more aware of the importance of helping those less fortunate than them through more involvement in volunteerism programs. In fact, surveys have shown an increase in student volunteerism. More than 3.3 million college students engaged in volunteer activities in 2005, up 20 percent from 2002, according to a report released by the Corporation for National and Community Service (Jaschik, 2006).

The best news about social responsibility is that because it's directed outward, it's perhaps the easiest component of emotional intelligence to change. As it changes, other skills tend to slipstream along behind it and fall into place.

Here's a typical example. A friend whom we'll call Alex experienced a bout of apathy, low energy, and general depression during his first year away from home at university. We suggested that he become a Big Brother to a fatherless boy who was giving his mom a hard time. Not only did the child's behavior improve beyond everyone's hopes, but the weekly outings helped remedy Alex's fit of the blues. His self-regard improved, he was better able to set priorities, and he entered with renewed enthusiasm into campus life.

Being socially responsible has a demonstrable upside: it tends to pay off big and sometimes unexpectedly for modest effort. By helping others, you often gain more meaning in your own life. By focusing on the more serious problems and dilemmas of others, you gain new perspective on your own. This alone can be therapeutic.

And it can pay off in more tangible ways as well. Confirmation of this comes from an unexpected source: two professors based at the universities of Oxford and Vienna, who set out to discover why people cooperate with each other, developed a mathematical model that pinpointed the benefits (Nowak & Sigmund, 2005). We're probably programmed to put up with our relatives (this is known as *kin selection*, or the selfish gene), and if two people believe that they'll meet again, they are likely to at least make a stab at behaving halfway decently to each other. The challenge, though, was to figure out what drives the good Samaritan—someone who helps another person with no expectation of being helped in return at some future date. The explanation seems to be that word of your good deed will spread. Others will hear about it, view you as a kindly and altruistic individual, and be far more likely to do you a good turn when the time comes.

You can think of social responsibility as a series of pebbles thrown into the water. The ripples can spread in unexpected ways. Let's look for a moment at Sam and Janet, two college students both trying to get into medical school. Both were conscientious students, but Sam tended to live and die by his schoolwork, staying up late and putting in too much extra time on assignments for his own good. Janet, in contrast, felt it important to involve herself in all sorts of community activities, acting as a Big Sister and volunteering at an AIDS clinic and at a mental health treatment center for emotionally disturbed youth.

In time, Sam began to feel he was getting stale at school— treading water by exerting himself more and more, but getting no further ahead. He felt, rightly, that he'd dedicated himself to his education, but began to suspect that his grades didn't reflect this contribution—in other words, his grades weren't much better than those of other students who studied more efficiently and in a more focused manner.

Meanwhile, Janet's activities were doing her a world of good. First and foremost, she felt that she was contributing to the betterment of society. Her personal involvement set her apart and gave her a real sense of fulfillment. As well, her outlook changed when it came to the inevitable aggravations at school and home—things that Sam, conversely, took hard. A minor setback in one of his projects was immediately magnified into a full-blown disaster. Janet saw things in a different way. She knew what real disaster looked like, having witnessed it firsthand in the lives of those she helped.

As well, word of Janet's activities got around. As a volunteer at the AIDS clinic, she met a number of doctors who were on faculty at the medical school that was her first choice in schools. They were impressed by her initiative and dedication. She also met some interns and faculty at the children's treatment center who provided her with valuable information and coaching for her application to med school. Janet benefited in a number of ways from her volunteering. She became more knowledgeable about real-world medical issues, networked with like-minded people, increased her self-confidence, met professionals who would provide references for her medical applications, and developed a more professional attitude.

● But What About Group Projects?

In addition to volunteer or philanthropic activities, social responsibility also encompasses your ability to contribute to your classmates, groups, teams, or campus clubs. Social responsibility involves everything from doing your fair share of the work on a team project, to honoring your residence hall rules about quiet hours, to reaching out to others on campus who may need help. Being a good team member on a group project does *not* mean that you volunteer to do all the work because you don't trust others. Nor does it mean that the group has to adopt your ideas. Sometimes an idea offered by others, even if it is your second or perhaps even third choice, may be the one idea that everyone else in the group supports enthusiastically. If the group's decision fulfills the project objective, well-developed social responsibility would require you to put your personal preferences aside and follow what the group supports. And well-developed social responsibility requires that you contribute your fair share to make the project a success, even if there is a group member who you know will do your part if you don't do it. Why not take advantage of such a situation where someone will do your work for you? Two reasons: first, you'll develop a habit of trying to determine how others can serve you rather than vice versa, and second, if others do your work for you, you won't learn very much or become prepared for the future.

A corollary of this is that excellent leaders can compromise and put their preference aside, when the group or team's decision is also appropriate. Doing so solidifies team spirit, is evidence of grounded flexibility, and demonstrates that good leaders are also good followers.

● Seinfeld and the Good Samaritan

Is the biblical story of the good Samaritan a bygone theological homily? Not at all. Just as individuals clearly derive important benefits when they exercise social responsibility, so society itself has moved toward viewing helping others as a necessary component of community life—not a luxury, an indulgence, or an extra.

You may be familiar with the once-popular TV show *Seinfeld*. This award-winning show, one of the longest-running series on television, was ostensibly about "nothing." The four main characters—Jerry, Elaine, George, and Kramer—were depicted as self-centered and self-absorbed. Each episode showed them navigating the idiosyncrasies of their lives.

The final episode of the Seinfeld television show had an interesting plotline even for a self-confessed show about nothing. In this program, Jerry and his friends fail to help a person whom they see being held up by a gunman, and they are promptly charged under a fictitious good Samaritan law (in reality, a *duty to rescue* law). While on trial, the self-absorbed quartet are forced to watch a parade of the moral misdemeanors they'd committed throughout the preceding seasons.

But a very real law of this type was passed in Israel in 1998. It obligates citizens to help another whose life is in danger or who faces great risk to safety or health, as long as that help can be reasonably safely given. France and Germany have enacted similar laws. These laws don't compel citizens to risk their own lives—say, to rush into a burning building in order to save the occupants—but they must at least summon the fire department. Our ancient and collective understanding demonstrates that these actions on behalf of the common good are the glue that binds our society together. A high level of social responsibility means a better, more fully functioning emotional intelligence.

Being successful is not a solo activity. Real success comes from being a valued, contributing member of a social group. Caring about and sharing with others, no matter how rich or poor you are, gives real meaning to your life and your success.

Reflection Questions

1. What activities have you thought about that could help others in need?

2. How do you currently contribute to a team, school group, or other group?

3. What skills do you have that a volunteer agency would desire?

4. How might helping others benefit you?

In *The Student EQ Edge: Student Workbook* you will find a number of exercises that can help you excel in this area.

The Decision-Making Realm

This realm of emotional intelligence concerns your ability to use your emotions in the best way that helps you solve problems and make optimal choices. Success in this area means that you can grasp problems and devise effective solutions, deal realistically with situations, and manage impulses that may disrupt effective decision making.

Figure Part 5 Decision Making and Emotional Intelligence

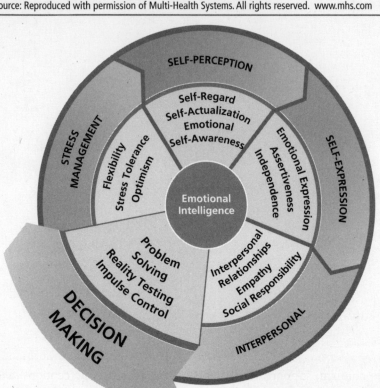

CHAPTER 12

Reality Testing

There are some people who live in a dream
world, and there are some who face reality; and
then there are those who turn one into the other.
—Douglas H. Everett

Definition: "Reality Testing is the capacity to remain objective by seeing things as they really are. This involves recognizing when emotions or personal bias can cause one to be less objective. Reality testing involves the active search for objective information to confirm, support, justify, and validate feelings, perceptions, and thoughts. Strong reality testing skills allow one to keep things in the proper perspective and experience things as they really are, without fantasizing, daydreaming, or attaching wants, desires, and ideals to a context. An important aspect of reality testing involves the ability to concentrate and remain focused when presented with emotionally evocative situations. In essence, reality testing is all about perception, clarity, and objectivity" (Multi-Health Systems, 2011, p. 6).

● Overreacting

As they passed in the hallway, Dinah smiled at Dr. Jenkins, the professor in her history class. Dr. Jenkins did not smile back. "Oh, my gosh," thought Dinah, "she doesn't like me. That's all I need. I must have done something to offend her. What am I going to do?

I hate it when people don't like me. She must have graded my term paper low."

Dinah's reality testing was compromised by unsubstantiated fears. She was unable to accurately and objectively judge her interaction with Dr. Jenkins; instead, she catastrophically interpreted it as confirmation of her worst fear: she was a person whom others didn't like and was likely to fail. Had she been more objective and analytical, and less haunted by a basic sense of insecurity, she might have recognized that Dr. Jenkins was not slighting her but was preoccupied with her own concerns.

● Be Objective

A police officer's job is not an easy one for any number of reasons. One of the major challenges is dealing with, say, three witnesses to a car crash, who commonly will produce three radically different versions of the event, leaving the cops to sort out what actually happened.

This same phenomenon unfolds daily in every human interchange. An old saying captures it well: there are three sides to everything— yours, mine, and the truth. When we experience an event, how close do we come to perceiving matters as they really unfolded, rather than coloring them with our fears, wishes, and prejudices and a host of defensive or offensive emotions? Discerning the difference between the way things are and the way we fear they are or hope they might be is the essence of reality testing.

How do we go about this necessary task? It involves a search for objective evidence that will guide our thoughts and perceptions. As well, reality testing is the capacity to read situations accurately, to size up what's going on. At its most sophisticated, it allows us to tap into a group's emotional currents and power relationships, the shifting political alliances and allegiances that swirl beneath the surface. Reality testing lets us tune in to a situation while keeping it in a broader and accurate perspective, without excessive fantasizing or daydreaming. It also enables us to concentrate and focus on ways of coping with what we discover and to keep our emotions in check, uncolored by excessive fear.

People with a strong capacity for reality testing see the world around them in an objective, clear-eyed manner. They are quick to recognize where problems exist and can perceive opportunities when they come into sight. Those who have weaker reality-testing skills either keep their heads in the sand to avoid facing problems or can see (and magnify) only risks and, as a result, are unable to take advantage of opportunities.

Don't Fear the Worst . . .

Let's see how reality testing plays out in one or two scenarios. First, we'll eavesdrop on Ben and Neil as they take a break at Starbucks. Ben is on the boil about the new coach of the football team: "This guy isn't one of us; he doesn't understand what goes on here. They parachuted him in from Florida. I don't know what to make of him, but I do know he's moving too fast. Now he's going to make everyone re-earn their positions, he's putting in all new plays, and he's making the team do more conditioning work. He's been here a month, and he's turning the team upside down. All these changes are getting to me. I don't know if I can stay with the team, I'm not happy about it. I like this team, but I don't know if I can take the constant pressure he's putting us under. How about you?"

Neil, having taken all this in, replies, "I don't know much about the new coach either, but I've got friends in Florida, and they say he seemed pretty fair. I'm not all that concerned. Why should I be? My defensive line has been doing really well, so why should he tear it apart? I don't think there's been a problem with my performance, so why should he get rid of me? Anything can happen; maybe he wants to bring in new players. But I've been here a while, and I made lots of tackles last year. I can't see why he would want to cut me. I haven't got my head in the sand, but I think there's a future for me with this new coach. I'm not going to screw it up by spending all my time worrying about what he's trying to do. I can handle change as well as the next guy. It doesn't threaten me; it's more of an opportunity. Actually, I feel pretty good about football and the coach these days. But if he did cut me, then I'd look for another school that needed a good defensive lineman."

How would you rate Neil's capacity for reality testing? His views are well thought out, well argued, and based on a pragmatic assessment that seems to be supported by the evidence—neither his defensive team nor his position is in peril. He's willing to work with the new coach, and he intends to remain a valuable player, but he is confident that if he's cut, he'll be able to deal with it. He's unfazed by the prospect of change, and he will probably continue to function as effectively as before. Ben, on the other hand, has given way to fearful fantasies, has begun to catastrophize for no valid reason, and will only end up increasing his level of stress, which will interfere with his ability to play effectively—and may even result in his getting dropped from the team.

● . . . But Take Off Those Rose-Colored Glasses

In Ben's case, his baseless dread interfered with his ability to lucidly assess his situation. But other people who are deficient in reality testing rush to the opposite pole, adopting a naive, starry-eyed attitude, in spite of mounting evidence that all may not be rosy.

Nowhere is this reaction more prevalent than in the field of romance. Love is blind, and many a relationship (especially when it begins) finds both individuals painting their partners in idealized terms—as in this monologue delivered by Anna on the subject of her new boyfriend: "I know you think I'm nuts, but I really love him. He's changed, he really has. I have faith in him, and I know that my love has made a difference. Okay, he used to run with a bad crowd, but what do you expect when he got shuffled off into all those foster homes, and there was that time when he was arrested. And I know he hasn't been able to keep a job, but that's just because others don't understand him. And he's older now . . ." But why continue? Anna's reality-testing skills obviously need work; she has her head in the sand and is denying very real evidence that her new boyfriend is trouble.

Whether you're forging a relationship (or trying to turn a difficult one around), assessing the magnitude of a problem, or evaluating the benefits of an emerging opportunity, seeing the situation as it truly exists is crucial to success—but if you misread the information you're receiving from your environment, you're at a disadvantage from the start.

A clear, unblinkered reading of your environment leads to success because it brings with it capacities for identifying and addressing problems and recognizing and building on opportunities. Finely honed reality testing also allows you to read a group's emotional climate and the power relationships at work. It is a complement to self-awareness, which gives you the capacity to take your "internal temperature"; reality testing allows you to measure "external temperature."

● Some Common Problems Students Face with Reality Testing

One of us, Korrel, has been a college professor for over 30 years and as a result can predict all of the reality testing mistakes students might make. Read the lists that follow, see which behaviors most closely match you, and then try to change your way of examining the facts.

Catastrophizing, Predicting Doom and Gloom

Those of us who tend to worry too much can easily find reasons why bad things will happen. Do any of these sound familiar to you?

- Someone doesn't speak to you, and all of sudden you doubt their friendship or, even worse, assume they hate you.
- A coach yells at you for being out of position, and you worry about losing your place on the starting lineup.

- The B+ on the first test of the semester surely means you won't make an A in that class this semester. And you really need that A, or you definitely won't get into graduate school (even though you have a 3.7 GPA).
- Your older friend's rejection letter from her preferred college makes you doubt your ability to get in, even though you have higher grades and better standardized test scores.

And About Those Rose-Colored Glasses

Just because you want something to be true doesn't mean that it *is*!

- A student skips half the classes, doesn't turn in homework, and misses the first test. He shows up at the professor's office two days before the final, asking what he can do to pass the class.
- Your dating partner is consistently rude and inconsiderate of your feelings. When you ask to spend time together, there's always something more important for him or her to do. You hang on to the relationship because you love this person and know that she or he will change.
- You're a freshman on a superb lacrosse team, one full of juniors and seniors who won last year's national championship. You think you should start, though, because you were a high school All American and most of them were not.
- You think that you can hold a 30-hour-a-week part-time job, take five difficult college courses, play intramural sports almost every day, and be involved in three campus clubs. You're surprised when you end up having to pull an all-nighter the night before the first big test of the semester and still make a D.
- You ignore swollen and tender glands, too busy with life to make time to see a doctor. You're sure the glands will return to their normal size and are shocked to learn six months later that you have a serious illness that will cause you to drop out of school and have surgery.
- You know your bank account is low but don't check your balance before going shopping with friends.

Sometimes we cannot discern whether we have over- or under-reacted until after a situation becomes clearer. In the meantime, ask yourself a simple question: If 100 people faced the situation I face, how would they interpret the facts and what behaviors might they engage in? Or think about one of your parents, a pragmatic friend, or a trusted advisor: what might that person say about the situation you are facing? Although it can provide temporary relief to ignore something that scares us or that will involve lots of hard work, the relief is short-lived. On the other hand, there's no reason to cause yourself undue stress by exaggerating, engaging in irrational beliefs, or otherwise expecting doom and gloom to befall you.

Reflection Questions

1. Would others be more likely to describe you as an ostrich—with your head in the sand, oblivious to the world around you—or Chicken Little, the fictional character who proclaimed "The sky is falling!"? Explain.

2. Think about your family when you were growing up. What did they teach you about how to face reality? Did some of them model being an ostrich? Or Chicken Little?

3. If you tend to be Chicken Little, ask yourself: what's the worst possible outcome in this situation? Then realize that the worst possible outcome *rarely* happens and adjust your thoughts to a more realistic outcome.

4. If you tend to be an ostrich, ask yourself: what will I gain in the long run by remaining clueless? (There are no doubt short-term gains, like less pressure or not having to hear bad news, but the long-term negative consequences can be much more severe.)

You can practice developing your reality testing even more by referring to the exercises in *The Student EQ Edge: Student Workbook*.

CHAPTER 13

Problem Solving

It isn't that they can't see the solution. It's that they can't see the problem.
—G. K. Chesterton, 1935

Definition: "Problem Solving is the ability to find solutions to problems in situations where emotions are involved. Problem solving includes the capacity to understand how emotions impact decision making. Problem solving is a complex and even multiphase process. It is not about neutralizing emotion, but about using emotional information to enhance the process of recognizing a problem, feeling confident in one's ability to work through it, defining the problem, generating a solution, and implementing the plan. The appropriate application of emotional information can help identify potential pitfalls, inspire the recruitment of help, and even expedite the solution by evoking feelings of confidence. Problem solving is about understanding the impact that emotions have on the decision making process and using those emotions most effectively" (Multi-Health Systems, 2011, p. 6).

● Same Problem, Different Strategies

Susan, a law school student, had trouble working her way through the reams of documents that were required as part of her civil litigation practice course assignments. She could eventually pull everything together and see the big picture if she stuck with it, but more often she felt like giving up after two or three attempts of trying to organize and assess it all. Her quiet and somewhat less self-assured classmate An, on the other hand, was more persistent. As she reviewed her case documents, she would determine the issue and formulate one strategy, then try another if the facts and documentation failed to support it, then another, and so on. She chose not to give up, seeing her work assignments as a challenge. If she hit the wall and grew frustrated, she'd look to her next option—calling on someone for help. An had a list of classmates and professors she could count on to point her in the right direction. They would discuss the assignment, which helped her cut through the clutter and determine the key issues in ways that made it easier for her to proceed.

In another five years, chances are that An will have proved more successful in her career, thanks to her approach to problem solving. Notice that one of her skills, common to most people with a high EQ, is her ability to keep herself motivated, even when obstacles get in the way. Using emotion to motivate yourself, regardless of the nature of the challenge, is characteristic of people with well-developed emotional intelligence skills.

Susan's tendency to give up is connected to her propensity for responding to difficult situations by quickly feeling lethargic and unmotivated. She then begins to engage in negative self-talk: "Oh, this is all too much! Just look at me, what a dummy I am. I've made two attempts, and I still cannot get it right! I just always screw up!!"

If Susan were to use the A-E model, covered in Chapter 2, to "dispute and debate" her self-talk, she would be on the road to becoming less down on herself and less lethargic, and she could be far more motivated to successfully return to the task at hand.

Another important emotional skill is knowing when to call on the advice and expertise of others. The key is not to throw up your hands and ask that person to solve it for you immediately, which would render you dependent, but to seek aid from diverse sources who'll assist you in reaching your own conclusion.

There are many possible emotional reactions to problems—frustration, which may make us want to give up; anxiety, which may make us jump to a conclusion too quickly; or anger that the problem even exists, which distracts our focus from the problem to those we perceive to have created the situation. The next section covers the six steps of problem solving that you'll need to master in order to excel at it; you'll also need to know how to recognize what emotion the problem has stirred and either dampen that emotion or use it as motivation to help you move forward.

● Six Steps for Solving Problems

Never has it been more important to focus on problem solving. In workplaces everywhere, supervisors are asking their employees to come to them not with difficulties as they may arise, but with solutions in hand, ready to be implemented. A competitive economy demands that we be problem solvers, not problem reporters or collectors. So if you begin practicing good problem solving now, that will help you succeed in your academic work and later on will likely make you more attractive to employers as a new hire.

Among the pioneers of social problem solving as an intervention are psychologists Thomas D'Zurilla and Arthur Nezu. They have published dozens of research studies demonstrating that training people in better problem solving can greatly influence their ability to deal with problems in every area of their lives: work and career, finances and personal property, health and behavior, relationship and family (D'Zurilla & Nezu, 1999).

They have defined problems as being either (1) a single time-limited event, such as being late for an exam, fixing a jammed printer, or dealing with an acute illness; (2) a series of similar or related events, such as dealing with a disgruntled roommate or a family member who is very critical; or (3) more long-term, such as coping with chronic pain, loneliness, or boredom.

There are also two categories of problems: interpersonal and technical. Note that most problems fall into the interpersonal category. Even with technical problems, however, there is usually an interpersonal component and a role for emotions.

Consider for a moment the case of Ed, a student who got a part-time job taking school ID pictures but cannot work the computer equipment attached to the camera very well. Suddenly he's faced with a long line of impatient students waiting to get their photos taken. Not only are the students getting frustrated while waiting, but they have to be in class soon. As a result of not being competent in this part of his work, Ed is slow and makes many errors, and the students who need their photo IDs become increasingly frustrated and then irritated with him.

As their impatience mounts, they begin pressuring him to hurry up and get the photos done. Under such pressure, his anxiety increases and interferes with whatever skill set he has—making his output even worse. What began as a technical problem soon also became an interpersonal difficulty.

Next time you encounter a problem, view it as a challenge to be overcome, an opportunity to be seized. Each time you have the chance to beat a problem into submission, grab it and go. With practice, the better you'll become, by bearing these steps in mind:

1. State the case. Examine the problem, describing it as accurately and realistically as possible. Try looking at it from other people's points of view, to make sure that your perspective isn't unduly narrow. Part of being objective involves being aware of the impact of your emotions. Our emotions often color our view of problems we encounter. That doesn't mean you should become unemotional; rather, be aware of your emotions and the biases they create for you in your problem solving.

2. Generate alternatives. Think of as many solutions and approaches as you can. This is a brainstorming session, so accept that some of your ideas won't hold water. At this stage, don't evaluate your ideas—just let them come. Again, think of ways that other people might tackle the same dilemma.

3. *Evaluate each alternative.* When you've got all your options firmly in mind or—better still—down on paper, look at each one and consider the probable outcome. Prioritize them, from best to least favorable. Also, do a gut check. Pay attention to how the potential solution *feels* to you. Sometimes we reject options because they just don't feel right. You don't need to explain why; that alone can be important information. Pay attention to the reverse as well. Some solutions just feel better for us. If it feels right, then you may be moving in a good direction.

4. *Choose the best option.* Now is the time to take the plunge, recognizing the risk involved. No one can predict the success or failure of a given course of action with 100-percent certitude. Gain confidence from the knowledge that you assumed the risk and took action based on sound information gathering and an analytical process.

5. *Implement your solution.* Press on without getting bogged down in what-ifs and maybe-we-should-haves. Perhaps you'll have to make adjustments along the way, but resist the temptation to go back to square one. Give your chosen strategy a chance to work. Remember, settling on it rather than your other choices was the hard part. So reward yourself—pat yourself on the back for moving beyond the quagmire of indecision.

6. *Assess the outcome.* Evaluate whether your solution has solved the problem. If it has, great. If not, begin this process again. When the problem seems to be of a technical nature, do not overlook any interpersonal difficulties that may have emerged as a result of that technical issue.

Now let's see how these techniques play out when applied. Linda, a very personable and congenial young woman, came close to finishing her nursing certification, but decided instead to join the army and train as a medic. Although aware of her lack of formal education, she had a wide variety of interests and a keen, inquiring mind. In fact, she ran into trouble in the army because she kept challenging the drab and lockstep routine. "Why do we have to have to clean our bedrolls three times a day?" she'd ask. "Wouldn't it be better to clean them once, and then wrap them up in plastic? Then we could get on to other stuff." Her superiors viewed these very sensible suggestions as borderline insubordination, with the result that Linda eventually switched to the navy, which she found far less regimented and much more to her liking.

In time, Linda married Jack, who served in the marines. When she resigned from the navy to start a family, Linda became concerned about the family's suddenly decreased income. She said nothing directly to Jack, who liked and was very adept at his military duties. Still, she began to subtly prod him into thinking about the possibility of civilian employment and the higher salary he would make.

After the birth of their second child, Linda began working part-time with the Red Cross, organizing blood donor clinics at various corporate headquarters. Pretty soon she had a plan in mind. Everywhere she went, she chatted with a wide range of employees and, if possible, senior executives, asking them every question she could think of about their firms. After a clinic was wrapped up, she'd stay a while in the staff cafeteria, where people were pleased to talk to such an interested visitor. In time, she'd personally investigated and individually rated dozens of computer and software firms. She also got a gut feeling from each organization as to how the culture felt to her.

Thus Linda had identified the problem—finding a great place for Jack to work as a civilian. She studied the problem during her own employment—finding out about the different companies in the vicinity. She brainstormed by coming up with numerous questions to ask at each workplace, and she carefully recorded her findings for later reference. The next steps would involve proposing solutions, selecting one for implementation, and monitoring the outcome.

One day, Jack—unaware of all these activities—took Linda out for dinner and announced that he'd come to the conclusion that it would be wise for him to investigate a change of career. Without missing a beat, Linda brought out her notebook, which the two of them examined and discussed for several nights. Fortunately, she had the interpersonal finesse to pull this off without bruising her husband's ego. On the contrary—he was delighted and flattered that she'd saved him so much research, legwork, and doubt. In no time, they'd narrowed his choices down to three companies that they both felt strongly would suit his personality and abilities. Jack applied to all three, and eventually got the job of his—and Linda's—dreams.

Notice how Linda used her emotions to energize her action. Instead of worrying about their financial situation or being mad at Jack because he wasn't ready to make a career move yet, Linda channeled her emotions into a positive outlet.

● Externalize, Visualize, and Simplify

Taking a slightly different approach, let's look at externalization, visualization, and simplification, the three rules of problem solving formulated by Marvin Levine, author of *Effective Problem Solving* (Levine, 1993).

Externalization involves displaying the information you're working with. Write things down or draw a graph to define more complex relationships. That way, you'll have all the elements in front of you.

Visualization might include imagining yourself going through the various steps involved in dealing with a problem before you carry them out or picturing the outcome of a possible solution. A variation on this technique has proved very successful in helping professional and Olympic-caliber athletes. We have them rehearse in their minds the most challenging and typically encountered aspects of their sport and conjure up a clear mental image of themselves performing at peak, eluding opposition players and scoring points. They can do this anywhere, anytime—on the team bus en route to an arena or as they go to sleep the evening before a game. And you can too. By preparing to meet obstacles as they arise, you'll be much better prepared for the real thing when it comes along.

Finally, simplification involves breaking the problem down to its simplest common denominators. If you focus on the most relevant information, keeping things as specific and concrete as possible, it becomes easier to get a grip on even the most seemingly convoluted difficulty.

How does this work in practice? Let's consider Darlene, a sophomore student who had many different interests and had difficulty picking a major. The online course descriptions were of little help, so she went through the externalization, visualization, and simplification process. First, starting to externalize, she wrote down in as much detail as possible the sort of work she'd eventually like to do, knowing that her choice of major could affect her ability to get hired in certain jobs. Then she came at the problem from different angles, thinking about the part-time jobs she'd had in the past and what she'd liked or disliked about them. This exercise helped her identify what had given her the most satisfaction in the working world and in life.

Next, continuing with her externalization, she began to think about all her current and previous fellow students, as well as her friends and acquaintances. Some were obviously happier with their courses than others, and she tried to analyze why this was so. Then she thought about what others had (or might have) said about her in her previous courses. Were her memories and perceptions in tune with their probable readings? Did she strike them as happy and fulfilled?

Then Darlene tried to visualize herself in all sorts of different jobs that in some way caught her interest. She ran through the entire gamut: jobs that involved a high degree of interaction with others, solitary jobs, jobs that involved technical skills that she had or could perhaps acquire, jobs that required artistic flair, jobs that took place indoors and out, and even jobs that she could perform at home. As she visualized, she paid attention to her gut feelings—the internalized emotions she associated with each option, as well as the self-talk connected with these emotions that might also be interfering with her performance.

She learned from this visualization that she was primarily interested in and emotionally tuned into creative work, rather than something highly technical. She liked working with others and didn't want to be tied to a desk or a cubicle. And an unexpected theme emerged: she was happiest and most at peace with herself when she was involved with art.

This narrowed her choice of major to art, art history, or a related field. Now she had a smaller number of majors to investigate. But was art a job? Of course it was, and it could be analyzed too using the same process.

She started this exercise with externalization: making a list of every position associated with art history, painting, galleries, and art museums, describing them in detail. She thought about her résumé and visualized how she'd present herself in an interview; she recalled past experiences that were at all relevant to each job category. Having noted the pros and cons of each, she selected a few that seemed appealing: an internship at a major art gallery, a position where she could teach art to children, and a similar post with an art museum. She did as much research as possible, visiting the library and reading all sorts of trade magazines, calling anyone she knew who had contacts in the three fields, and paying personal visits to prospective employers. By the time she graduated, her knowledge and enthusiasm had paid off: she was hired by a local gallery and soon became indispensable to its operation.

Our advice, then, is to take heart from Darlene's experiences. Problems are normal events, part of everyday living. Everyone goes through them, so don't take them too personally or imagine that they're aimed at you alone. Successful problem solvers see them as challenges to be overcome or learning experiences that will lead to strength and growth. By starting with a positive approach and putting your emphasis on their solution, the rest of the steps involved will be that much simpler, easier, and more effective.

● Using Emotion and Innovation to Solve Problems

Problem solving, as we've seen, is associated with being conscientious, disciplined, rational, methodical, systematic, and perseverant. The key is a desire to do your best in the face of doubt or adversity—to confront problems rather than avoid them.

But people who successfully solve their problems have two other capacities. First is intuition—commonly known as *hunches* and *impressions*. The trick is not to follow intuition blindly or give it too much credit, but to explore it in a logical and realistic way. In fact, intuition can be an early warning signal, identifying problems that haven't fully emerged but are beginning to edge onto the scene. If you can pick up on these almost subliminal signals—and then examine them pragmatically and methodically rather than dismissing or over-looking them—you'll have a head start when the problem lands with both feet.

Successful problem solving is also bolstered by innovation— the capacity to come up with fresh new ways of viewing the issue at hand and brainstorming alternative solutions. Like intuition, though, innovation must be tempered by a clear-headed calculation of the risks involved in these unusual approaches.

Emotion plays an important role in your ability to solve problems. Research has found that when you want to work on detail-driven problems, it's best to be in a serious or slightly sad mood (Hughes, 1998). When we're sad, we tend to pay more attention to detail. On the other hand, when brain storming or trying to be creative, do you think a bad mood or good mood would help you the most? Most of us turn on favorite music, go to a peaceful location, or do something else to help us get our creative ideas flowing.

How do we get into the right mood for solving problems? Well, there are a number of different techniques, but one that is fairly easy is through music. You can pick the right music to get you into the mood you need. For example, one of us, Steven, motivates himself to write by listening to Billy Joel, Van Morrison, Supertramp, or Amy Winehouse. Music can not only motivate you (think of the *Rocky* theme and exercising), but it can put you into the mood you need for better problem solving.

In sum, the most adept problem solvers have a vital edge because they can identify obstacles that might prevent them from attaining their goals in a family, social, or workplace setting, and they overcome them by a blend of intuitive and logical means. Those who don't have this capacity often fail to see the obstacle until they run into it—or, if they recognize it, they become flustered or demoralized. They cannot correctly spot the problem until it throws them for a loop, and they wind up stymied in their desire to achieve what they want.

Reflection Questions

1. Think of a problem you are facing right now in your life. Analyze the problem using the six steps. What is your conclusion?

2. Many athletes solve the "problem" of performing well under pressure by using visualization and simplification to control their strong emotions during a competition. How might using those help an athlete perform better? How could you use visualization and simplification to promote academic success?

3. Think about a past problem that you handled well and one you did not handle well. Analyze what you did right and where you got off track. Be sure to pay attention to what emotions were driving you during those events and how you responded to those emotions.

To practice some exercises that could help you use emotion more effectively in solving problems, consult *The Student EQ Edge: Student Workbook.*

CHAPTER 14

Impulse Control

I can resist everything except temptation.
—Oscar Wilde, *Lady Windermere's Fan*

Definition: "Impulse Control is the ability to resist or delay an impulse, drive, or temptation to act. It involves avoiding rash behaviors and impetuous decision making. Impulse control entails a capacity for recognizing and accepting one's desire to react without becoming a servant to that desire. Difficulties in impulse control are manifested by low emotional threshold, impulsiveness, loss of self-control, and unpredictable behavior" (Multi-Health Systems, 2011, p. 6).

● "But Impulsiveness Helps Me"

Following a presentation on emotional intelligence to a group of business executives, several members of the audience approached one of us (Steven) to continue the discussion. One man, accompanied by a slightly younger woman, waited impatiently for his chance to speak. When his turn came, he began by admitting that he agreed with much of what we'd said, but took great issue with one point. According to him, we were miles off base when it came to impulse control.

He himself was very impulsive, he said, and always had been. If he hadn't been, he believed, he'd never have gotten anywhere in life.

He alluded to the millions of dollars he'd made and mentioned other equally successful entrepreneurs. Controlling their impulses would have dragged them down and held them back. Snap decisions were his life's blood; he was renowned for them, and he wouldn't apologize to anyone. He trusted his own intuitions, his own judgment. Nor was he afraid of acting as quickly as he made up his mind; he didn't let anyone stand in his way.

This was interesting logic, and it seemed to impress the members of the audience who overheard his comments. But it called for some follow-up on our part. We asked if he'd ever lost out on a business deal because of his impulsiveness. Of course, he replied; that's the way the world works. You win some, you lose some.

Well, then, we wondered, on the personal side—was he married?

"Three times."

"Any kids?"

"Yes, four."

"Do you get to see them often?"

"Sure, every couple of months or so. What does that have to do with anything? Anyway, about impulsiveness—I just thought I'd let you know." With that, he turned and joined the departing crowd.

When he left, his companion remained behind for a minute or so. She identified herself as his second in command at the head office.

"You're right, you know," she said. "I have to work with him. He walks in in the morning and starts to snap at everyone in sight. It puts them off; they're demoralized before they even start their day. He wants them up to speed—his speed. He flies strictly by the seat of his pants, and nobody else gets a chance to wear them. A lot of the time, he's right—but when he's wrong, he's wildly wrong. I've seen it happen time and time again. I can handle him, but then I have to turn around and make sure he hasn't bludgeoned the rest of the staff into submission, or left them in the dark about what he's up to. His personal life is another story, but there you are."

All pretty much as we'd suspected—and as you guessed when you saw his replies to our questions. Fortunately for him and his company, the impetuous businessman was smart or lucky enough to have hired the ideal second in command, whose career appeared to consist largely of compensating for his weaknesses. Her patience, calmness, thoughtfulness, and superior interpersonal skills held the office together, while he went on his pyrotechnic way. That's a good fit, while it lasts—although how long she'll be able to carry such a heavy burden is debatable. But just imagine how much more he might achieve in both his working and personal relationships if he were able to operate less impulsively.

Here's another example. Stacy was a very bright science student with aspirations of attending medical school. Although her freshman grades weren't as high as they should be, she knew that she was smart enough to pull her grades up to where they needed to be. In any event, she felt that her freshman grades wouldn't matter that much anyway.

It was now the weekend, and her chemistry and physiology midterm exams were coming up on Monday. Her plan had been to spend the weekend studying. As she was getting ready to start her chemistry review, she heard the ping of an email arriving in her inbox.

It was a notice about a big fashion sale at the nearest discount mall, just a couple of hours from her college town. She had been planning to spend the weekend studying, but the prices at the sale looked too good to miss. She decided that if she left early Saturday morning, she could shop all day Saturday, work her part-time job Sunday and still have study time Sunday night. After all, she had been getting B's in her courses all semester without applying herself very hard.

Did she make the right decision? Well, that depends on what her real goal was. Probably not if it was to get into medical school. Her attention was easily distracted from the job at hand—studying. Even if she had stopped working and just read the email, managing her impulses well would have led her to conclude that the sale, although exciting, could wait for now. There will be plenty of opportunities in the future for sales, but this was her chance to get the grades she needed for her future. The ability to put off short-term gains for our long-term goals is a critical part of impulse control.

● Look Before You Leap

Note that the businessman in the true story we first presented credits impulsiveness for his success—but muddies the waters by talking about trusting and acting on his true instincts. No one suggests that effective impulse control involves stifling or disregarding valuable gut feelings. Rather, it's the capacity to look before you leap—to manage a wide range of volatile emotional states and urges wisely and coolly.

We know that people have trouble with impulse control when others describe them as rash, hot-headed, impatient, or (at best) mercurial. They have a low tolerance for frustration; they're fine one minute and difficult the next. They tend to make poor decisions under pressure and spend money unwisely. Their love lives are hyperactive but go nowhere because they can't sustain a relationship. They don't act in their own best interests; they get carried away by the moment. The "instinct" referred to by the businessman is in truth usually a series of knee-jerk responses to events.

Individuals with effective impulse control, in contrast, have the capacity to think first rather than responding reflexively. It gives them mental space for weighing alternatives and assessing options so that their actions and expressions are reasoned and well considered. This leads to wise decision making and responsible behavior. Plans made after a period of reflection always have a much greater chance of success. Who, after all, is going to be more apt to achieve their aims—people who don't pause to consider the facts, but respond immediately to any idea or thought that pops into their heads, or those who calmly plan their words and deeds, remaining unperturbed even under trying circumstances? Who is going to be more adept at turning around relationships that have gone sour, dealing with upset friends, and listening thoughtfully and respectfully to an upset partner? It's no contest, is it? People who exercise healthy impulse control—while still retaining flexibility and spontaneity, so that they don't come across as rigid or a stick-in-the-mud—will remain cool under pressure and will come out ahead of the game every time.

Each time we hear of an outburst of road rage, we know that we're dealing with serious impulse control impairment. (Of course, the use of alcohol and other drugs plays havoc with our ability to keep ourselves in check.) Partner abuse and date rape are among its other more tragic manifestations. The majority of lapses occur in less dramatic ways—but they occur daily in most people's lives.

In any discussion of impulse control, it's tempting to center on the failure to deal with anger and aggression. No doubt these feelings and behaviors are among the most likely to get us into big trouble—but we don't think you'll have all that much difficulty thinking of occasions when someone you know has overstepped the bounds of friendship and resorted to bulldozing and intimidation; given in to a desire to purchase something for no good reason (and perhaps with insufficient funds in the bank); or simply taken an undue risk based on insufficient knowledge and consideration of the outcome. Whenever we leap before we look, we may be acting impulsively.

How can we guard against doing so? By reviewing our ABCs— our *activating* events, *beliefs*, and *consequences*. All of us are prone to behave impulsively when our thoughts and feelings are heating up. We feel we've been unfairly criticized, so we lash out. We see an opportunity that's too good to ignore (and probably too good to be true, but we don't take the time to recognize that fact), so we try to grab it at any cost. We want instant retaliation or instant gratification, as the case may be. What are we really doing? We're not only leaping before we look, we're leaping directly from A to C. Feelings are translated into action with the speed of light. There's no opportunity to bring logical evaluation to bear, to ponder the Bs, let alone the Ds and Es described in Chapter 2. As a result, we respond reflexively, rudely, and inappropriately, alienating the people we want to win over and, in so doing, undercutting our chances of success in attaining our goals.

● The Impulse Gate

You'll recall our overenrolled class scenario, during which Brett flew off the handle, threatened the professor, and stomped out of his office—and, as a result, never got into the class—whereas John, the far more savvy student, achieved his aims. Brett—and anyone else who has severe problems with impulse control—also has a defective emotional safety valve called an impulse gate. Here's how it works, in the context of the A-E model.

We've discussed how the *consequences* (C) of an *activating* event (A) and our intervening *beliefs* (B) involve both feelings and behaviors; that is, our emotions give rise to a course of action. Here's where the impulse gate comes into play. Picture a classroom and a student walking into class late. When the teacher responds, imagine a little gate that swings open and closed in the teacher's head, controlling the flow of impulsive feelings. Based on the A-E model, the *activating event* is the student's arriving late in class. One teacher's *belief* interprets this as disrespect for the teacher (an irrational belief, until the teacher knows the real reason for the late arrival) and, acting impulsively, the teacher snaps at the student—the *consequence*. But another teacher may *believe*, based on a rational view of the facts, that the student has a time management problem, and so will calmly tell the student to be on time for the next class or it will be counted as an absence—setting clear boundaries for the student as the *consequence*.

● The Marshmallow Test

All of us, as reasoning and reasonably self-aware people, have the ability to practice impulse control—even though, for some of us, it's a bit late in the script. The human infant has no impulse control at all. Babies are remarkable though fairly straightforward pieces of work. When their bladders are full, they urinate; when frustrated, they scream. Then they start to observe and listen to their earliest emotional coaches—a fancy term for parents.

Sometimes the lesson takes hold, but sometimes it doesn't. A precedent is set early on. One of the more enduring illustrations of this fact was a study conducted in the 1960s by the psychologist Walter

Mischel (Mischel, Ebbesen, & Zeiss, 1972) at Stanford University—the so-called marshmallow experiment.

Mischel's experiment involved a number of four-year-old children. Each child was seated in a room that contained a chair, a table, and a single marshmallow. The person who was conducting the test informed the child that he or she had to run an errand, and made an offer the kid might (or might not) refuse. If the child wanted to eat the marshmallow immediately, that would be okay. But if the child waited until the adult returned, the reward would be a second marshmallow.

The kids made their choices, and Mischel and his colleagues (1972) noted the results, which were interesting in themselves. Two-thirds of the children managed to hang tough and earn the second marshmallow. The rest did not. But that wasn't the end of the experiment. Because they were mostly the children of Stanford professors, graduate students, and employees, Mischel was able to locate them twelve to fourteen years later, when they were about to graduate from high school. At this point, he gained access to their academic records and asked their parents to evaluate how successful they had been in and out of school. What do you think he found?

The kids who had gobbled up a single marshmallow were having a few problems. As a group, they were less adept at making social contacts and more prone to be stubborn and indecisive. They yielded readily to frustration as well as temptation. Those who had put their gratification on hold—and by doing so, doubled their pleasure with a second marshmallow—were more successful: they showed more social skills, exhibited superior coping mechanisms, and, in general, were ahead of the game. This was reflected in their grades. They were, simply put, better students, and they had scored remarkably better on their SAT tests (Shoda, Mischel, & Peake, 1990). It sounds incredible—but the ability, at age four, to wait for a second marshmallow was twice as accurate a predictor of a kid's future SAT score as the child's IQ. Remarkably, the researchers were able to locate many of the original participants as adults and once again examined various aspects of their success in career and relationships. Do you want to guess what they found? If you're thinking that those who could delay gratification during the preschool years were more successful adults, you'd be correct (Mischel, Ayduk, et al., 2011).

We're sure that if you think about it, you might recall a politician or two who has fallen from grace as a result of poor impulse control. You might even think of a number of athletes, rock stars, and movie actors who have given in to their impulses and suffered the consequences.

A more recent study drives this point home in a much larger scale. We are now learning the seriousness of the effects of poor impulse control over decision making throughout the lifespan. A study carried out in New Zealand followed 1,000 children from ages 3 to 32 (Moffitt et al., 2011). The children were tested on a number of dimensions of self-control from the beginning—using observations, self-reports, and parent and teacher reports—and throughout their childhood, adolescence, and well into adulthood.

The bottom line of Moffitt and her colleagues' (2011) findings was that children with lower self-control were three times more likely to develop multiple health problems, struggle financially, or be convicted of a crime. In one example of this, 13 percent of children with high self-control were convicted of a crime by aged 32 compared to over 40 percent of children with low self-control. Also, multiple health problems showed up in 27 percent of low self-control children as opposed to 11 percent of high self-control kids. The study focused on self-control, factoring out intelligence, social class, and mistakes made as teenagers.

The researchers identified several gateways—what they called "snares"—encountered by low-self-control children in their teenage years that increased the probability of the outcome findings. For example, poor-self-control children were more likely to start smoking at age 15, drop out of school, or become teen parents. According to the researchers, self-control not only helps us control how we react to what's happening right now, but also allows us to think about the future and how we plan to get there (Moffitt et al., 2011).

We commonly associate lack of impulse control with anger and aggression. However, we've seen students struggle with other aspects of impulse control, such as overeating, overdrinking, partying before studying, and overspending. Unfortunately, there are many ways to give in to our impulses!

● Managing Your Impulses

People with effective impulse control look before they leap, consider before they act, and are able to resist and delay the urge to react in a knee-jerk fashion. Those with difficulty controlling or delaying impulses are burdened by a low tolerance for frustration and vulnerability to stress, and they behave in compulsive, arbitrary, and thoughtless ways. They tend to have difficulty controlling their anger and so are hot-headed, tempestuous, and given to abusive outbursts, rage reactions, or explosive and unpredictable behavior.

Now think of an individual with good impulse control and one with poor impulse control, comparing them with the preceding descriptions. Again, individuals who respond immediately to any idea, thought, or impulse that enters their heads; who do not have the time to consider the facts or information; and who respond to frustration with tempestuous outbursts are not going to experience success in life. Individuals who consider aspects before reacting, plan instead of lunging forward, weigh pros and cons, and remain relatively unperturbed and calm even under trying circumstances will be successful. They'll be better at turning around relationships that have gone sour; dealing with demanding and unsettled clients; and listening thoughtfully to significant others who are upset.

Impulse control should not be confused with inflexibility. People with healthy impulse control can still be flexible and spontaneous. If someone with what seems like highly effective impulse control comes across as stiff and inflexible, this is more a reflection of a deficiency in the EI component of *flexibility*.

Reflection Questions

1. Do you consider yourself a patient person? Explain your answer.

2. What sorts of temptations tend to lead you astray (for example, food, video games, spending money on clothes)?

3. How could you be more in control of your impulses?

Consult *The Student EQ Edge: Student Workbook* for some exercises to increase your impulse control.

PART 6

The Stress Management Realm

This realm of emotional intelligence concerns your ability to be flexible, tolerate stress, and be optimistic. Success in this area means that you are able to remain calm and focused, to constructively withstand adverse events and conflicting emotions without caving in, and to see the light at the end of the tunnel. At school these skills are vital if you customarily face tight deadlines or must juggle many demands on your time. At home, they enable you to simultaneously maintain a busy schedule and be mindful of your physical health.

Figure Part 6 Stress Management and Emotional Intelligence

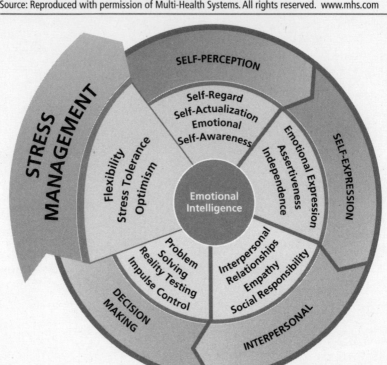

Flexibility

CHAPTER 15

*It is not the strongest of the species that survive,
nor the most intelligent, but the one most responsive
to change.*
   —Charles Darwin

Definition: "Flexibility is adapting emotions, thoughts, and behaviors to unfamiliar, unpredictable, and dynamic circumstances or ideas. This component of emotional intelligence refers to one's overall ability to adapt and tolerate the stress that accompanies change. Flexible people are agile and capable of reacting to change with minimal adverse effect; they are open to and capable of change, and tolerant of new ideas, orientations, and practices" (Multi-Health Systems, 2011, p. 7).

● More Business, Please

Dhara, an above-average student, was a year away from graduation. Besides the basic requirements in math, English and history, she had managed to take only business and accounting courses at college. Dhara's college only required one social science course for graduation and Dhara chose economics, the social science required for business majors. Her advisor recommended she take a course in psychology, sociology, or some other social science field to broaden her education. Dhara declined. When her advisor asked why, Dhara replied,

"I don't see the relevance of it. I only want courses related to business. That's all I'm really interested in."

Her advisor noted that employers were beginning to ask about interests and skills other than business and accounting during interviews and that she would be at a disadvantage getting a job. And a class in the social sciences would help her better understand other people—an important skill in the business world. Again, Dhara refused to budge.

Her advisor recommended she at least think about it overnight. Dhara replied, "I don't want to take any other course. I'm not interested in any of those things. I'll just get a job that only uses business skills."

Dhara did eventually find a job in the business world. Unfortunately, it took her longer than most of her peers to get hired. Her lack of other interests and narrow range of courses made her less desirable to employers. More and more organizations are looking for well-rounded people who are open to new ideas and to change.

Yesterday's Leaders

Business leaders who insist on keeping everything the same risk the future of their companies in today's world. This was not the case 100 years ago. This type of leadership was fairly common back then. An example can be found by looking at one of the icons of corporate leadership during the first half of the last century—Henry Ford. Being steadfast and staying the course were significant contributors to Ford's early success. However, there came a time when flexibility, willingness to change, and listening to others would be even more important.

As Lee Iacocca told the story in *Time* (Iacocca, 1998), Ford stayed loyal to the model T for way too long, refusing to build any other models and offering only one color—black. His obstinacy almost cost him his business. It wasn't until Ford introduced the Model A in 1927 that he offered any choice. By then, General Motors was gaining ground rapidly.

Sticking with the status quo at that time gave Ford's biggest competitor, General Motors, the break they needed to take significant market share. It was Ford's son who stepped in and finally insisted on bringing out new models (such as the Model A) needed for the continued survival of the company.

The other key aspect of this leadership style is that these leaders were driven by the past. They looked at the past to guide their future. What seemed to work before should continue to work again. This of course supports the need to be consistent but does not support ultimate success!

● Today's Leaders

On the other hand, let's look at how one of the 20th century's icons of corporate success—Bill Gates—faced a changing business landscape. Gates has always projected enthusiasm about new technologies and their potential to improve our lives. But some people have forgotten that, when it came to the early days of the Internet, Gates was decidedly pessimistic and slow off the mark.

In the early 1990s Gates talked about how Microsoft spent several million dollars looking at the potential of the Internet. He concluded that the best commercial use would be for video-on-demand (which people could already get via cable and satellite transmission), and that the bandwidths required would be insufficient until the year 2010. As a result, Microsoft chose to take a pass on the Internet.

Then something happened that changed everything. Silicon Valley veteran Jim Clark got together with a recent University of Illinois computer science graduate named Mark Andreessen. In Clark's kitchen they created a small company with a plan to simplify and speed up access to the then-little-known World Wide Web. They called their enterprise Netscape. As soon as their little company went public, it changed the landscape of initial public offerings—it also changed the world as we knew it. As documented in *Time* (Gelernter, 1998), the World Wide Web had emerged. Java was developed by Sun

Microsystems, and it was clear that internet browsers were necessary for doing business. With one bold move by an innovator, Netscape, Microsoft was lagging behind when it came to a new, cutting-edge technology.

And Microsoft, in the public's mind, meant Bill Gates, who in numerous forums had staked out a position that now looked untenable. He was captain of Microsoft, and old-style captains of industry have traditionally gone down with their sinking vessels. At best, they'd find ways to shore up and continue to defend their positions— because the worst thing a leader could do would be to publicly change his or her tune. Being inconsistent was worse than being wrong; it could be seen as weakness and waffling under pressure.

So what did Gates do? After all, he was already one of the richest human beings on the planet. Would he stick with his decision to pass on the Internet? Or would he risk publicly changing his mind? Would he base his decision on what others would think of him? Was he concerned about his ego? Come on—do you really think Bill Gates would make that kind of decision based on what people would think of him?

Gates turned a multi-billion-dollar organization around, and went flat out after the Internet. Microsoft Explorer was developed and eventually became the world's most widely used web browser.

What spurred Gates to move forward after all? Like many of today's successful leaders, Gates was and remains more concerned with success than with what people might think of him. He is driven by the future and its opportunities, not by the past or his ego. He values learning from the past, but he also realizes that preserving it can waste energy. Worrying about others' opinions, being consistent, or keeping the status quo were yesterday's virtues, but in today's fast-paced business world they are the kiss of death. Successful leaders put their egos behind their missions, move forward with the times, and aren't afraid to alter their positions as necessary.

In the future, so will successful employees in every field. Today's teenagers can expect to change careers—not just jobs, but careers—six times before they retire. Many of tomorrow's employment opportunities don't exist yet. You and your classmates will do things we simply can't imagine, changing and upgrading your skills on a constant basis. So you must start to practice being flexible now!

Consider the story of Lamar. He was an engineering major and a member of a fraternity, and he played club soccer for his university. Each semester he met with his advisor, Lamar refused to sign up for any 8 or 9 AM classes (he was too sleepy from studying) or classes that began at 2 or after (he would miss soccer practice) or any that ended after noon on Friday in case he wanted to go out of town for the weekend. His advisor pointed out that Lamar would have to change at least one of those criteria in order to meet all his engineering requirements and remain a full-time student. But Lamar refused to budge. "I know there have to be classes I can take that fit my schedule. I'll take a look at the schedule of classes later and let you know what I find."

Lamar looked, and he couldn't find anything that was still open that met all of his criteria. So he waited until the start of the following semester to fill his course load, hoping that classes held at the times he wanted to take them would come open. Sometimes they did, but because Lamar was just a sophomore, an upperclassman always had priority. Lamar quickly fell behind in meeting his requirements and had to go to summer school two years in a row.

Is not having to get up for a 9 AM class worth the cost in time and money Lamar had to pay by going to summer school? Most of us would say no. And he still had to take courses his junior and senior year that were scheduled at times he didn't like. In other words, his inflexibility gained him nothing!

Or take Sasha. She was a star on the basketball team at her school and gained the attention of college coaches with scholarships to offer. Sasha played the point guard position in high school, but most of the college coaches thought she would be a better fit for the shooting guard position in college. Her high school coach encouraged her to move to the shooting guard position for her senior year so she could develop her skills there. She refused. Each of the college coaches recruiting her asked her how she would feel about being a shooting guard in college. She told the coaches that she was a point guard and that was what she wanted to play.

Sasha had a good senior season in basketball and expected the scholarship offers to come pouring in. A few offers came her way, but not from the bigger schools where she really wanted to go. She texted a couple of the coaches to find out whether they were going to make a scholarship offer. She was shocked to find that almost all of them had already offered the shooting guard scholarship to someone else. But what about point guard? she asked.

You can probably guess the answer. The coaches did not see her as a fit for the point guard role in college and weren't willing to offer her a scholarship to play that position. Sasha ended up going to a school much lower on her list, and after one season—in which the coach promised she could play at point guard—the coach moved her to the shooting guard slot. Sasha inquired about transferring to one of the schools that had first recruited her, but at that point none of them were interested.

● Flexibility Can Be Learned

Flexibility involves being able to train yourself to reinterpret unexpected situations that may at first inspire gloom or alarm. These range from the merely annoying (the five-minute traffic delay, having to share a bathroom in college) to the major and life-altering (for example, upon graduation you refuse a great job because you don't want to live in that city and then cannot find a job in your favored location that requires a college degree).

Inflexibility represents an extreme form of the homing instinct— we become overly attached to familiar ways of thinking and behaving. We can change this, although not without disruption and a period of adjustment. Consider something as simple as not being able to buy your favorite jeans, but settling for a substitute brand instead. At first it will feel odd, which you'll interpret as discomfort. Then it will start to feel normal.

Or take the case of first-year roommates who find they differ about whether to bunk their beds. They both become so entrenched in their opinion that it ruins their relationship and they spend a miserable semester together. Or take the case of a senior who insists on applying to grad schools she will not get into because her GRE score is too low. Using the A-E model can help you become aware of your irrational beliefs (*only brand X jeans are acceptable; my roommate is rude because she won't do things the way I want to; I must attend only the most prestigious school*). It can help you unlearn long-standing inflexibility and understand why you haven't been able to think about doing things a different way.

Emotional self-awareness will help too. Sometimes we fear change, and that's why we're rigid. One way to overcome this resistance is to use imagery. When you are confronted with the possibility or even the near certainty of some change in your life—changing schools, starting a new class, traveling to a different country—try not to panic. Start off by imagining the change taking place. See yourself entering the new lecture room or visiting one of the famous cultural sights; imagine how the situation will play out.

As you watch the scenes in your mind, keep calm. Picture yourself following the new situation, taking part in it, looking for new challenges or adventures. By running through the change and seeing yourself calmly adapt to it, you'll be more aware of opportunities that might arise. You may see yourself meeting new people, being less stressed, learning new things, or enjoying yourself! By visually exploring changes before they occur, you might just make it easier to adapt to these changes.

Here are two other simple strategies for becoming more flexible. Pick a routine that you almost always follow and then change it. Do you always eat the same thing for breakfast? Follow the same route to school? Arrange your clothes the same way in your closet? You may wonder how changing any of these things could help you. But if you're so uncomfortable with these changes that you resist them, then larger, more consequential events will have more power to upset you. Another strategy you can use is to make plans with a friend to do something and then, at the last minute, change your plans to a different activity. Better yet, ask your friend to change the plans and not tell you until the last minute. You'll find that some changes can be exciting, and other changes, which you may have feared, turn out to be harmless or just mildly frustrating. The more you practice adapting to small changes now, the better you will adapt when larger events, especially those you don't control, are forced upon you.

● Be Open to Change

In sum, the flexibility component of emotional intelligence concerns our overall ability to adapt to unfamiliar, unpredictable, and fluid circumstances. Flexible people react to change without rigidity; are able to change their minds when the evidence suggests that they're mistaken; are open to and tolerant of different ideas, orientations, and ways of doing things; and can smoothly handle multiple demands and shifting priorities.

Remember, though, that flexibility doesn't equal impulsiveness. Impulsive people typically react in an arbitrary manner, without sufficient thought, rather than in response to new and valid information. In contrast, people who lack the capacity to be flexible are resistant to new ideas and incapable of adapting. They cling to old behaviors in novel situations, even though their actions are clearly insufficient and ineffective.

Nor is flexibility equivalent to letting others push you around. Some people stand their ground, refusing to give an inch because they don't want to be seen as weak or don't want to give another person too much control. Your flexibility has nothing to do with other people. But it has everything to do with your ability to weigh information, think about the value of adaptation or change, and then make a decision to do something different. It really doesn't matter whether the change is your idea or someone else's idea. If you believe that making the change (with grace, *not* kicking and screaming) will benefit you in some way, then make the change!

Remember also that flexibility is tied to reality testing. If you can't read your environment accurately, you'll be hampered in picking up new signals that ought to lead you to appropriate responses. A football quarterback, for example, had better be highly flexible. He may have a particular plan in mind when the ball is snapped, but he must depart from it if he sees that the action is unfolding in a different way. Were he to stick to the agreed-upon play at any cost, regardless of what was happening on the field, he'd be doomed to failure.

Why Be Flexible?

Flexible people have the capacity to smoothly handle multiple demands, shifting priorities, and rapid change. Particularly in today's business environment and in a globally interconnected world, flexibility helps drive success because it allows you to take advantage of new information as it arises, adapt to change as it occurs, work with people of other cultures with ease, and respond to shifts in priorities.

People who lack the capacity to be flexible continue to practice old behaviors in new settings where they may prove ineffective and inefficient. They are resistant to new ideas and, being unable to adjust to changes, are unprepared when new and different ways are required. As a result, opportunities for success slip through their fingers. Graduation is delayed, relationships challenged, work progress stymied, or promotions lost.

Flexibility is built on twin foundations: a strong sense of reality testing and an ability to manage stressful situations. At this point, it makes sense to revisit your reality testing capability—because if you can't assess what's going on in your environment you'll have difficulty adapting your responses to new information. For example, course changes that affect your scheduling can't be ignored or misinterpreted. If you're blind to them, you could create conflicts that interfere with other courses that are important to you.

Another key to flexibility is self-awareness, which allows you to tap into unrealistic fears (typically, concerns about losing control or being pushed around) and damaging self-talk. If you can identify and deal with these impediments, your innate flexibility will grow.

Reflection Questions

1. When was the last time you resisted change? How did that situation work out for you? Think about conflict you may have experienced, opportunities lost, or other setbacks that occurred. If the situation worked out well, do you believe that will always be the case?

2. When was the last time you embraced change? How did that situation work out for you? What coping mechanisms did you use to help you deal with the stress the change created?

3. Pick one routine and change it for a week. At the end of the week, look back and consider how you reacted to making this change. Did you become more comfortable as the week progressed?

For helpful exercises in increasing your flexibility, consult *The Student EQ Edge: Student Workbook.*

CHAPTER 16

Stress Tolerance

It is not stress that kills us. It is effective adaptation to stress that allows us to live.
—George Vaillant, 1954

Definition: "Stress tolerance involves coping with stressful or difficult situations and believing that one can manage or influence those situations in a positive manner. This component of emotional intelligence is multifaceted: one's stress tolerance depends on being equipped with the necessary and relevant coping skills, maintaining a belief that one can handle the situation, and feeling confident that one can have a positive impact on the outcome. Stress tolerance is very much related to resilience and, when coupled with optimism, is a strong indicator of one's ability to effectively deal with problems and crises (as opposed to surrendering to feelings of helplessness and hopelessness). When stress tolerance is low, anxiety is likely, which can have negative effects on well-being, concentration, and ultimately performance" (Multi-Health Systems, 2011, p. 7).

Too Much Stress

Kevin burst into his residence hall room and frantically began shuffling papers on his desk. "Where's my credit card? I just found out that I was supposed to buy a book for this class, and we have a quiz on the first reading tomorrow. I'm due at work in 15 minutes, and I've got a paper due tomorrow that I put off because the restaurant hadn't scheduled me for tonight. They're understaffed tonight, so I told them I'd work because I need the work to pay for my tuition. Since my dad lost his job, my parents haven't been able to pay for it."

While Kevin was searching, his roommate, Akeem, asked what he could do to help. Akeem knew how much stress Kevin was experiencing now that he'd had to increase his hours at the restaurant so much. Kevin had always made good grades and been well-organized. Now it seemed to Akeem that Kevin was always racing around, creating even more stress for himself because he didn't have good coping strategies to manage the stress.

"You could go pick up that book I need from the bookstore," Kevin replied.

After more searching, Kevin uncovered his credit card and called the bookstore. He gave them his card number, but the charge was rejected. Kevin realized he'd put off paying his last bill because of a tuition payment and now his credit card payment was overdue.

Kevin hung up, muttering under his breath. Now he would owe Akeem for the book, so he made a mental note to go by the ATM machine the next day. He went to the closet to find a white shirt and black pants, which he was required to wear at the restaurant. He found a pair of pants, but there were no white shirts. He remembered then that he had put off doing laundry because he had been so busy working those extra hours. He dug a white shirt out of the dirty clothes pile. It had a few small stains on it, but it would just have to do.

Kevin arrived at work 10 minutes late and got chewed out for being late. When the manager noticed his dirty shirt, he told Kevin to go buy a new shirt at the store next door. Kevin told the manager he didn't have any cash and he couldn't use his card.

"Well then, you don't have a job," replied the manager.

Kevin really needed to be able to pay his bills, so he asked for a second chance. The manager told him to come back the following night with a clean shirt or not come at all. Kevin went home and tried to work on his paper, but his attention drifted. He gave up and went to bed, setting his alarm for 6 ~AM. But he couldn't go to sleep because he kept thinking about everything that had happened that day. His anxiety grew as the night progressed. This wasn't the first night lately that he hadn't been able to sleep. And the more sleep he lost, the more disorganized he seemed to become.

Kevin was experiencing a bout of major stress—and understandably so. He had gone from working a couple of shifts a week at the restaurant to working five or six days a week. He didn't want to drop any classes because that would delay his graduation, and now that he was paying his own tuition, he needed to graduate as soon as possible. But many students face the same situation Kevin faced and handle it better because of their well-developed stress tolerance skills.

Kevin's loss of sleep and disorganization were getting out of control, so the next day he went to the doctor. Kevin found out at his doctor's visit that his sleeplessness and confusion were stress related. Loss of sleep, excessive worrying, sweating, racing heart, confusion, memory problems, and other symptoms all can result from stress, yet we sometimes mistake these symptoms for a physical disorder.

Stress overload is one of the most common maladies of our time. Stress, especially too much of it that we don't control well, has been proven to have an enormous impact on our bodily functions—chiefly our heartbeat, breathing rate, and blood pressure. Stress also creates cognitive problems such as mild memory loss and disorganized thoughts. Over the long term, a person's emotional equilibrium, or ability to manage stress effectively, will affect the person's physical health. Poor health is stressful in itself, making ineffective stress tolerance a vicious cycle.

We may think we know what stress means and how it affects our lives. But even if our understanding is correct, we have difficulty doing something concrete about it amid our increasingly hectic schedules, school responsibilities, family obligations, and other pressures. The more centered you are, the better you'll be able to absorb life's blows, and the healthier—both physically and mentally—you'll feel.

The Evolution of Stress

Our understanding of stress has changed dramatically over the past three decades. In fact, the term did not originate in psychology or physiology, but came from physics. It referred directly to a mechanical force acting on a body. The reaction to that stress was called *strain*.

The notion of stress was first applied to animals and humans in the 1930s, when evolutionary scientists demonstrated how, in the past, threatening situations had caused states of physical arousal. Outside events or perceived danger primed the body for a "fight or flight" response. If early humans (or lions and tigers and bears) had elected to fight, it was critical that they had what it would take to ward off their opponent. The alternative (for humans or smaller creatures) was to make a run for it.

These automatic physiological responses were crucial for our primitive ancestors, and we are their inheritors. But such deep-seated biological impulses can be a mixed blessing for us today. When both our minds and our bodies instinctively react to a barrage of present-day stress, the result can be devastating. Of course, our responses are somewhat more varied than fight or flight.

In the 1960s, Dr. Hans Selye (1976) identified what he termed the "general adaptation syndrome"—our innate methods for coping with stressful events. Basically, he believed that we go through three stages: alarm, resistance, and exhaustion. All of this is more or less automatic, hard-wired into our genes. However, Selye believed that conscious interventions to better process these three stages could modify their impact. These interventions underpin effective stress tolerance techniques, some of which are outlined later in this chapter.

The Indicators of Stress

As with many other components of emotional intelligence, the first step in confronting stress is to engage your self-awareness and look for physical and mental sensations. Which ones apply to you? You might feel wound up, wired, or overwhelmed; experience tension in your neck, back, and shoulders; or suffer from headaches, dizziness, or shortness of breath. Sleep patterns may be disrupted, and you may experience loss of appetite, heartburn, or a variety of aches and pains.

Under stress, our mood turns sour, and we have to fight off depression and anxiety. Thoughts run along the lines of "This is too much to bear"; "I just can't face it anymore"; "How do I get out of this?"; "I wish my problems would all just disappear"; "Can't somebody do something to help me?"

As for behaviors, stress is usually apparent both to the person who's suffering from it and to an astute or even casual observer. When you're under pressure, perhaps you can't sit still. You pace to and fro and wring your hands or run your fingers through your hair. Or you may go to the other extreme: a tendency to sit gazing into space, flopping like the proverbial potato in front of the TV for hours on end, or retiring early to bed, where you stare at the ceiling. And some people, students included, turn to alcohol or other drugs to abate the sensations of stress. Although there may be short-term abatement, using any type of substance to control stress is considered a destructive coping technique.

If you take a minute to run through these admittedly negative responses to stress, and write down any others that you may have experienced—physical sensations, emotional state, habitual thoughts, and observable actions—you'll have a clear picture of your personal stressed-out profile.

● Keep Your Perspective

Effective stress tolerance serves as a preventative measure, helping to protect us from excessive worry, ulcers, and anxiety attacks. It involves a repertoire of suitable responses to trying situations. It's the capacity to be calm and composed, to face difficulties without getting carried away or hijacked by strong emotions. It allows you to tackle and take control of problems one by one, rather than surrendering to panic. As we've seen, the alternatives are less than attractive.

James O. Jackson, a senior writer and editor at *Time* magazine, is one of those rare professionals with an admirable threshold for stress. The nature of his business finds him facing a barrage of last-minute assignments, yet he's able to concentrate, assimilate vast amounts of information in mere hours, and produce beautifully written prose. All the while, he somehow manages to keep his sense of humor, has time for the problems of others, and meets erratic behavior and unreasonable expectations on the part of his frazzled colleagues with unflappable equanimity.

How does he do it? In writing to the authors, he explains, "It helps to have been raised in New Mexico, where the only stress is imported by visiting Texans, New Yorkers, and Californians." The key, he says, is to be assured of what you can do, do the best you can, and don't let anyone or anything nudge you into unnecessary frenzy. Of course, as we feel more confident, we expand our horizons. Most important, according to Jackson, is a sense of perspective: "What will it all mean in 100 years, or 100 days or 100 hours? Today's magazine is tomorrow's birdcage liner." And, with typical self-deprecating wit, he points out the value of laziness: "Lazy people find quick, easy ways to get the job done." This from a man who has run field bureaus in Bonn and Moscow, was the first American journalist to interview Mikhail Gorbachev, wrote a spy thriller in his spare time, and enjoys gardening at his Massachusetts summer house (James O. Jackson, personal communication, May 25, 2004).

Jackson's formula centers on three key elements: the capability to plan a course of positive action to limit and contain stress; the ability to maintain an optimistic attitude in the face of sudden change and negative experiences; and the capacity to feel that you have control or at least influence over stress-inducing events.

● Don't Be Your Own Worst Enemy

Stressed-out feelings are very often stoked by the A-E model described in Chapter 2 and by self-sabotaging self-talk. It is very easy to catastrophize the situation, along the lines of "I'm going to have a nervous breakdown. It's absolutely impossible for me to do this." Exaggerated beliefs such as these are guaranteed to keep the vicious cycle of stress running at full throttle. It's difficult—if not impossible—to address the true external cause of your stressful feelings without first getting those feelings under control.

Let's go back to Kevin, the stressed-out student trying to make ends meet, and take a look at his A-E model. His activating events are clear: he's juggling a course paper, a part-time job where he's increased his hours because of his dad's unemployment, responsibility for paying his own tuition, and a full load of demanding college classes; he arrives at his part-time job late, in dirty work clothes, so his boss wants to fire him; he doesn't have a textbook he needs; and his credit card is refused because the payment is overdue. He then describes the consequences: he's tense, anxious, overwhelmed; his mind is racing, he's losing sleep, and lack of sleep is destroying his powers of organization and concentration. He doesn't know which way to turn; he fears for his health.

Now Kevin must look at the beliefs that conspire to make him feel overwhelmed. *If I don't buy a textbox by tomorrow, I'll fail the quiz and start the course with a bad grade that I won't be able to pull up. If I don't get my credit card account straightened out, I'll have to work even more hours, and I can't handle the ones I'm working now. And getting fired will mean I have to drop out.*

Holding these beliefs just makes the emotional (more anxiety) and physical (more lost sleep) consequences of stress worse. But what if Kevin disputes or challenges these beliefs? Instead of focusing on the worst possible consequences, he can be more optimistic. He still has enough time to improve his grades, even if the first quiz doesn't go well, and his boss is giving him another chance at work. He has the money to pay his credit card bill; he just needs a better system for remembering to do that, and Akeem has offered to help. By framing his reaction to these admittedly serious problems in a different way, Kevin may well find a way to deal with them.

The first step in combating feelings of being overwhelmed and powerless, which are associated with being stressed out, is to regain control. Simply writing down all the many situations with which you are dealing moves you from a passive position to an active stance. Psychologically, this shifts the emphasis from your being a helpless victim of circumstances to an active agent in mastering these circumstances.

Next, combine related pressures into a single category. Kevin began by writing down the amount of school work he had, the full class load, the rushed deadlines—all of these he listed under "school-related stressors." Next, he wrote down the other simultaneous pressures to which he was exposed: problems with part-time job, dealing with laundry (getting work clothes ready), getting to work on time, and the need to work more hours to pay for his tuition. All of these went under the category of "part-time job issues."

The process of writing these down made the stressors more concrete, and in doing so, more manageable—far more than the amorphous feeling he previously had of being bombarded by ill-defined issues.

The third step is to take on the stressors in "bite-sized" chunks. For example, take one problem only, and address it. In reflecting on this, Kevin realized that most of his school problems were not the result of insufficient time; rather, he wasn't using his nonwork time constructively He could handle this by not spending so much time surfing the net or watching TV now that he had to work more hours. This would give him more time for studying and preparation of coursework. Although money was also an issue, by better managing his time, he'd get to his job on time (in a clean shirt!) and not jeopardize his income. Another option was to ask the manager to give him more weekend hours and fewer shifts during the middle of the week. Again, the idea that there are alternatives—whether they work out or not—psychologically gave Kevin a sense of control over what previously had felt like an uncontrolled downpour of demands.

Kevin might also try to prioritize which "bite-sized" tasks he was going to address first, based on what seems to be the most important, what seems to have the shortest timeline, or what would be the easiest to successfully manage.

While doing this mental planning, Kevin might also pay attention to activities that could diminish his sense of physical and emotional exhaustion. He could get involved in a physical activity like running, a sport, or working out—all of which, through their release of endorphins, will have a destressing effect on Kevin's physical and psychological symptoms of being stressed out. Listening to the right music during his free time would also have a tranquilizing effect on his mood, thoughts, and behavior.

Resolving to stay in touch with his family and close friends at other schools more often by text, video calls, or phone calls could also help him reduce stress, while strengthening his relationships and providing social support.

Kevin can handle his credit-card stress by leaving the credit card in his desk drawer and using it only in emergencies. He resolves to pay for everything with his debit card, which will help him limit his spending to necessities only, thus freeing up more money for tuition payments.

Going through this exercise, Kevin's panic subsides, he perceives a number of sensible courses of action, his mood brightens, and his stress—while still present—begins to feel more controllable.

Can you strengthen your resilience to stress and actively increase what might be called your hardiness? Indeed you can. Stress tolerance can be learned (as we'll demonstrate later on in this chapter). Once learned, it offers relief and improved health in both the short and longer term. That, in turn, allows us to become more flexible and adaptive when further, more severe hardships come our way.

The attempt to understand the relationship between negative events and our ability to cope with them has a long history. As early as 1915, Freud was postulating what he termed a "defense mechanism," a largely unconscious process involving deep-seated internal repression and rationalization as a reaction to anxiety (Freud, 1915). But Freud's theories were updated in the late 1970s by researchers who believed that, on the contrary, stressful situations usually unleash conscious strategies or styles that people under stress have developed over time to suit themselves.

This is good news for those who wish to handle stress better. If Freud had been correct, we would have to probe for and uncover unconscious processes by means of extensive therapy—an arduous prospect. But if stress can be eased (or worsened)—sometimes instantaneously—by those affected, depending on what they tell themselves and how they behave, then the condition is much more amenable to improvement on an individual basis.

● Dealing with Stress

If we do not develop stress responses to demanding and challenging situations, we always run the risk that the emotional experiences of anxiety, panic, or hopelessness will erode our ability to reality test, problem solve, and behave with confidence and certainty. Our physical symptoms—chronic tension, shortness of breath, and so on—will deplete our sense of vitality and make it difficult for us to concentrate and focus. All of these debilities will make it less likely that we can be successful.

In short, if we "cave in" to minimal environmental demands, we will not have the presence of mind, the hardiness, or the resilience to behave independently and assertively, and all of this will undercut our attempts to successfully manage stress. Individuals who do not have good stress tolerance tend to fall apart or become overwhelmed in two ways: some feel highly anxious and agitated, flustered and worried, helpless and hopeless, demoralized and apathetic; others may not experience what they recognize as uncomfortable emotional states, but may develop physical symptoms of insomnia, rapid heartbeat, breathing difficulties, nausea, diarrhea, unrelenting headaches, or unexplained rashes.

Take the case of the star basketball player standing on the free throw line, all alone with the game hanging in the balance. Does getting flustered help the player make the free throw? What about having your heart rate surge, providing more energy than usual to the shot, probably making it go long? Does that help? What about feeling anxious about the team losing if the free throw is missed? How in the world can we expect a young athlete to *not* respond to the stress in that situation? After all, does the athlete really have control over his or her body in this situation?

The answer is yes, assuming the athlete has maintained good stress tolerance practices, has the basketball game in perspective, and has visualized this situation before during practice (remember visualization from Chapter 13 on problem solving?). It helps to prevent overreaction to stress as well. Although some degree of stress is normal and expected in this situation, many athletes step to the free throw line and calmly (or at least with a calm demeanor) make the shot. Others, however, take extra bounces of the ball, let out a heavy sigh, or fidget while waiting for the ref to give them the ball. And many of them miss the critical free throw. We're not saying that managing stress is easy, but we are saying that practice makes perfect (or almost perfect)—just like with free throws.

Individuals who have developed the ability to tolerate stress do not develop the stress-related symptoms, but rather stay calm and focused under pressure. They do not visit their difficulties on others. They have the capacity to relax and wind down emotionally. Those who tolerate stress well are also described as hardy and resilient. They can present themselves with confidence, think clearly, and assess their environments realistically.

Of key importance is that you develop positive coping strategies that have proven to be successful: exercise, meditation, yoga, social support, hobbies, and biofeedback have all been proven to help manage and relieve stress. Likewise, there are coping mechanisms that some people use—such as overeating, drugs, cigarettes, alcohol, excessive shopping, and playing endless computer games—that can be detrimental to effective stress tolerance and result in other problems as well.

Stress tolerance is linked with success because it brings with it the capacity to focus and weather storms without allowing unpleasant feelings or disturbing bodily symptoms to interfere with moving forward and reaching a goal. Without the capacity for stress tolerance, we find that reality testing, problem solving, flexibility, and impulse control are all eroded. And as these abilities are undermined, individuals become less and less able to function successfully.

Reflection Questions

1. List your major stressors right now.

2. Now categorize them into groups, as Kevin did with "school issues," "part-time job issues," and so on.

3. Now, identify one or two small steps you can take for each of these categories. As you successfully implement those strategies, scale up your coping strategies.

4. Identify two or three things you are willing to engage in daily that will help reduce the impact of stress. Pick things that relax you (from yoga to talking with a friend) and make sure you build in daily time for these.

For some very specific exercises and assignments you can do to better manage your stress, consult *The Student EQ Edge: Student Workbook.*

CHAPTER 17

Optimism

The optimist proclaims that we live in the best of
all possible worlds, and the pessimist fears this is true.
—James Branch Cabell, 1926

Definition: "Optimism is an indicator of one's positive attitude and outlook on life. It involves remaining hopeful and resilient, despite occasional setbacks. Optimism assumes a measure of hope in one's approach to life. It is a positive approach to daily living and a significant component of resilience and well-being" (Multi-Health Systems, 2011, p. 7).

● Lessons from a Candy Man

Reuben Rodriguez was a vice-president of human resources at Group IMSA, a $1.6-billion manufacturer that, with 2,600 employees, is among the largest 25 firms in Mexico. In his position as an export sales manager, he was having trouble closing a deal with a major client, who looked as if he might be ready to take his business elsewhere. Reuben was perplexed and upset; he grew more worried by the day. He couldn't focus on his work, and his personal life began to suffer. Defeatist thoughts threatened to overwhelm him for the first time in his career. Then, as he told the authors, a seemingly trifling incident drove home to him the positive power of optimism and the negative effects of dwelling on the downside (Reuben Rodriguez, personal communication, February 15, 1999).

One Saturday morning, in the midst of Reuben's most stressful period, a traveling vendor came to his door with an order of fresh strawberries for Reuben's wife. The vendor was accompanied by another shabbily dressed man, carrying a tray of fruit candies whose virtues he kept pitching whenever the conversation lagged. Reuben fended him off at first—but when the man persisted, Reuben lost his temper. "Don't you understand?" he shouted. "Can't you hear? I don't want any candies. Go away and stop bothering me. Learn to get the message—no means no!" With that, Reuben took possession of the strawberries and slammed the door behind him.

But he'd slammed it so hard it popped open, and he had to go back and close it again. This time, he overheard the two men as they walked away. The strawberry vendor was trying to cheer his friend, but the candy vendor didn't need cheering. "No problem," he said. "This guy is going to be my customer next week. Just wait and see. He's in a bad mood today, but sooner or later he'll buy."

Reuben stood on the doorstep, as a mental lightbulb came on. Here he was, the highly trained professional with a college education, receiving a lesson in salesmanship 101 from an unexpected source. The peddler had showed persistence, optimism, and generosity of spirit. On a day when everything had gone wrong, he had seen future opportunity. In fact, the opportunity materialized at once. Reuben called to the man to come back; he bought some candies and tipped him lavishly. "You have no idea how helpful you've been," he told the vendor.

So the vendor made his sale—but did Reuben? In fact, he didn't, but he accepted this setback and went on to achieve greater success. He'd learned a lesson that stayed with him—one that he applies to this day while training his employees. Optimism has nothing to do with how rich or poor you may be. It's an inner resource—the ability to believe that even though times may be rough, with renewed effort they'll improve; that failure and success are to a great degree states of mind (Reuben Rodriquez, personal communication, February 15, 1999).

● Turn the Three Ps Around

Like assertiveness, optimism is very often misunderstood. It's not a tendency to believe that things are going to turn out for the best no matter what. That inclination reflects a weakness in our reality testing, and also abdicates our part in the equation—risky behavior that can blind us to the real challenges that must be faced and overcome. Nor is it the capacity to indulge in a perpetual pep talk—to keep repeating positive things about yourself. This too can lead you up a blind alley.

Rather, optimism is the ability to stop thinking or saying destructive things about yourself and the world around you, especially when you're suffering personal setbacks. And it's also the ability to stay positive and persist, as the candy salesman did, even when things aren't going well. True optimism is a comprehensive and hopeful but realistic approach to daily living.

The psychologist Martin Seligman has discovered three major attitudes that distinguish optimists from pessimists (1990). First, they view downturns in their lives as temporary blips in the graph. The bad times won't last forever; the situation will turn around. They don't feel doomed to walk through an unfolding disaster movie of sadness, disappointment, and underachievement. They see troubles and difficulties as delayed success, rather than outright and conclusive defeat.

Second, they tend to view the misfortune as situational and specific, not as yet another manifestation of a long-standing and inescapable doom that permeates every aspect of their lives. Thus even a really bad experience can be examined and dealt with individually—it's not the last straw. Third, optimists don't immediately shoulder all the blame. If their examination turns up external causes for what is happening, they take these into consideration.

This is in contrast to the three Ps of pessimism: *permanence, pervasiveness*, and *personalizing*. Pessimists will tend to experience each and every setback as just the latest in a long line of past and, quite probably, future failures (pervasiveness) that they're fated to suffer for the rest of their lives (permanence). Any lapse will be seen as yet another example of how they screw up everything all the time (personalizing). Why do bad things keep happening? Because pessimists decide that their own incompetence or ineffectiveness is to blame (Seligman, 1990).

The optimist turns those three Ps around—not by some so-called power of positive thinking, but by using the A-E model to dispute inappropriate self-blame and feelings of helplessness. Consider Chang, who lost a good job opportunity after getting caught in a traffic jam that made him late for a crucial interview. If he were a die-hard pessimist, his responses might be: It figures. Nothing has gone right for me in a long time (permanence). No wonder this happened; every part of my life is messed up (pervasiveness). I'm an idiot for starting so late and taking that route (personalization).

In contrast, if Chang took an optimistic view, he might respond like this: Ugh, what a downer. But I've got another interview next week. (The outcome, although undeniably unpleasant, isn't the end of the world.) Bad luck—but I've missed appointments before, and I'm not on the breadline yet. (The present situation is unique, not a reflection of how things "always" turn to ashes, and it needn't be repeated.) It wouldn't have made any difference which route I took; the whole city's gridlocked. (An external force played its part.) Note how optimism is closely tied to the ability to dispute irrational beliefs that lead to negative feelings and behaviors.

It would have been a mistake for Chang to try to blame all his woes on heavy traffic. That would have been looking for excuses, an abdication of all responsibility for how things turn out. The traffic was a factor, to be sure, but he could have gotten up at the crack of dawn and played it extra safe. Perhaps he will the next time around. Pinning all the blame on external factors is just as bad as pinning it all on ourselves. The healthy approach lies somewhere in between the two extremes.

Consider an example Korrel experienced with a student who came to her office to inquire how she could do better on tests. When

Korrel suggested the student try different study techniques, the student responded, "Well, nothing will help" (pervasiveness) "if you're giving multiple choice tests. I can't do those" (personalization).

Korrel then gently replied, "Then your grade won't change."

The student looked puzzled.

"It sounds as if you've already given up and believe you will never be able to do well on multiple choice tests. If that's what you tell yourself, then it will probably come true. You have to decide that you can learn to do well on this type of test and then practice strategies to help you do well."

This student, who got an F on the first test, went on to earn a B– in the course. The question type and test difficulty did not change, but the student's attitude did. It's all about how you frame things.

● Flexible Optimism Versus Blind Optimism

Another danger is the tendency to put on rose-colored glasses. If our attitude is too positive, it may lead us into uncritical assessments of a given situation. That's why optimism is tied to reality testing—our ability to read our surroundings accurately. Seligman (1991) uses the term "flexible optimism" for this grounded-in-the-real-world hopefulness and distinguishes it from "blind optimism"—an essentially pie-in-the-sky and un-self-critical approach. Blind optimists are in denial—for them, no problems exist, and success can be obtained against impossible odds and in the face of logic. They also overlook or skate around the cost of failure.

As an extreme example, if you spend large sums of money buying lottery tickets, you marginally increase your chances of winning, but the odds remain stacked against you and the price of losing increases because you've devoted even more of your income to a fool's errand. Sometimes a child can see what the blind optimist cannot—it's time to back down and take another approach. Generally, these are times when the potential cost of a particular decision is enormously high, even if the risk involved may appear to be somewhat low.

Given these distinctions, how can we increase our sense of realistic or flexible optimism? Adversity and disappointment strike us all, but our responses vary. An optimistic approach is vital for enhancing resilience—the capacity to bounce back from frustration or failure. Why do optimists experience life's inevitable downturns so differently from the way pessimists do? Both, over the long haul, probably encounter the same number of defeats (although pessimists, because they expect the worst, are perhaps looking for trouble, and find it more often). One answer is that the difference lies in what optimists say to and about themselves following an adverse event—the self-talk identified in our A-E model.

As noted earlier, everyone responds to various events with specific thoughts, which drive feelings and behaviors. Pessimists tend to follow a particular cycle. Their thoughts are angry or hopeless—they want something, can't get it, and are convinced that they never will. Remember the student who "could not do" multiple choice tests? Not surprisingly, the resulting feelings and behaviors are sadness, guilt, helplessness, passivity, and inaction or (worse) destructive action.

The optimist guards against these feelings and behaviors by breaking the cycle of destructive signals that get passed down the line when misfortune strikes, and replacing them with more appropriate ones. Think of this as recording over an existing tape. The result is enthusiasm about new alternatives, confidence that renewed or alternative efforts will succeed, creative planning, goal-oriented activity, and healthy living.

● Give Yourself a Break

Keep in mind that it's always advisable to look for plausible alternatives. Pessimists head straight for the worst-case scenario and, as explained earlier, take it personally. For example, consider a student who spoke up in a student government meeting, to find that no one even acknowledged her comment. What does she do next? She shuts down, folds her arms, and says to herself, "No one values my opinion.

I'll never be a good leader." And so on. To appreciate how counter-productive these thoughts are, imagine someone else saying those things to the student. The comments would be considered offensive, and the student would leap to her own defense.

What might have actually been happening at that meeting? Maybe a whole lot of people were talking at once, and only the person beside her heard the comment—and didn't agree with it. Maybe it's time to reassess. She should focus on what's temporary and change-able (*I'll wait for the noise from other speakers to abate*); specific rather than all-encompassing (*This is a controversial topic, and the other students all have strong feelings they want to express*); and above all not personal (*People have listened to my comments in other meetings; no one is listening to anyone else either*).

Alternatively, she could wait for a time to support someone else who makes a comment similar to her opinion, thus reinforcing her beliefs. This is called the "so what?" technique, and should not be scorned. You got the worst grade in class? You got turned down for a job or by someone you had asked out on a date? Well, so what? Try your best to let it go. Recognize your legitimate feelings of dis-appointment, but don't let them debilitate you. Use the setback to spur yourself on. Take another class—perhaps one more suited to your skills and interests—and you'll score higher. Another com-pany or organization may recognize your talents; another applica-tion will yield the result you seek. As for finding the love of your life, even a host of rejections doesn't mean that there's no one who's right for you. Romance is a mysterious endeavor at the best of times; you never know when Mr. or Ms. Right will come around the corner, and you'll be better prepared if your head isn't buried in a sand pile of pessimism.

Even if some of the negative thoughts that crowd your mind have some degree of validity at the moment, you can move on, taking steps that will enable you to handle similar situations better in the future. Try not to repeat your mistakes. It's surprising how many people—especially those with pessimistic tendencies—continue to bang their heads against the wall, perhaps as a way of punishing themselves for not being able to attain success in one particular task. This leads nowhere. We aren't counseling you to give up in the face of adversity. We are saying: take a time-out, step back and look at yourself objectively, and don't force yourself to do something over and over if you know that it's not one of your strengths. That realistic self-examination is a strength in itself, and will lead to brighter days.

So how can you give yourself a break? Here are some examples that might help you. Think of a student who gets a bad grade on a paper but believes she will do better next time and vows to use the writing center to help; or the student who loses an election in student government but vows to stay involved in student issues and build a better case for next year's election; or the athlete who loses a starting role on the team to an older player but thinks about the playing time he will get and future opportunities to start; or the senior about to graduate who chooses to do everything recommended by the career center even though the job market is horrible. You may be able to come up with similar examples in your own life, and then consider the upside—or opportunities you may have as a result of what seemed like a defeat.

● Advantages of Being Optimistic

In his book *Learned Optimism*, psychologist Martin Seligman (1991) details a number of scientific research studies that show that optimistic people live longer, have fewer illnesses, and have lower blood pressure. They tend to be more successful in all their activities. And, as you'll learn in an upcoming chapter, optimism can even be a better predictor of college GPA than SAT scores! Is any of this surprising? Not really.

Realistic optimism is the ability to look at the brighter side of life and maintain a positive attitude in the face of adversity. It is a positive approach to daily living. Optimistic people recognize when they are in difficult situations, but they have a positive view of how things will turn out—based on recognition and acknowledgment of their own skills, the capacity to actively address problems, and the ability to recall other situations in which they have successfully overcome obstacles. In this way, realistic optimists differ greatly from those individuals who maintain an unrealistically positive outlook *despite* objective evidence that they are confronted with very difficult and real problems. These people are not realistically optimistic; they have significant difficulties with their reality testing. They keep themselves blinded to the very real problems they face by maintaining a head-in-the-sand attitude.

Here's the difference between realistic optimism and blind optimism for a student. Suppose you were assigned a 25-page paper that required multiple scientific resources and evidence to support your conclusions. And let's suppose that the longest paper you've completed previously was 10 pages. The realistic optimist would begin thinking about how to tackle the paper, what resources are available to help (librarians to help guide a literature search, writing center to help organize ideas, office hours to meet with the faculty member to discuss the paper) and then begin work on the project, tackling a little bit at a time. Though the work is hard, this first student persists and continues to believe the end product will be good.

The blind optimist, in contrast, discounts the enormity of the task, tells others it's no big deal because he's a good writer, and begins working on the paper the weekend before it's due on Monday. Blind optimism looks a lot more like living in a fantasy world, whereas realistic optimism is just that: optimism that takes into account the realities of the situation.

Optimistic people are resilient and hardy; they face adverse situations with a realistic "can do" attitude. Rather than feeling hopeless, giving up, or turning away from difficult situations, they persevere: they are tenacious; they keep trying. They are also flexible—they try different approaches. These qualities fuel their success.

Reflection Questions

1. Spend a day listening to family and friends, writing down optimistic thinking (like that shown by the candy salesman) and pessimistic thinking (like that shown by the student who "couldn't do" multiple choice tests). What did you hear more of: optimism or pessimism? What patterns did you notice among your family and friends that you believe are influencing you?

2. Write down something bad that happened to you recently. Then write out three statements you told yourself at the time that *contradict* any tendency to permanence, pervasiveness, or personalization.

3. Do a quick search on Google Scholar or in your library's database. Find three abstracts that relate optimism to some positive outcome.

For some helpful exercises and assignments on how to build your own optimism, refer to *The Student EQ Edge: Student Workbook.*

General Well-Being

This area of emotional intelligence concerns your ability to enjoy yourself and others and your overall feelings of contentment or dissatisfaction. As you can see in Figure Part Seven, well-being, which mainly encompasses happiness, surrounds all the other realms. We see happiness as a facilitating factor of emotional intelligence. It can affect all the other areas. Happier people tend to perform better in the various realms than people who are unhappy in their lives.

Figure Part 7 Happiness and General Well-Being

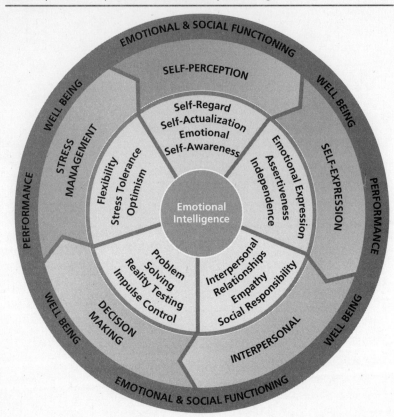

CHAPTER 18

Happiness

Rules for Happiness:
something to do,
someone to love,
something to hope for.
   —Immanuel Kant
The more you praise and celebrate your life, the more there is in
life to celebrate.
   —Oprah Winfrey
Happiness is no laughing matter.
   —Richard Whatley

Definition: "Happiness is an indicator of emotional health and well-being. It is characterized by feelings of satisfaction, contentment, and by the ability to enjoy the many aspects of one's life" (Multi-Health Systems, 2011, p. 8).

● Do You Enjoy Life?

Andrew awakes thinking, "Another day of school, school, school. Oh well, gotta get up." Walking to class, he thinks, "The sun's too bright. I should have brought my sunglasses. Oh well, I'll be in class soon." On campus, he puts in his time, talks with his friends, daydreams in class, skips another class, but keeps his eye on the clock, waiting for the time to go back home. When invited to join a number of friends for dinner, he thanks them and takes a rain check, saying there is a sports program on TV he has his heart set on watching.

Jamal, on the other hand, awakes, peers out his dorm window at the blue sky and sunshine, and thinks, "Looks great out—a bright sunny day."

Walking out of the building, he heads down the street, gazes up, and notices the first change of tree leaves, beginning the fall season. "Wow, those colors are awesome," he muses. At school, he spends some time joking with his friends and, although he is looking forward to a sports program on television later that evening, when invited to join his friends for dinner, he replies, "I was going to watch the sports special tonight, but this sounds even better!"

Unlike Andrew, Jamal felt pleasure at the beginning of a new day, appreciated seemingly small things like a blue sky, and had both a jocular ease with friends at school and a sense of spontaneity that allowed him to change his plans and actively and joyously participate with his friends at dinner. He had a sense of vitality about, and pleasure in, life. Jamal, in effect, lived by Oprah's quote at the beginning of this chapter. The more you find to celebrate in life, the happier you will be.

Happy people have a sense of cheerfulness and enthusiasm about them and a strong capacity to enjoy life, have fun, and be spontaneous. They take pleasure in the small things in life.

In contrast, individuals whose capacity for happiness is diminished rarely feel delight, tend to be inhibited in their style, and seldom show spontaneity. At the far end of this spectrum, people who lack happiness may exhibit symptoms typical of clinical depression: a pervasive feeling of sadness and glumness, a pessimistic outlook, significant guilt over what seem to be minor transgressions, suicidal thoughts, and bodily symptoms of sleep disturbance and weight loss, among other things.

The capacity for happiness is not an isolated ability. It influences and is influenced by other abilities, such as reality testing, self-regard, self-actualization, interpersonal relationship, and optimism. If, for example, your capacity for reality testing is compromised and you tend to evaluate the environment around you through dark-colored glasses, always "making a mountain out of a molehill," chances are your capacity to feel happy will be impaired. On the other hand, accurate reality testing combined with a strong sense of self-regard and self-actualization will positively influence your capacity for happiness.

How so? Self-actualization indicates we are pursuing and achieving meaningful goals, something that should boost our self-regard—unless we are too self-critical. Happiness partly comes from the pleasure of knowing we have done something well. Happiness also multiplies when we have others in our lives with whom we have strong, caring bonds (interpersonal relationship). There's nothing like a best friend or partner to turn to in good times or bad, knowing the person will be there for you. Finally, happiness is related to optimism. Believing you will succeed at something or successfully manage a difficult time in your life breeds the kind of positive energy that fuels our happiness. How many people do you know who think bad thoughts—like Chicken Little did running around shouting "the sky is falling" in the well-known children's story—and simultaneously experience happiness? Pessimism and happiness just don't mix well.

Broadly speaking, there are two reasons why some of us wind up feeling unhappy. First, we hope that we will obtain something we desire, or expect that something good will happen to us. When these hopes or expectations do not materialize, we feel disappointed. We may then start to believe that it is our destiny to be forever unsuccessful or unfulfilled. Second, we expect or fear that something bad will befall us. When these fears are realized—and all of us do occasionally have bad things happen to us—we once again sink into resignation and helplessness.

But there's good news: if we modify our wants and expectations, we can temper both the sense of resignation and the resultant sadness. Through reality testing, we may be able to shift our goals so that they're more appropriate and attainable. Of course, if they're in fact appropriate and we still can't attain them, we'll be forced to either give them up (which is bound to make us feel sad in the short term) or come at them from another direction by using problem-solving skills—a valuable technique because to abandon hope of achieving what you want may well reflect a pessimistic attitude or faulty problem-solving. And when we do have the inevitable setback, being surrounded by a support network of friends and family can help ease the disappointment.

● Nature or Nurture?

The pursuit of happiness ranks right up there with the search for love and the quest for eternal truths as one of the most riveting preoccupations of humankind. Because North Americans have both time and money on their hands, achieving happiness is a growth industry. Each publishing season, a new batch of book titles speaks to our individual and collective yearning to feel content. Meanwhile, academics and scientists are doing their part. Each year for the past two decades, more than 1,000 scholarly articles have sought to dissect our quality of life and our chances at self-fulfillment.

This is nothing new. Many ancient philosophers believed in the search for happiness, known by them as *hedonism*. In their view, this was a noble goal, the highest and best use of our time on earth. These days the word has fallen into disrepute, and we think of hedonism as a primarily selfish activity—a short-term scramble for more or less instant gratification. Happiness, in contrast, is seen as a more desirable, more all-encompassing, and far more worthy aim. Recall how the philosopher Kant defined happiness in this chapter's opening epigraph: something to do ("work" that provides self-actualization), someone to love (interpersonal relationships), and something to hope for (optimism about the present challenges and future possibilities). Pursuing happiness, as defined by Kant, is a worthy goal.

But how to attain it? In 1996, a remarkable possibility was raised by two researchers at the University of Minnesota (Lykken & Tellegen). They released the results of a study of 2,310 pairs of identical and fraternal twins, which found little variation between the self-reported satisfaction levels of those twins who were raised together and those who were raised apart. Happiness, the scientists surmised, must be partly genetic—somewhere between 44 and 52 percent inherited. The medical and psychological communities took a skeptical view of the so-called happiness gene, and things quieted down for a while. The consensus was and remains that, although we may be born with some kind of predisposition toward being happy, whether or not we actually achieve the state itself depends more on external factors and our reactions to them.

● Money Does Not (Necessarily) Equal Happiness

Happiness seems to have relatively little to do with material well-being. The Hungarian-born American researcher Dr. Mihaly Csikszentmihalyi (1999), who has spent much of his career putting happiness under the microscope, has several insights to offer. According to his findings, people worldwide tend to describe themselves as more happy than unhappy. We'd expect, for example, that anyone who's fortunate enough to live in a country that's economically prosperous and politically stable would be ahead of the game, and this is true to some degree—Swiss and Norwegians report a higher level of happiness than Greeks and Portuguese report. And when the Irish and the Japanese are asked whether they are happy, more of the Irish answer yes. In the United States, studies have consistently found that about one-third of people surveyed say they're "very happy," whereas only one-tenth of people describe themselves as "not too happy." The majority choose the description "fairly happy"—that is, slightly above what they'd imagine to be the average.

Since the 1960s, an international group of social scientists has been collecting data in 50 countries for a project called the World Values Surveys (World Values Study Group, 1994). These surveys found that happiness levels increase in direct relation to economic development until a country achieves prosperity roughly equivalent to that of Ireland. Past that point, there seems to be hardly any direct link between prosperity and happiness. The Values Surveys also found that a sudden financial gain—as, for example, a lottery win—can boost happiness for a few months, but that over a ten-year span it has no impact on happiness.

When the University of Illinois psychologist Ed Diener and his colleague David Myers at Michigan's Hope College reviewed a host of other studies for a *Psychological Science* article titled "Who Is Happy?" they found little difference based on gender, race, and age, and only a small relation between riches and life satisfaction. In the United States, billionaires are only slightly happier than people with average incomes. Personal incomes may have more than doubled between 1960 and the late 1990s in constant dollars, but the proportion of people who described themselves as happy has remained stable. That is, once you're above the poverty line, more money contributes less and less to the happiness mix. More important, according to their research, were traits such as self-esteem, sense of personal control, optimism, and extraversion (Myers & Diener, 1995; Diener & Biswas-Diener, 2002; Diener & Seligman, 2002).

Happiness Comes from the Inside Out

How can we actually increase our happiness level? As we've seen throughout this book, what we *do* concretely affects how we *feel*. If we're strong and active, we're more likely to be happy. If we can achieve a reasonable quality of life, even in relatively modest circumstances, we'll be happy. If we develop goals that give our lives meaning and we keep mentally and physically alert, we'll be happy. It's important to have dreams and take risks in life, no matter how humble the dreams and modest the risks.

The love and companionship of friends, romantic partners, and family certainly enters the picture. Although we can be happy in private moments of reflection and during solitary activities, most of us feel better when we're with others. Individuals with a large social network—those with strong interpersonal skills—tend to be happier than those with few personal contacts. A state of withdrawal does not lead to happiness, which may partially explain why extroverts are happier than introverts. That having been said, achieving happiness really does hinge on yourself alone. Stephen R. Covey (2004), the renowned business writer and trainer, was convinced that long-term happiness comes from the inside out—by our controlling our own lives and directing our short-term desires to higher purposes and principles. Simply put, happiness must be built from within. Covey went on to explore the folly of trying to change the world—let alone your marital partner or your children—without first recognizing and changing the role you yourself play, which is plainly the first step toward real fulfillment and happiness. Covey's beliefs about happiness coming from within are verified in study after study about what produces happiness.

Another factor in the happiness mix is a person's ratio of expectations to accomplishments. Setting goals is fine, but if you set your sights unrealistically high, you may fall short and fall into unhappiness. Even those who accomplish the most may not necessarily enjoy their achievements, simply because they are unable to satisfy themselves. For example, Asian students who come to North American schools frequently achieve excellent grades but are less content than classmates who are doing less well (Saw, 2011; Wong, Brownson, & Schwing, 2011). Why? Because the demands they place on themselves are even higher than their formidable accomplishments. Again, one's perception and the ability to set a realistic frame of reference are key to achieving happiness.

Some students strive for high marks in order to please their parents. But the joy of discovery and learning in courses that were chosen out of interest can often be more rewarding than a good grade. Many students have reported happiness from giving their best effort in a challenging situation even though they didn't get public recognition. Their most memorable moments may have come from playing in a school band or orchestra, being part of a great football or basketball team, or contributing to the school paper. When recent graduates return to campus, they often talk about the one or two classes that challenged them the most—the exact challenge they needed to feel a sense of accomplishment; not surprisingly, they also talk about the elevated confidence that followed. Let's consider an example.

Although this was his first year at a new school, Trevor wanted to become president of the student council because he thought it would give him a higher profile, offer him an opportunity to meet new kids, and help him to be seen as a figure of importance. He discussed this with his dad, who pointed out, "I think it's a great idea that you want to contribute. However, you've been at this school for only a couple of weeks. Most of the other kids have been there for a couple of years. I think chances are good that you may not be successful. Not because you're not a good candidate or haven't got what it takes, but because people just haven't had the opportunity to get to know how good you are. Maybe it would be better if you did something else, where you could still contribute, but where your success doesn't depend upon being elected by kids who don't know you. Then, when they get to know you, you'll have a better chance next year."

Trevor listened to his dad and thought the advice was good. He modified his goal: instead of running for school council, he volunteered for the school newspaper, which would put him into contact with lots of kids and allow him to lobby for school issues and display his name in a byline once every other week. He felt good about his decision and ultimately was happy with the experience he had on the newspaper.

Think what would have happened if he had run for president of the school council, given his newness. Chances are he would have been defeated and would have felt quite sad as a result. However, by reexamining and readjusting his goal, he was able to focus on one that was attainable and from which he experienced a fair amount of enjoyment.

Clearly happiness is tied to reality testing. Happy people are able to take pleasure in what they have done and can do, rather than being driven to think that they should or must do more. They don't dismiss or denigrate their achievements. If they become unhappy, whatever the reason, their self-awareness enables them to note their change in mood, to understand what caused it, and to set about solving the problem in an upbeat way. They're resilient because they have a track record—a trajectory of success that motivates them, providing a source of energy and enthusiasm. This not only propels them along a positive course but also draws others to them, ensuring those all-important relationships that keep us happy. If we're satisfied with our life and not particularly envious of anyone else's, it's much easier to build strong and lasting relationships.

The Wonders of Flow

The idea of wholehearted participation and dedication seems to be integral to happiness. Csikszentmihalyi, Abuhamdeh, and Nakamura (2005) noted that many people, while engaging in certain activities, become so focused and absorbed that they reach a heightened state of consciousness, an almost euphoric state of mind. This can happen while they are writing or painting, playing sports, or going for a walk on a beautiful day. It occurs unexpectedly, sometimes during something as prosaic as cooking or doing a math problem or rearranging your room. The key element is total involvement—being really involved in the activity.

Csikszentmihalyi and colleagues call this phenomenon "flow." The flow state of mind occurs most often when you engage in tasks that demand intense concentration and commitment, when your skill level is perfectly attuned to the challenge posed by the endeavor. As well, the task must entail a clear-cut goal and offer immediate feedback.

In studies over the past 30 years, Csikszentmihalyi and colleagues (2005) have found that most of us generally live our lives at two extremes. We're either stressed by work or other obligations or bored by spending leisure time in passive ways; we jitter in response to a given day's bumps and grinds or collapse in front of the TV. Somewhere in the middle lies a happier, more satisfying life.

And a longer one. As a final inducement, research has proven what many of us have suspected—happier people live longer, whereas miserable people die younger (Veenhoven, 1984). That in itself may be enough to spur us to take the first steps toward learning new skills, reaching out to others, and looking for happiness within ourselves and in what we do.

● Benefits of Happiness

Happy people have an infectious, buoyant mood. They are pleased with, receive joy from, and show enthusiasm at play and work, and their attitude infuses their relationships. Happy people tend to have a trajectory of success in both play and work because they are pleasant to be with and, as a result, easily attract and build relationships with others. Their happiness motivates themselves and others and provides a source of energy and enthusiasm that is lacking in their counterparts. Additionally, people who are happy show the kind of resilience necessary to overcome minor and, at times, major setbacks. Their sense of satisfaction with their lives offsets feelings of envy and greed that have a sabotaging effect on building relationships and motivation.

People who are chronically sad, on the other hand, have little energy or enthusiasm. They experience difficulty getting their work done at school and in the context of their relationships. Their chronic glumness tends to make others avoid them and leaves them without a social support system to help them attain their educational or personal goals.

A final and important word about this side of the happy-sad continuum: as noted earlier, some people who seem sad may in fact be suffering from a clinical depression. The good news is that, of all medical illnesses, depression is probably the most eminently treatable through appropriate medication and counseling. Recovery rates can run as high as 95 percent—much higher than for diabetes, ulcers, or heart disease. However, because many people associate depression with "weakness," and because for many years it has been stigmatized as a "mental" illness, many avoid treatment that could be so helpful. And, depression is no more a sign of "weakness" than are other medical diseases such as diabetes or hyperthyroidism.

The signs of depression are many and varied, but here are some of the warning signals. Over the past few weeks, have you felt:

- Continuously down and glum?
- That you've lost interest in activities that previously gave you pleasure?

- That you don't want to hang out with friends?
- Uncertain, helpless, or pessimistic about your future?
- That you would be better off if you didn't wake up in the morning?

Physical manifestations are also important. For example, have you found that:

- You have difficulty falling asleep or staying asleep?
- You wake up at odd hours and can't fall back to sleep?
- You have trouble getting up for class?
- Your appetite seems to have diminished?
- You have suddenly lost more than five pounds?

If you affirmed three or more of these warning signals from either list or both lists combined, it would be wise to consult your physician or a trained counselor. Or, if the above list sounds like a friend, encourage that person to get help.

Reflection Questions

1. What goals am I pursuing that, if I reach them, will make me feel happy?
2. Who do I enjoy spending time with? How can I further develop that relationship?
3. Who is my support network? Who do I turn to when things aren't going so well?
4. Which of the epigraphs that opened the chapter resonated the most with me? Why?

To try out some exercises in increasing your happiness, consult *The Student EQ Edge: Student Workbook*.

PART 8

Putting It
All Together

You've learned about the various facets of emotional intelligence and, we hope, have come to believe how valuable a high EQ can be. But you don't have to just take our word for it. The next four chapters explore research about how EQ predicts educational outcomes, career success, leadership effectiveness, and, finally, how we may fare in all those areas that give life more meaning, such as sustaining fulfilling relationships and taking good care of our health.

CHAPTER 19

EQ and Student Success

We hope that throughout this book we have conveyed that success in any field rests on a number of emotional intelligence factors. Through-the-roof scores in one or two categories of emotional intelligence don't necessarily guarantee the job of your dreams, a meteoric rise on the organizational chart, millionaire status, or the realization of your fondest personal dreams.

Rather, think of success as the result of a mix of several competencies, some of them unexpected. For example, successful engineers—the most pragmatic bunch you can imagine—are distinguished by high scores in self-regard, optimism, stress tolerance, and self-actualization; the success of human resources professionals, who many may think should excel at interpersonal relationships, in fact depends even more on self-actualization; and, to cite a recent survey, 68 percent of 150 information technology executives in the nation's 1,000 largest companies stated that they believed "soft skills" were more important now than they were five years ago (Dizdarevic, 1996). Suffice it to say that no component of emotional intelligence exists in isolation. All are interrelated; all are valuable and may be brought to bear to enhance your chances for success.

In the previous chapters, we presented various examples of how emotional intelligence works in real life. In these final chapters we want to present some of the research that's been carried out on emotional intelligence in selected areas—education, the workplace, and leadership, as well as health, lifestyle, and relationships. We'll also give you some examples of how emotional intelligence applies to "star performers"—that is, people who have excelled in some area.

We will briefly describe research studies in which groups of people were tested in order to profile these stars, as well as some individual case studies. At Multi-Health Systems (MHS) we have tested the emotional intelligence of more people in the world than anyone else—more than two million people from over 72 countries. Our data were the world's first to explore the relationships between emotional intelligence and sex (Mirsky, 1997), age (Carey, 1997), and culture and race (Sitarenios & Stein, 1998a). The studies and individuals in this chapter highlight some of the first work directly examining the role of emotional intelligence and performance. Some studies used the EQ-i Youth Version, which was developed for work with children and adolescents aged 7 to 18.

● EQ and College Graduation

Imagine if we could predict who will complete their college education. Surprisingly, it is not academic ability that separates who will graduate from who will not. In an interesting set of studies with hundreds of college students, Dr. James Parker and his colleagues at Trent University in Canada have come a long way in helping us understand college retention. In one study they tested all incoming students at a small Ontario university for their EQ. They also had the college GPAs of all the students. They found a significant relationship between their EQ and grades at the end of the first year (Parker, Summerfeldt, Hogan, & Majeski, 2004).

They continued to follow these students throughout their college years. The main reasons students dropped out of college were to change their program of study and because they were experiencing personal, economic, or health problems. The main personal problems tended to be difficulties forming new relationships, problems changing existing relationships (living apart from loved ones), difficulties learning new study habits, and problems learning to be independent. There were consistent findings that emotional intelligence scores were significant predictors of which students dropped out of college (Parker et al., 2004).

In another study, which included close to 1,500 students attending four universities located in Mississippi, North Carolina, and West Virginia, Parker found nearly identical results (Parker, Duffy, Wood, Bond, & Hogan, 2005). A strong link was found between academic achievement and several dimensions of emotional intelligence. Specifically, the academically successful students had greater interpersonal, adaptability, and stress management abilities, as well as overall emotional intelligence. According to their research, these skills are what students need in order to be successful in forming new relationships, modifying existing relationships, learning new study habits, adjusting to increased academic demands, and learning to live more independently.

● Does Emotional Intelligence Help You Get Through College?

There have been more studies demonstrating the importance of emotional intelligence in students who successfully complete college. And they seem to be pointing in the same direction. Here is yet another.

Larry Sparkman (2009) at the University of Southern Mississippi tested 783 students with the EQ-i and followed up by looking at enrollment status, graduation status, and cumulative college grade point average. The best predictors of college completion (or graduation) were the emotional intelligence scales of empathy, social responsibility, flexibility, and impulse control. Of these scales, the strongest predictors were social responsibility, followed by impulse control and empathy. Interestingly, too much flexibility got in the way of completing college. A certain amount of routine and discipline is required to complete assignments, prepare for tests and exams, and make it to class on a regular basis, suggesting that moderate flexibility combined with strong impulse control are keys to success.

Cumulative college grade point average was best predicted by self-actualization, social responsibility, and happiness. There was an interesting qualifier here as well. Very high scores in independence and interpersonal relationship tended to be associated with a lower grade point average. So students who are unwilling to seek help from tutors, counselors, or professors and are too busy with their many friends and a full social calendar may be at a disadvantage in getting better grades (Sparkman, 2009).

In addition to the emotional intelligence scores, high school grade point average was a good predictor of continued enrollment, college grade point average, and graduation; and ACT scores predicted both graduation and college grade point average (Sparkman, 2009). To conclude, both academic and EI measures can predict college performance and ultimate graduation.

● Can EI Help First-Year College Students?

Many of you will be relieved to hear that something besides your SAT or ACT score may better predict how you'll perform those first few semesters in college. Schulman (1995) found that University of Pennsylvania first-year students' scores on optimism were a better predictor of first-semester GPA than SAT scores. And Mann and Kanoy (2010)—in a diverse sample of students from across the United States and Canada—found that first-year college GPA could be predicted by optimism (believing you will succeed and persevering when things get tough), self-regard (knowing both your strengths and weaknesses), impulse control (resisting that temptation to play when you need to study), and problem solving (leveraging emotions to help you solve problems). And it doesn't matter whether you are an honors student or an athlete. Jaeger (2004) sampled athletes, honors students, and students enrolled in a first-year experience program; in all groups, higher emotional intelligence correlated with higher GPA for first-year students.

First-year college students face multiple stressors, including an increased level of academic expectation, a higher degree of independent learning, and, if they live on campus, adjusting to shared living spaces, noise, and different opinions about what's acceptable. Enhanced EI skills help students navigate these many changes, whether they are managing money so there's enough to buy textbooks or developing meaningful relationships.

● Can College Students Increase Their Emotional Intelligence?

The simple answer is "yes." We now know how important emotional intelligence is for getting through college. One question that frequently comes up is whether or not you can improve emotional intelligence in college students. A study completed at the University of Hawaii by Kelly Chang (2007) evaluated a program designed to improve the emotional intelligence of college students.

In the study, two groups of students—79 in a treatment group and 74 in a control group—were assessed for their emotional intelligence using both the EQ-i and the MSCEIT. The program used behavioral self-modification techniques that included training in assertiveness, empathy, self-regard, and emotional management. After the training there were significant increases in tests scores for the treatment group and no change in scores for the control group (Chang, 2007). We hope that these types of training programs will become more integrated into college courses, especially in light of studies confirming that incorporating emotional skills content into first-year experience courses enhances retention (Schutte & Malouff, 2002).

● Are You an Adult Learner?

Does emotional intelligence affect the way that adult students learn? Do academic programs need to take into account various "nonacademic" factors? A study done in Phoenix, Arizona, by Colston (2008) looked at what role EI might play in adult learning. Colston investigated academic achievement among 115 male and female adult nontraditional undergraduate students. They were all administered the EQ-i, among other measures, and their GPA was noted.

In this group of learners there was a significant relationship between EI scores and their performance based on GPA. Learners with a higher EI score were found to also have a higher GPA. The study made some suggestions about how EI could be integrated into the curriculum to benefit these learners.

Many adult learners take a significant portion of their college credit hours online. It's not surprising that students with higher emotional intelligence perform better in online courses than those with lower EI (Berenson, Boyles, & Weaver, 2008). Students taking online courses have to be highly disciplined, highly motivated, and able to work independently. Self-actualization, independence, reality testing, and impulse control all are essential to performing well in most online classes.

⬤ What About Other Cultures—and High School Students?

Research on emotional intelligence hasn't been confined to North America. There have been a number of studies carried out around the world. For example, researchers in Iran, at Mahabad Azad University, Al-Zahra University, and Tehran Azad University, used the EQ-i with Iranian high school students (Sadri, Akbarzadeh, & Poushaneh, 2009). They tested 40 male students and randomly assigned them to treatment or control groups. The experimental group went through a 12-session training program in emotional intelligence. At the end of the program both groups were retested with the EQ-i. Only members of the group receiving the training showed a significant increase in their scores.

One study, looking at adolescent EI and its relationship to other factors—such as academic achievement and ability to cope with stress—was completed in Bahrain. Jihan Alumran and Raija-Leena

Punamaki (2008) tested 112 adolescents in the Bahraini school system to explore these factors. Among their main findings was the fact that gender, but not age, was associated with levels of EI and the coping styles of these adolescents. EI contributed to the variance in all three coping styles that were looked at. Here, as in many different cultures around the world, the EQ-i helps us better understand our ability to deal with others.

Adding to the international research on EI, a study from Mexico looked at adolescence from a different perspective. Instead of looking at what goes wrong with teens, this study, from the University of Guanajuato, looks at what differentiates highly popular teenagers from those who are less popular. Zavala, Valadez, and Vargas (2008) were interested in why some adolescents are more socially accepted by their peers than others.

Through a series of surveys they were able to identify 62 adolescents who were rated among the most popular in their peer groups. These teens, with an average age of 13, were administered a number of tests including the youth version of the EQ-i. The researchers also tested 331 other students who were neither high nor low in their level of popularity. The more popular teens were significantly higher in their emotional intelligence scores. Interestingly, the researchers also measured social skills, which were not universally higher in the popular group. The authors raise some interesting questions and propose a number of ideas for helping adolescents to become more popular by improving their emotional and social intelligence skills.

● Can EI Be Used to Prevent Problems for Students?

We've often been asked what can be done in the way of early intervention with emotional intelligence. Can we detect early warning signs in kids before problems get out of hand? That was part of the focus of a study carried out with the youth version of the EQ-i (EQ-i YV) at the University of Arkon. Amanda Rovnak (2007) tested 684 students in seventh and eighth grade across 19 schools in Ohio. She found that the EI scores were important predictors of academic and mental health issues. Her findings show that by using an inexpensive screener we can use early detection to help intervene when there's a good chance of problems down the road.

Along the same lines, an interesting study was carried out at West Virginia University looking at college students and binge drinking (Dulko, 2008). What role does emotional intelligence play in the problems caused—both to oneself and to others—through the misuse of alcohol?

In this study, which looked at 309 undergraduate students, Dulko (2008) found that emotional intelligence played a significant role in predicting the impact of binge drinking. The number of binge drinking consequences (getting sick, getting into fights, and so forth) was related to the student's overall score in EI. That is, the higher the student's EI, the fewer negative consequences of binge drinking the student experienced. The specific factors of emotional intelligence that predicted outcomes in this area included intrapersonal (self-perception and self-expression), stress management, and interpersonal skills. So by intervening and improving EI skills in college students, we may be able to lessen the negative consequences associated with binge drinking.

What about another addictive behavior, excessive gambling? As you may have noticed, with the widespread use of the Internet there have been increases in gambling addiction. Would emotional intelligence help protect young people from getting in over their heads with gambling? That's a question that Bar-On and Parker (2000) looked at in different samples of adolescents. They used the EQ-i: YV with two groups—209 13- to 15-year-olds and 458 16- to 18-year-olds.

Basically, they found that emotional intelligence scores were a good predictor of addiction-related behaviors in both groups of adolescents. They went on to discuss some of the implications of these findings in setting up preventative programs for youth at risk for gambling addictions (Bar-On & Parker, 2000).

And an American study looking at middle school students found a connection between emotional intelligence, discipline problems, and school grades. The study, carried out by Karen Kohaut (2010) at Widener University, used the EQ-i Youth Version and compared it with students' final grades for the year and the number of discipline referrals taken from school records. She found significant relationships between the youth's emotional intelligence scores and both academic performance and number of school discipline problems, with higher EI predicting fewer discipline issues and better performance. Interestingly, she found no difference between student's ethnic or racial origin and their EQ-i YV scores.

What about the malady called procrastination that almost every student experiences at some point? We know the tendency to procrastinate can create enormous anxiety, poor sleep and eating habits, and, typically, less than one's best potential performance. It's not a surprise, then, that Deniz, Tras, and Aydogan (2009) found that students with lower EI scores, particularly on adaptability (factors like problem solving and reality testing) and stress tolerance, were more likely to procrastinate.

● EQ and the Teacher

Now that we've explored the relationship between emotional intelligence and student performance, what about the people who teach you? Just think about the various teachers you've had over the years. What made a few stand out as great mentors and teachers? And how would you describe the ones you really didn't like? In fact, one of the most frequently asked questions at our lectures is "What makes a great teacher?"

In response, we've administered the EQ-i to thousands of teachers, and we're often asked to give presentations and workshops to teachers' groups and to schools as part of their professional development programs. For example, consider our work with a medium-sized private school. Each year, the school identifies the five top-rated teachers through an evaluation of and presentation by all teachers (including a case study of a student who's excelled in their class) to an administrative committee, outlining what their classes have accomplished over the school term. As part of our work, we tested the EQ-i of the entire staff of this school and compared their results with the evaluations of the administrative team (Stein & Sitarenios, 1997).

We found that these top teachers scored significantly higher than the other teachers in several categories, but we were mildly surprised by which categories these were. We often ask teachers to identify what they believe to be the most important factors in their work, perhaps by describing the best and most effective teachers they themselves had when they were young. But the factor that emerged as the most important in our study—emotional self-awareness—never made the top of their lists (Stein & Sitarenios, 1997).

Why would emotional self-awareness stand out as critical for teachers? Because, as we've seen, being in touch with your emotions is the first step toward managing them effectively. Students will arouse emotions by intentionally or unintentionally pushing the teachers' hot buttons. The more a teacher can maintain a steady emotional state, the better. Emotional self-awareness also informs a teacher about what aspects of teaching are the most and least pleasurable. Emotional self-awareness can help teachers persist through the less pleasant tasks, keeping themselves motivated for the more pleasurable aspects of teaching. Emotional awareness also helps them do their best, week after week, in handling a classroom full of students with wildly varying needs, abilities, interest levels, and attention spans.

In another study (Stein & Sitarenios, 1997), we administered the EQ-i to 257 elementary and 157 secondary-school teachers. We also asked them to rate their own perceived performance on the job. Thirteen percent of the elementary teachers rated themselves as average or below, 60 percent considered themselves average, and 27 percent claimed to be above average. What EQ factors differentiated these three groups? The biggest difference was their scores when it came to optimism; the teachers who proclaimed themselves better than average were significantly more optimistic than others. They also scored considerably higher in problem solving, self-actualization, stress tolerance, and happiness. When we repeated this procedure with secondary-school teachers, we found that the factor that set the more self-reportedly successful educators apart was self-actualization— the ability to enjoy their duties to the full, to get involved in extracur- ricular activities, and to constantly strive for excellence—followed by problem solving, self-awareness, and happiness.

But what about ineffective teachers? At the elementary level, you might guess that they were lacking in optimism, but you'd be mistaken. The factor that limited their success was a lack of impulse control, which led to problems with their temper, lack of patience, and poor organizational skills. At the secondary level, teachers who were less satisfied with their performance were distinguished by their low scores in flexibility. An excess of rigidity is not the way to an adolescent's heart, and the surest way to guarantee that your message doesn't get across is to follow the rules at any cost, without bend- ing and with a focus on enforcing discipline and maintaining your authority. For some teachers, flexibility is the most difficult ability to achieve, but it's necessary. Winning the battle for students' hearts, over the long run, will get teachers much further than fighting over who's the boss on a given day (Stein & Sitarenios, 1997). We suspect that, in or out of the classroom, highly regimented environments are increasingly becoming a thing of the past.

In addition to these studies of EI and teachers, there has also been interest in the emotional intelligence of leaders who work with children and youth, but not necessarily in a traditional teaching role. Karen Jerome (2010) at the University of Oklahoma conducted a study with 203 Department of Defense program managers who worked with children and youth. These professionals have a signifi- cant effect on the children in their care and can be very influential in shaping their future. The program managers were tested for emo- tional intelligence and leadership style. Jerome found that the EQ-i was a strong predictor of leadership style for these professionals.

● EQ and the School Principal

In addition to looking at students and teachers, researchers have sought to determine what makes an effective school principal. We now have some ground-breaking studies of school principals.

An ambitious study of leadership in education was carried out by Howard Stone, James Parker, and Laura Wood (2005). In this study, funded by the Ontario Ministry of Education and Training in Canada, 464 principals or vice-principals from nine different school boards in the province of Ontario were tested with the EQ-i. Two hundred and twenty-six of the participants were elementary school principals, 84 were elementary school vice-principals, 43 were secondary school principals, and 57 were secondary school vice-principals.

Their immediate supervisor and three staff members also completed a specifically designed leadership questionnaire regarding each participant. The twenty-one items related to leadership ability measured two broad categories: task-oriented leadership (for example, "comes well prepared for meetings") and relationship-oriented leadership (for example, "seeks consensus among staff members"). Building relationships and getting things done are widely accepted as two key components of leadership. A "leadership score" that included scores of supervisors and staff was calculated for each participant. This was used to identify "below average" (20th percentile or lower) and "above average" (80th percentile or higher) leaders (Stone et al., 2005).

What factors would you predict differentiate the highly rated principals? Do you think they are friendlier or higher in interpersonal relationships? Are they more assertive and therefore more direct with their staff? Well, if that's what you think, you're partly right. The above-average leadership group scored significantly higher on emotional self-awareness, self-actualization, empathy, interpersonal relationship, flexibility, problem solving, and impulse control. Interestingly, these skills were equally important for males and females, principals and vice-principals, and elementary and secondary principals. Stone and his colleagues concluded that training programs should be established that develop these eight critical areas of EI in elementary and secondary school leaders.

There have been other studies that consider the role of emotional intelligence in school leaders. These often ask whether school leaders who are emotionally intelligent are more resilient and better leaders. That was the focus of Bumphus's (2009) study at the University of Southern Mississippi. She tested 63 public school principals and surveyed their respective professional colleagues. They were sampled from across five states—Florida, Georgia, Louisiana, Mississippi, and Texas.

She found that emotional intelligence was a big part of a principal's resilience and good leadership. General mood on the EQ-i (optimism and happiness) was a strong predictor of resilience. Good leaders had higher scores in intrapersonal (self-perception and self-expression) and interpersonal scales (Bumphus, 2009).

And the investigation of emotional intelligence doesn't stop at the level of school principal. There's also been research looking at school district superintendents. Richard Hansen (2010) carried out a study that started out surveying 1,019 school superintendents in the states of Michigan, Indiana, and Ohio. He ended up getting a response rate of 13 percent from these superintendents who were tested with the EQ-i as well as a measure of transformational leadership and other questionnaires. As in other studies that we will see in Chapter 21, The Role of EQ in Leadership, he found a strong link between emotional intelligence and transformational leadership (leadership that inspires others to follow) among these professionals. And like others, Hansen found no differences in emotional intelligence due to age, race, or gender.

CHAPTER 20

EQ and Work Success

No matter what type of career you may be considering, the chances are excellent that emotional intelligence will help predict how successful you'll be. From surgeons to journalists, sports stars to fighter pilots, and successful sales people to the chronically unemployed, EI is predictive of who succeeds and who doesn't. But before you can be successful in a career, you must first get hired. Let's start with those who cannot get a job. Then read about the careers you are interested in and see what EI characteristics you might need to develop!

● EQ and the Job Challenged

First, let's consider those who generally struggle with finding employment. Rose-Marie Nigli (1998) at the YWCA in Toronto collected EQ-i data on a large sample of chronically unemployed people between the ages of 18 and 50. Their lowest scores were in assertiveness, optimism, emotional self-awareness, reality testing, and happiness. Scores were also below average in self-regard and independence. Put a different way, these people had a hard time getting noticed and expressing thoughts (lack of assertiveness); got discouraged more easily (lack of optimism); had a hard time understanding their own emotions, such as anxiety about interviews (lack of emotional self-awareness); probably had more difficulty sorting out which jobs best matched their skills sets, thus giving them the best chance to get hired (lack of reality testing); and, when they did get an interview, probably projected less happiness. No wonder they stayed unemployed!

Continued failure reinforces these underdeveloped emotional skills, creating a chronic situation. Notably, however, individuals in this group scored higher than average on empathy and social responsibility. Perhaps receiving government assistance increases one's awareness of and consideration for others who are less fortunate.

About 50 of these individuals participated in a six-week skills enhancement group that focused on increasing assertiveness, being more realistic in job choices, and improving general life skills (such as coping with challenges and being more optimistic). The group had classroom instruction, life-skills training, and vocational-management and/or technical-skills training. More than 90 percent of the participants found work following the training. When they were retested on the EQ-i, their scores showed significant increases on several scales. The skills that changed the most were assertiveness, reality testing, and emotional self-awareness (Nigli, 1998).

● EQ and Air Force Recruiters

Perhaps the largest study ever undertaken that looks at the role of emotional intelligence and work performance was with the U.S. Air Force (Handley, 1997). Back in 1996, the Air Force identified a problem with its recruiters—the people who choose the young men and women who'll be suited to military life. The trouble was, recruiters were coming and going with discouraging regularity; the turnover rate was sky-high—approximately 50 percent. Each person who had been selected was trained and very often relocated to another city or to a far-flung military base. If that person didn't stay at the job and function as he or she was supposed to, it meant the Air Force was throwing money away. To be more precise, every "bad hire" was costing the Air Force about $30,000 (in 1996 U.S. dollars). Of course, there were also human costs involved—including the strain on the recruiters' families, who were forever pulling up stakes.

Lieutenant Colonel Rich Handley, the head of the recruitment project, called us in and asked us to administer the EQ-i to 1,171 recruiters stationed at bases around the world, to see if we could relate their scores to success on the job. To get an accurate measure of that success, we wanted to know first, how they viewed their own performance, and second, how well they met the quotas that had been assigned for their particular region.

Having administered the EQ-i and other tests so many times, we're well aware that self-rating has its limits. A person may say that he or she is doing great, and that may or may not be the strict truth. On the other hand, when people say they're not doing so well, that usually proves to be the case. Having obtained the EQ-i results, as well as the claimed and actual performance ratings, we analyzed the results and found that 45 percent of the recruiters' self-reported success was accounted for by their scores in the 15 components of emotional intelligence (Handley, 1997)—a much stronger relationship than has been found in other studies that rely on cognitive intelligence.

With regard to their actual performance, it was found that many of these same components came into play. The five factors that were most likely to translate into success on the job may surprise you. In order, they were assertiveness, empathy, happiness, self-awareness, and problem-solving. Those recruiters who scored high in these categories were 2.7 times more likely to succeed, and of the 262 recruiters who scored highest on the EQi assessment, 95 percent met or exceeded their quotas (Handley, 1997).

The study also shed new light on several possible factors that the Air Force thought might have contributed to the turnover problem. A recruiter's base of operations—where he or she was stationed—had no direct relation to success. Nor did gender, ethnicity, education, age, marital status (although marital satisfaction was found to be related to job success), or the number of hours worked. Indeed, those recruiters who admitted to working the fewest hours were the most successful (Handley, 1997).

All these results made sense. First, assertiveness is highly desirable in a sales environment, and a recruiter's task is essentially the task of selling the military to civilian prospects. The Air Force was surprised to learn that empathy played a role (it had concentrated on improving the recruiters' interpersonal skills, but not empathy per se). Empathy, as we've seen, is the ability to read and respond to the emotions of others. The successful recruiters were able to bring it to bear, adjusting their presentations accordingly and—not incidentally—not wasting time on unsuitable candidates, which is why they could get the job done more quickly. Happiness is straightforward enough, as is self-awareness. Superior problem-solving skills were of real value because the recruiters frequently worked alone, isolated from their supervisors or coworkers.

What happened next? The Air Force quickly reorganized its recruiter-training program to address the determinants of success identified by the EQ-i. It then ordered a customized computer version of the EQi assessment, which has been used as part of the selection process for new personnel ever since. The responses of potential recruiters are compared with a database that contains the results of the initial 1,171 tests. Additionally, prospects take part in a structured EQ-i interview that we developed to confirm the areas of strength or weakness pinpointed by the self-report instrument.

In fact, our work was cited in a report to a U.S. congressional subcommittee, which compared the recruiter selection processes adopted by various branches of the armed forces (United States Senate, 1998) and concluded that only the Air Force used measures to evaluate the interpersonal skills of potential recruiters during the screening process, and, as a result, their recruiters were more than twice as effective as other branches of service. The report compared the cost of hiring a recruiter with the cost of the computerized assessment and noted that the computerized assessment was purchased for less money than it took to hire *just one recruiter!*

And what's happened in the meantime? A follow-up study—also submitted to the congressional subcommittee—found that, after a year of using the EQ-i and the specially developed EQ-i interview to help select new recruiters, the retention rate for this position had increased by 92 percent worldwide, at a cost savings to the Air Force of an estimated $2,700,000. The U.S. Government Accounting Office praised the Air Force screening system (United States House of Representatives, 1998a) for its cost-saving measures. And, in case you're wondering, yes—we've begun working with the Navy and the Army on similar projects, tailored to their specific needs.

Top Guns

Imagine having to convince fighter pilots aboard one of the most technologically sophisticated aircraft carriers, the USS George Washington, that emotional intelligence is relevant to success. Using your visualization skills, picture in your mind the "ready room," where fighter pilots are briefed. Picture also a senior medical officer, who introduces a lowly psychologist named Steven Stein to a highly skeptical audience of men, some of whom had been through the first Gulf War and couldn't care less about emotional intelligence. Empathy does not appear to be one of their strong points, and the psychologist is forced to draw on his deepest reserves of optimism.

Fortunately, one of the navigators is vaguely familiar with the notion of emotional intelligence and wants to hear about it. The psychologist begins by accidentally stepping on the fighter crew's emblem painted on the floor (and must pay a $2 fine), but recovers and launches into his presentation—basically, that emotional skills are important, particularly in life-and-death situations.

By the end of the afternoon, against all odds and expectations, the entire crew had completed the EQ-i, and several stayed behind to talk about emotional issues related to their job experiences. We were impressed not only with their superb technical skills, but with their wide range of interests and backgrounds. All of them had a college education, but the disciplines varied from history to mathematics to engineering to English literature. In fact, not one of them was sure how he'd been picked for his elite position, and several remarked that they'd certainly have qualified for civilian jobs that would pay far more than their present earnings. On the other hand, in civilian life you can't fly an F-14.

Steven thought he knew how the majority of the pilots would score on the EQ-i. To his surprise, he was slightly off base. First, they were among the highest-scoring groups we'd tested up to that point in time. They would be expected (along with entrepreneurs, physicians, and members of other "elite" occupations) to do well when it came to self-regard, and so they did. But their answers in this category (and in emotional self-awareness) showed them to be free of arrogance, over-confidence, or blind faith in their abilities. In other words, because they knew exactly how good they were, they had absolutely no need to exaggerate (Stein & Sitarenios, 2000).

They also scored well when it came to reality testing (a good thing when they have only a fraction of a second to decide whether or not to fire at what may or may not be an approaching enemy) and to impulse control (again, a vital attribute when pushing the wrong button can spell the difference between life and death for others and for yourself).

They also excelled at stress tolerance, as well they might—but they weren't hesitant to pinpoint the cause of their greatest anxiety. Steven asked them (and don't forget, most had seen live combat in the Persian Gulf) what frightened them the most. They said they could handle bombing missions and the sight of an enemy plane or missile with aplomb; their major worry was coming "home"—landing on the pitching deck of the carrier at night (Stein & Sitarenios, 2000).

● EQ and the Oval Office

Moving from the theater of war to the political arena, let's see how emotional intelligence affects our elected leaders. And lest you think that we want to discuss politics, we don't. Emotional intelligence strengths and weaknesses affect all politicians, regardless of their views on the issues or their success in world affairs. Politicians, after all, are human.

Consider the case of a U.S. president in the 1990s. Bill Clinton's indiscretions (his affair with intern Monica Lewinsky while in the White House) are now receding from memory, but they may yet endure as the hallmark of his term in office, pushing aside his many achievements. The question repeated over and over at the time was why did Clinton behave that way?

Not that he is the only politician who has ever committed indiscretions. Other examples include politicians from all over the world and from all political parties such as Italian prime minister Silvio Berlusconi, presidential candidate and senator John Edwards, New York governor Eliot Spitzer, Governor Mark Sanford, Mayor Marion Barry, Governor Arnold Schwarzenegger, and numerous others. Do these politicians harbor a self-destructive streak that perpetually pushes them toward irresponsible acts? We certainly wish that we could administer the EQ-i to some of these politicians. But in the absence of their EQ results, we can make one or two educated guesses about the emotional intelligence levels of these politicians.

For example, we'd expect that, like the majority of successful politicians, Bill Clinton would score high across the board, particularly on interpersonal skills. He'd also likely do well when it came to stress tolerance, empathy, and social responsibility. His style indicates that he's a strong "people person" who's maneuvered his way through many political and personal minefields. His empathic abilities are clear; whenever he speaks, listeners feel as though he's communicating and connecting directly with them alone.

Clinton's Achilles' heel is equally clear: in his personal life, he's had difficulty exercising impulse control. This shortcoming finally led to a national scandal and political firestorm. Whatever his feelings about Monica Lewinsky and numerous other women, it's obvious that he'd have been far wiser to keep his impulses in check, as he himself admitted in numerous apologies to the American people.

But still—because of his charisma and interpersonal flair—he survived these incidents. Even after the report submitted by Special Prosecutor Kenneth Starr (U.S. House of Representatives, 1998b) was made public—when Clinton's very public humiliation was being paraded on the newscasts night after night—his approval rating among voters never dropped below 60 percent.

As we've said, Clinton is certainly not the first politician (nor will he be the last) to get into hot water due to faulty impulse control or other EI shortcomings. Now for a Republican example: Richard Nixon resigned in disgrace after faulty decision-making skills led to the Nixon-authorized break-in at the Watergate Hotel and then to the even more damaging cover-up that resulted in several of his top aides serving prison sentences for their role in it. Yet we continue to witness headlines from around the world exposing leaders who engage in extramarital affairs while calling for a return to family values, or who are discovered skimming profits or improperly accepting monetary benefits, having just won an election on a house-cleaning platform. It could be that these leaders lack the kind of reality testing that would help them understand that many of these dalliances or deceptions eventually become public.

Perhaps out of a sense of self-preservation (not a component of emotional intelligence, but a long-standing prime political imperative), very few elected officials are keen to take the EQ-i—or, if they are willing, to have the results made known. One who dared is Bill Vander Zalm, the former premier of British Columbia, Canada. Not only did he cheerfully complete the test, but he also agreed to talk about his scores as part of a Canadian Broadcasting Corporation (CBC) television program about our work, and he gave us permission to publish his scores in this book (Vander Zalm, personal communication, May 22, 1999).

Vander Zalm was, and remains, a flamboyant personality. He was forced to resign his premiership in the wake of a conflict-of-interest scandal. When we tested him, he said that he had nothing more to hide and was interested in learning what, if anything, the EQ-i would reveal.

And what exactly was that? Vander Zalm achieved his highest scores in the intrapersonal (now referred to as self-perception and self-expression) and interpersonal realms. The "average" EQ score is 100; Vander Zalm was quite high (or significantly higher) in several categories, scoring 126 in independence (in keeping with his reputation as a leader who stood up, took charge, and led his party to victory), and 123 in both self-regard and happiness. Clearly, his defeat (about which he joked while completing the questionnaire) did not diminish his capacity to enjoy life—he continues to this day to exhibit an upbeat demeanor, at least in his public persona.

Vander Zalm's lower scores are equally revealing. For example, he did not (to put it charitably) excel in problem solving—a shortcoming that plagued his government and led to his being labeled a person who shoots from the hip, only to shoot himself in the foot. Another low-scoring category was, as expected, impulse control, in which he managed only 86.

We don't know whether Vander Zalm will rival Clinton's legendary resilience and will spring back to life, phoenix-like. Our advice, if he hopes to reenter public life or gain elected office again, is to work on his two most deficient areas of emotional intelligence. He'd do well to stop and reflect before he speaks, refrain from answering questions unless he's sure of his ground, and rely on solid advice to sort out reasoned approaches to the tough issues, rather than winging it on his own. If he can do all of this, he stands a decent chance of putting the past behind him and reestablishing a positive public image.

● "He Shoots, He Scores!"

In the 1990s the Toronto Maple Leafs, once the pride of the National Hockey League, had racked up several bad years, not only failing to win the Stanley Cup championship but even missing the playoffs altogether. Suddenly, in the 1998–99 season, they were on a comeback, moving from 25th to 5th place in the standings, and ensuring themselves a playoff berth.

But they'd paid a heavy price, and the team had suffered a number of injuries, relegating several of their top players to watching from the bench. This situation became critical by the third game of the second-round playoffs against the notoriously physical Pittsburgh Penguins, and the Leafs, having assessed their bench strength, came up with a bold and unusual plan. They brought in an 84th-round draft pick named Adam Mair, who'd never played an NHL game in his life and had been biding his time with the Leafs' development club in eastern Canada.

Mair skated onto the ice at the Igloo, Pittsburgh's home arena. No one in the full-house crowd noticed him—otherwise, he'd have been roundly booed, along with the rest of the Toronto players. But the television commentators were struck by his almost unprecedented arrival; they spent a moment speculating on his likely fate at the hands of the Penguins, and they scheduled a between-periods interview with whatever was left of him when Pittsburgh got through welcoming him to the big time.

Instead, Mair made himself known at once. He scored a goal, becoming only the second player in Maple Leaf history to debut in the playoffs and put a puck in the net. (For trivia fans, the first player to do so hit the ice in 1948.)

We don't wish to appear smug about it, but we weren't in the least surprised by Mair's performance. Why? Because one of us had tested his EQ, along with the EQ of 28 other Maple Leaf prospects, at a preseason training camp (Stein & Sitarenios, 1999). With Mair's permission (Adam Mair, personal communication, August 15, 1998), we're sharing his EQ scores, which stood out from all the rest and marked him as the most likely to succeed in whatever he attempted.

His overall score was very high, indicating excellent general adjustment. When we tested him he was only 19, but his highest component score was in reality testing, indicating that he had a keen sense of his situation, which would prove helpful in accepting his developmental-club status. If you're suddenly selected by a major league team, it's easy to indulge in unrealistic fantasies. Next week you're sure, you will be a league-leading goal scorer, adored by all and paid in keeping with your status. The idea that you have a lot to learn gets lost in the shuffle, which impedes your necessary development. But not so with Mair. Instead, he spent his time well, working hard, polishing his skills, and preparing for his chance.

His second-highest score came in problem solving—an important predictor of success for any athlete. Knowing how to use your emotions to guide your ability to think on your feet in the middle of ever-shifting circumstances—deciding whether to pass the puck or shoot from a less-than-ideal angle, meanwhile avoiding a swarm of defending players—can spell the difference between victory and defeat. Superior players hone these responses by means of the visualization technique, mentally rehearsing how to overcome obstacles as they arise.

This returns us to the importance of emotional intelligence in a particular field. Any hockey player who's taken at all seriously by an NHL scout or coach is on a certain plateau, in possession of a certain level of athletic talents and skills (which are, of course, miles beyond what most of us could ever hope to command). He's got strength and stamina; he's good at the game. But what will enable him to become great?

As one of us continued to test the Maple Leafs' draft picks over a two-year period, we identified several components that seemed to be directly linked to success in professional sports. Many people would identify stress tolerance, and it's in the running, but by far the most vital factor was optimism (Stein, 2000). When a team loses by a narrow margin, the player who gets angry, blames others for the loss, or goes into a tailspin from which it takes him three more games to recover is not professional material. Instead, his attitude had better be "Well, if we'd only had a few more minutes, we could have made it. And here's what we're going to do next time around." The ability to learn from mistakes and misfortunes differentiates the stars from the rest of the pack.

Another, perhaps unexpected factor is happiness. We'd thought, as we set out to test the hockey prospects, that this would surely be the happiest time of their lives. The dream of making it to the NHL was within their grasp; they'd been chosen over hundreds if not thousands of their peers from all over North America, Europe, and the former USSR. But for many of them, happiness remained elusive (as did a berth on the team), whereas those who were genuinely glad to be getting their chance tended to perform at a higher level (Stein & Sitarenios, 1999).

By the way, we also identified one component of emotional intelligence that had a negative effect on sports success. This was independence. Players who went their own way tended to underachieve; at this early stage in their careers, they'd have been better advised to learn the team's system, heed the coach, and listen to and follow directions to the letter (Stein & Sitarenios, 1999).

Another athlete we tested is Shirley Diertshi, a (previously) nationally ranked skier from Oregon. She and her three brothers were raised on the slopes, and Shirley achieved great success in both downhill and slalom junior competitions—until one weekend on Mount Hood when she was bowled over by another skier (in fact, by an instructor who'd been doing freestyle flips in mid-air and didn't see her and her companion ahead of him until it was too late). She was sent airborne by the impact and dislocated her hip. Six hours later, having endured excruciating pain while the ski patrol got her down the hill on a sled, she wound up in the hospital under general anesthetic. When she awoke, she demanded to get out of bed and back to training for the next weekend's race—a plan the doctor vetoed. In fact, as she related to the authors, he told her she might very easily have lost her leg, and she faced a long and agonizing rehabilitation (Shirley Diertshi, personal communication, August 21, 1999).

She remembers that every night she prayed that it would rain, so her brothers couldn't go skiing. To conquer these unworthy thoughts, she contacted her instructor at the Portland Art Museum and asked for hospital-bed assignments, practicing calligraphy ("every letter in the alphabet at least a million plus times") and developing the ability to focus on something completely different.

Her first day on crutches, she headed for the local Jewish community center and found the therapy pool. Soon she was swimming laps, and she was hired as an instructor and lifeguard. Then she got back her old job as a teacher's aide at a public school, walking there and back (a five-mile round trip) on crutches. Later still, when she could walk unaided, she began to run ("little did I know I had aerobic endurance genes"); went back onto the slopes, this time as an instructor; and wound up in New Zealand, where friends asked whether she'd like to join them in a marathon. Her immediate reply was "Sure, how far is it?" To give her an idea of its rigors, her so-called friends took her 14 miles out of town, dropped her off, and told her to come home under her own steam. A week later, in the actual race, she finished ahead of the expected winner, leading the organizers to suggest that she go back to Boston and try her luck there. The first time she entered that city's well-known marathon she came in 15th. The next, she led all the other American women and set a personal best of 2 hours, 39 minutes and 17 seconds.

Her note to us concludes:

> I didn't stop running then and I still run now, except now I coach others to reach their potential. My experiences motivated me to pursue further education in an area in which I could contribute to the betterment of other athletes, which is why I chose to attend graduate school to earn a Ph.D. in sports psychology. I had no idea I would travel so far, using the skills I'd developed— commitment, dedication, discipline and a willingness to work hard and hang in until reaching the finish. I'm currently teaching the psychology of exercise, health and wellness, and am coaching a cross-country and track team. I still have energy to burn, and I try to aim it in a positive direction, to encourage others to dream and to strive for their desires. (Shirley Diertshi, personal communication, August 21, 1999)

As well, Shirley has served as a consulting psychologist for the U.S. Winter Olympics team.

You should not be surprised to learn that Shirley's EQ-i results evidenced high scores in self-awareness, optimism, self-actualization, stress tolerance, and interpersonal relationships.

● Do You Want to Be a Better Athlete?

The EQ-i is widely used with athletes at both Olympic and professional levels of competition. An important question for developing
athletes may be how aware their coach is of the importance of emotional intelligence in nurturing athletic performance. One athlete
who is interested in this question is Leith Drury, who completed her
dissertation in this area at the University of Toronto.

Drury (2008) was interested in athletic coaches' perceptions of EI
and their influence in the coaching process. She surveyed 60 coaches
of elite adult athletes and administered the EQ-i to further explore
this area. She looked at both male and female coaches and individual
and team sports. In general she found that most coaches were unfamiliar with the concept of emotional and social intelligence. As well,
their coaching style tended to be focused on maintaining unilateral
control or power over the athletes they coached.

Some of the athletes rated their coach's EI using the 360 rating
form of the EQ-i. Interestingly, they saw their coaches quite differently from the coaches' own self-perceptions. The athletes' level of
satisfaction with their coach and the coach's type of relating styles
were strongly influenced by the coach's levels of emotional and social
intelligence. Drury offers many suggestions on how EI can be successfully integrated into the coaching-athlete relationship.

Another study looking at professional hockey players was carried out by Perlini and Halverson (2006). They tested 79 players from
24 different teams in the National Hockey League. They were also
interested in the role that emotional intelligence might play in the
performance of professional athletes. They found that the number
of years since the player was drafted was the strongest predictor of
performance, and draft rank was the weakest predictor of performance. This implies that those players that are able to stick it out the
longest—that is, have the most staying power—tend to do the best.
Also, being a top draft pick can be a bad omen. Perhaps the pressure

around being picked early can influence performance in a negative way by increasing the pressure on the player.

Interestingly, emotional intelligence had a role to play in these athletes' success. The researchers found that both intrapersonal competency (now known as self-perception and self-expression) and general mood were significant predictors of number of NHL points and games played (Perlini & Halverson, 2006). So it seems likely that emotionally intelligent players are more likely to have the staying power that leads to success as an athlete. This is something that professional coaches, scouts, and trainers in all areas of sports should note!

● Emotional Intelligence and the Financial World

Numerous studies have shown that emotional intelligence can be conclusively linked to workplace success in a variety of sales and financial careers. One of the first studies undertaken took place in Manila, the Philippines, in 1997 and was conducted by Joseph Hee-Woo Jae, then a graduate student at the local university (Jae, 1997). He administered the EQ-i to 100 frontline workers at the Planter's Bank, the country's fifth-largest financial institution. They also took a standardized IQ test, and their supervisors carried out and submitted independent work appraisals. When all the results were tabulated, the IQ test results accounted for less than 1 percent of their work appraisal scores, but their EQ scores could be linked to 27 percent of their success.

Another study that demonstrates the link between emotional intelligence and success on the job stems from our work with the Canadian Imperial Bank of Commerce (CIBC), one of Canada's largest financial institutions, and centered on the elite Global sales unit, once headed by Brian Twohey (Sitarenios & Stein, 1998b).

As head of Global Private Banking and Trust for the CIBC, Twohey believed that EQ skills are key to his team's performance. Its members are responsible for handling the accounts of wealthy clients whose investments transcend national boundaries. They must therefore be familiar with both Canadian and international tax law and (in short) a maze of rules and regulations. But each member of the unit is in essence a salesperson and has targets to meet. Their sales fall into two categories: those that have already been completed (or booked), and those that are waiting for certain events to transpire before they can be closed (known as "pipeline sales").

Twohey was extremely interested when we suggested that his team complete the EQ-i to see whether its findings might be used as a predictor of sales success. The results show conclusively that they can. Briefly, an individual's test scores accounted for 32 percent of his or her booked sales and 71 percent of pipeline sales (Sitarenios & Stein, 1998b).

Another well-documented example of the way emotional skills can be improved in a work environment comes from American Express Financial Service (Sitarenios, 1998). Kate Cannon, a lead executive, designed a very effective program to achieve this aim; she used the EQ-i to evaluate its effectiveness by comparing the test results obtained from 52 sales consultants with their subsequent performance. Not only did the salespeople's performance improve at work, but many of them also reported greater success in dealing with situations that arose in their personal lives. In Kate's group, the EQ factors that showed the most change—especially for those who initially scored rather low—were assertiveness, empathy, reality testing, self-actualization, and self-regard, as well as optimism.

Makes sense, doesn't it? When you're trying to sell something or (in the case of the collection agents we'll describe shortly) get something from someone, assertiveness comes in handy. Combined with empathy (the ability to understand others) and reality testing (the ability to determine whether you're really dealing with a potential customer or spinning your wheels), assertiveness takes you a long way down the road to success.

We know you're dying to hear about the collection agents, but hang on just a second. First, we'd like to mention insurance sales, a field we were drawn to because of a classic study conducted by psychologists Seligman and Schulman (1986) working with Metropolitan Life in New York. They not only administered personality and IQ tests to new employees but also designed a new test to measure optimism. They arranged to follow the employees' progress during their first year in order to gauge the effectiveness of Metropolitan's training procedures. At the end of that time, they found that the traditional tests (IQ and personality) did not predict success, but that the salespeople who scored high in optimism sold 33 percent more insurance than those who scored low. They also found that, after two years, the optimistic group members were more than 50 percent more likely than their lower-scoring peers to be thriving on the job. Optimism, then, seemed to be a strong indication of not only sales success but also an inclination to remain with the firm.

Naturally, when we began administering the EQ-i to workers in various fields, salespeople were high on our list. We found that optimism was still a predictor of success, but it wasn't right up there at the top. In our first study, we looked at 90 insurance sales people, broken into two groups—those who were doing well and those who were underachieving (Logan & Papadogiannis, 2007). Their scores varied significantly—with averages of 108 and 97, respectively. The factors that most set the two groups apart were, in order, assertiveness, happiness, self-regard, self-actualization, stress tolerance, and optimism.

We might expect that assertiveness would contribute to sales success. The better you can express your thoughts, feelings, and beliefs in a tactful way, the more your customers will view you as authentic and worth dealing with. It also works wonders when you come, as you must, to closing the sale.

Happiness may seem, at first glance, a less obvious factor, but ask yourself this: who wants to buy life insurance from someone who mopes around and behaves more like an undertaker? An upbeat disposition appears to take the insurance salesperson far, and allows him or her to cast the product (which, after all, is concerned with death) in a positive light.

As for self-regard, it imparts a sense of confidence and assurance, a sense that the salesperson knows the product inside out, but never gives way to cockiness. Dealing with stress is also an important part of the job description—but how many insurance companies actively seek to recruit people who possess these skills? Based on our informal surveys of audiences at our seminars, it seems that, despite the evidence, very few firms take advantage of these findings.

And now, as promised, EQ and collection agents. Several studies have been conducted in this field by Bachman, Stein, Campbell, and Sitarenios (2000). They collected data from debt collectors, those people entrusted to get others to pay overdue bills. What would you think it takes to be adept at this hard-nosed task? With visions of enforcers and well-muscled repo men dancing in our heads, we might think first of aggressiveness, toughness, and a willingness to be downright rude.

Wrong. According to the researchers (Bachman et al., 2000), the secret to success in recovering clients' money is to avoid destructive encounters. Bachman postulated the theory that two pairs of emotional intelligence factors could be key to this kinder, gentler strategy. He thought that emotional self-awareness and empathy would permit collectors to keep tabs on their own emotions while monitoring the debtors', thus keeping matters on an even keel. He also thought that impulse control and flexibility would allow collectors to negotiate without falling victim to the debtors' evasive, helpless, surly, or desperate comments.

To test these theories, the researchers administered the EQ-i to the best performers (as identified by their supervisors) and to their less successful coworkers. He was gratified to find that the group scores were 110 and 102 respectively, with the most effective collectors doing particularly well when it came to independence, stress tolerance, self-awareness, self-actualization, and optimism.

On closer inspection, the researchers found that the more productive group's scores were accounted for by not two but three pairs of emotional intelligence factors. The first was assertiveness and independence, which enabled the self-reliant collectors to work autonomously, secure in their ability to express themselves in a non-aggressive but highly effective way. The second was self-actualization and problem-solving, which enabled them to work toward fulfillment of their goals by means of time management, information processing, and enhanced communication and negotiation capabilities. The third was optimism and happiness, which imparted a stable mood that overcame the job's inherent stress, rejection, frustration, and disappointment.

Finally, the successful group coupled sufficient (but not too much) empathy with a rather elastic sense of impulse control. The right degree of empathy allowed these collectors to negotiate in a businesslike though humanistic way, without going overboard into excessive sympathy with a debtor's plight or, alternatively, with the client's rightful demands. A little less impulse control than average, it seems, allowed them to retain a sense of urgency—to maintain their edge and keep procrastination at bay (Bachman et al., 2000).

The results were twofold. Over a six-month period, it was found that the superior collectors raked in 100 percent of their quotas, compared with their less successful peers, who languished at 47 percent. After the researchers had created a statistical formula to help the firm select new recruits based on their findings, another study kept tabs on their performance over the first three months on the job. Remarkably, those who'd been hired on the basis of their high scores (as well as others, who'd been given special training) collected 163 percent of their quotas, while low scorers managed to come up with a still respectable 80 percent (Bachman et al., 2000).

● EQ and Journalists

Stein (1999c) had the chance to test another group of people who affect (for better or worse) our lives—that is, print and broadcast journalists. Journalists scored quite high in self-regard and optimism, but did somewhat lower in impulse control and reality testing (ominously, considering their job is to dig for the truth behind the headlines). Surprisingly, they also registered only average scores in empathy and social responsibility.

That final point puzzled a friend of ours, herself a journalist who had thought that most of her peers would be more overtly civic-minded. Her only explanation was that media people express their social responsibility through their work and are hesitant to involve themselves in their communities, for fear that their objectivity might be clouded if they later had to cover news events relating to these organizations. Interestingly, radio and television broadcasters tended to be more independent and optimistic than their print colleagues. They also showed an ability to be more self-directed and self-controlled.

● EQ Goes to Court

Another group we've had the opportunity to study in some detail is lawyers. In fact, we've administered the EQ-i to more than 130 criminal and corporate practitioners, as well as to judges. Overall, most of them tended to score in the average range, but some—the star performers—stood out from the rest. Among these, we'd like to mention two individual cases: Alan Gold and Don Jack.

Alan, as befitted a past president of the criminal lawyers' association in Canada, was cautious at first. He'd had occasion to attack a number of psychological tests in the courtroom and had given a number of expert psychological witnesses a hard time. Nonetheless, we persisted, and finally he agreed to complete the EQ-i (Alan Gold, personal communication, June 24, 1999).

When we met to discuss the results, however, Alan launched into a dismissal of the entire concept of emotional intelligence. He'd been a good sport, he said, but he doubted that any conclusions we'd draw from his answers would hold water.

So we decided to shift gears. We began by asking him to forget about the test, the questions, and the terminology that surrounds the field, and to go back to what he knew best. We asked him what makes a top-notch lawyer. Would he, for example, if he were charged with a crime, necessarily want to be defended by the person who ranked first in his or her graduating class?

"The smartest in class?" he replied. "You're kidding. No way."

Of course, we asked him why not. Surely that person would know the law inside and out. But Alan quickly set us straight. He said that knowing the law isn't all-important. Rather, it's a matter of knowing where and how to find out what you need to know—getting the answers to vital questions as they arise.

He also talked about the importance of communication: being able to get your point across quickly and understandably without wasting words or straying off topic, and of conveying an air of competence and confidence. He then remarked that in 80 percent of all cases, the lawyer's skill is probably irrelevant—that is, the issue is decided on points of law. In the remaining 20 percent, a lawyer can influence the outcome, but not always positively. In other words, a lawyer's performance can lose a case rather than win it.

Even though Alan had begun by attacking our field, what impressed us about him was his total lack of arrogance. He's at the top of his game, and as such he presents a challenge and a target to his adversaries, who quite often will make the mistake of going into full-blown attack mode. But he makes it a point never to respond in kind. In court, he's respectful, courteous, and businesslike, even if he dislikes the person on the other side.

This enables him to score points; if the opposition isn't in command of his or her emotions, Alan can turn it to his client's advantage. He keeps his cool, is always under control, and uses anger sparingly, for effect.

As well, visualization is an important tool in the legal arsenal. Alan sees a case unfolding in his mind before he sets foot in court (just like the athlete before a playoff game), dealing with crises before they happen and anticipating how his adversary might present an argument.

Not surprisingly, Alan's EQ-i score was significantly higher than that of the average lawyer. His individual component scores were illustrative too—highest in independence (as befits a senior partner in his own firm), followed by self-awareness and interpersonal relationships, assertiveness and problem-solving.

After we'd run this down, we asked Alan whether he saw the connection between reading other people well, being a good communicator, and being calm, courteous, in control, and confident—all components of emotional intelligence—and his success. He admitted that, despite his misgivings, perhaps our field made a good deal of sense after all.

Our second legal star performer is Don Jack, a corporate litigator who, when he took the EQ-i, had just been involved in a class-action suit against Bre-X, one of the most complex stock market frauds of the 1990s (Don Jack, personal communication, May 8, 1999). Our first impression was that he was a true gentleman. We were struck by his warm manners and sensitivity to others, but a mutual friend set us straight. "Don't be fooled," he said. "He's the person you want on your side." We later learned that in the courtroom Don's habitual courtesy is tempered by pit-bull tenacity, and witnesses have been reduced to tears by his probing examinations.

He, too, scored high on the EQ-i, excelling in self-regard, self-actualization, and stress tolerance. And although Don attended Oxford University, he too will tell you that it takes more than academic achievement to excel. One factor in his success is the ability to grasp the most complex picture, identify the most relevant details, and go for the jugular. He also sees the need to control his emotions and have a game plan, while reading the emotions of the judge, the opposing lawyer, and the witnesses on the stand. We'd compare his courtroom performance to that of the conductor of an orchestra, or perhaps a chess master who's always thinking a dozen moves ahead.

In an interesting series of articles published in the Canadian legal magazine *LEXPERT*, Irene Taylor, a reporter and consultant, profiled the emotional intelligence of some of Canada's top lawyers (Taylor, 2002).

High-performing lawyers were selected through a voting process that involved thousands of lawyers from across Canada. Irene profiled the top 25 corporate litigators, the top 40 under 40, the top 30 corporate deal makers, the top 25 women lawyers, and the top 25 general counsels. In each of these groups, the average EQ-i scores were significantly higher than those of our database of several hundred lawyers.

What are the emotional skills that characterize these star performing lawyers? Well, they differ somewhat depending on the type of lawyer. Although there were far too many findings to report in the space we have here, we'll highlight a few of the major findings. For example, when we think of top litigators, most of us think of pit bulls ready to pounce or scare the opposition away. Although the psychological profiling found them to be fiercely independent self-starters, they also emerged as sensitive, private introverts. Surprisingly, these attorneys are driven not by money or power, but rather by self-actualization and mastery, making a contribution, peer recognition, and winning "good" fights (Taylor, 2002).

The top litigators had higher-than-average emotional intelligence. Their key strengths were independence, optimism, reality testing, and stress tolerance. Their lowest scores were in flexibility, impulse control, and interpersonal relationships.

What about our top 40 under 40? These were an impressive crop of up-and-coming lawyers, destined for great things. Many of them had truly outstanding accomplishments, working with multi-billion-dollar accounts. What differentiated this group of young achievers? Well, factors such as birth order and family background were not significant. Also, these lawyers look different from the top litigators. They are more effective team players, less sensitive, and very pragmatic in action. And their motivation is different; rather than seeing law as a calling, they see it as a means to an end.

Emotional intelligence was a differentiator for this group as it is for other fields. These top litigators scored higher in EI than the general population and other lawyers, with three distinguishing factors. First, they were highly independent—self-starters with a great deal of initiative. Second, they had very strong stress tolerance—a great ability to work well under pressure. Third, they were very optimistic—able to see themselves get through the most challenging of situations (Taylor, 2002).

The next group, the top 30 dealmakers, represents a different type of legal professional. These are the skilled individuals who believe there is a solution for every problem—and they work until they find it. In interviews they were quoted using terms such as "adrenaline rush," "in play," "life-death choices," "one clear shot," "flanking tactic," "risk," "fun," "win," and other terms that characterize high risk–high reward adventures (Taylor, 2002).

There were three strengths that really characterized this group. First, they had high levels of self-awareness, really knowing their strengths and weakness. Second, they had high raw intelligence. Third, they had a very strong drive to succeed. Their highest areas of emotional intelligence were independence, stress tolerance, problem-solving, and optimism. Again, their overall scores were higher than those of the general population and other lawyers (Taylor, 2002).

We also learned a lot from Canada's top female lawyers. One of the big lessons we wanted to learn from this group was how they deal with work-life balance issues. As with the previous attorney groups, these women scored significantly higher than our general population and our lawyer normative groups. The three highest scores for this group were in independence, stress tolerance, and assertiveness. They were also very high in optimism (Taylor, 2002).

What advice did these female leaders give us on trying to balancing a demanding career and busy family life? Well, first, it's important to love what you do. If your work is not exciting and challenging, then it will be hard to easily navigate your time. Doing work you don't like is drudgery; it makes the time go slower and is not very enjoyable. Second, they recommend that women change their definition of success. They correctly point out that for most men, career is the measure of success. But successful women redefine the criteria, placing priority first on their roles of mother, spouse, and individual, and then on career. Imagine how difficult it is for male and female lawyers who rank career either first or second and still get outperformed by these women who rank their career fourth. Once again, EI separates the top performers from others in the same career.

Third, these female lawyers have come to realize that you can't have it all. So they pick their priorities and focus on only a few things at a time that they can really succeed in. In many cases, they learn to compromise and to develop new sets of rules. For example, when a client insists that certain information be compiled by the next day, they may show the client that only some of what they want immediately is important, and the rest of the information can be more carefully collected over a longer period.

Another characteristic of some of these women was to see adversity as a challenge. In more than one case, when they experienced difficult life challenges, they did not just resign themselves to accepting it, but rather took the bull by the horns and reorganized their lives and surroundings to deal with the challenges.

All of these higher performers kept physically active. In spite of their very busy schedules, they found time to run, hike, ski, and pursue other physical activities. They definitely were not couch potatoes.

Many of them also, at some point in their career, made a point of seeking out a mentor. They identified someone in their field for whom they had a great deal of respect and would use that person as a sounding board and adviser. The mentor provided invaluable help in achieving their career goals.

These women also mentioned managing their time well as a critical aspect of success. Although not all of them use the same time management techniques, they all seem to have perfected systems that work for their situation. After all, time management is the bottom line of work-life balance. One rule was mentioned as never to be broken: don't cancel family vacations (Taylor, 2002).

The last group of lawyers we'll look at are general counsel or in-house lawyers. There's been a move among many organizations to bring in their own corporate counsel. This is partly due to the high cost of sending all their legal work out and partly for the benefit of having a lawyer who understands the company's specific business issues. The trend toward corporate consolidations, global growth, an increasingly litigious environment, and the requirements of the Sarbanes-Oxley Act of 2002 have also contributed.

As in the previous groups, there are clear areas of strength reflected in their EQ scores. The highest scores, in order, are assertiveness, independence and stress tolerance (tied in second place), and problem solving. This means that as a group these are take-charge people who push to get things done. They are highly independent (in thinking, decision making, and action), can withstand high levels of stressful and tough situations, and are highly competent at working through complex issues (Taylor, 2002).

● EQ and the Power to Heal

We've also been able to test quite a number of physicians—who scored, alas, lower than average on EI compared with the general population. Their highest scores were in stress tolerance, flexibility, and reality testing; their lowest, in empathy, followed by happiness and social responsibility (Swift, 1999).

One of us was invited to be on a national radio show with the head of family practice at a major medical school to discuss our findings. The invitation was accepted with a degree of trepidation, fearing that she'd jump all over us or challenge our methodology. But she said she wasn't in the least surprised. In her opinion, medical schools are taking a bunch of intelligent and caring young people and ripping the caring right out of them. It's no wonder that holistic medicine is growing by leaps and bounds at the expense of more traditional disciplines, or that lawsuits against medical doctors have risen dramatically over the past 20 years, in large part because of a lack of communication between doctor and patient.

This lack of communication can have implications for patient care. In fact, a study by Peggy Wagner and her colleagues at the Medical College of Georgia helps shed more light on how this relationship plays out (Wagner, Moseley, Grant, Gore, & Owens, 2002). They tested the emotional intelligence of 30 physicians (including faculty and residents) with the EQ-i. They also developed a patient satisfaction scale that contained eight items and assessed patients' satisfaction with their individual physicians as well as their overall satisfaction with healthcare. They produced both a "total satisfaction" score and a "relationship satisfaction" score.

There were 232 patients included in this study, with an average of 7 patients rating each physician. Overall, the patient satisfaction scores were quite high, ranging from averages of 3.69 to 3.94 (out of 4) per item. There were no differences in satisfaction scores for male or female doctors, although there was a positive trend for satisfaction with faculty over residents.

There were no differences in EQ-i scores between faculty and residents. However, although female physicians scored higher than males in all scores, they were significantly higher only in stress tolerance. This is quite interesting because in the general population women tend to score lower than men on this scale (Wagner et al., 2002).

Comparisons were made between physicians of patients who were 100-percent satisfied and those who were less than 100-percent satisfied (138 out of 232 rated their physicians as excellent—4 out of 4 points—on all eight satisfaction items). The most significant finding on the EQ subscales was that physicians with higher patient ratings scored significantly higher on the happiness subscale. In other words, patients were more satisfied with doctors who were happy. The highest-rated doctors were also somewhat higher in social responsibility and optimism. Interestingly, as you will see later in this chapter, social responsibility and optimism are significant areas for leaders. The authors of the study suggest helping medical students learn the importance of personal happiness and life satisfaction as a starting point for EI coaching and intervention during training. So next time you see your doctor, you may want to see how happy she or he is.

Still on the subject of health, we might add that we've asked 3,829 people who took the EQ-i about their ability to cope with health-related issues. Of these, 2,715 thought they were dealing with them successfully, and 1,114 said they thought they could do better. As you might imagine, their scores differed significantly—those who felt they'd coped well averaged 10 points higher across the board. The skills and attitudes that most differentiated the two groups, in order of importance, were stress tolerance, optimism, flexibility, self-regard, and happiness (Bar-On, 1997).

Again, this is no great surprise. Illness is stressful, and the way we respond to it is in itself physiological and can compound our discomfort. We not only feel and act ill, but our reactions to the illness slow down our body's natural attempts to deal with disease. It's bad enough to be ill, but to stress ourselves out only compounds the problems we're experiencing. Optimism helps us get through this adversity, just as it helps us deal with other woes. Focusing on how well you can cope with illness and believing that it will eventually go away makes it easier to deal with. As does flexibility: rigidly refusing to do things that will help you get better will only prolong your misery.

While we're on the topic of those in the professions, another interesting call came to us from psychologist Dr. Dana Ackley, suggesting we explore the emotional intelligence of dentists. "How would emotional intelligence affect dental practice?" we asked.

Dana has been working with dentists for quite some time. In fact, he was working with the Pankey Institute in Florida, a world-famous training center for dentists. He wanted our help in carrying out a study looking at the relationship between the successes of the Pankey Institute for Continuing Dental Education graduates and their emotional intelligence. Together with dentists Drs. Irwin Becker and Richard Green of the Pankey Institute, he tested the EQ of 144 dentists who had completed training there. They also created a Survey of Progress (SOP) that evaluated dentists' actual practice following their training at the Institute. They found that emotional intelligence (as measured by the EQ-i) was directly related to success in implementing practice initiatives as identified by the SOP (Becker, Ackley, & Green, 2003).

They then identified the specific EQ factors that were most important, using a complex statistical (multiple regression) equation. The most important skills associated with dental practice success were emotional self-awareness, reality testing, assertiveness, and self-actualization. The investigators then related how these factors specifically contribute to successful dental practice (Becker et al., 2003).

For example, highly skilled professionals in technical fields such as engineering and dentistry tend to think of emotions as frivolous or unimportant. They want to appear objective. However, an objective dentist is not always what the patient wants. Denying that feelings exist does not help either. Here's an example: the dentist is tired at the end of a long day's work. The last patient of the day needs some unexpected dental procedures that exceed the time allowed, but the work needs to be done. The dentist, frustrated, may vent his or her frustration by being curt, maybe even impolite. The self-aware dentist knows that this kind of behavior is likely to upset the patient and could erode the dentist's long-range ability to influence the patient's dental health. Only by paying attention to and dealing with these internal cues can the dentist be more assured of a positive patient relationship.

● EQ and Law Enforcement

There has been a great deal of interest in the potential effect of emotional intelligence on policing or law enforcement in general. Sometimes questions would take the form of "What would the world be like if we developed emotionally intelligent police forces?" Well, it may have seemed far-fetched at first, but we've now seen some great progress in this area, thanks to the work of Special Agent Tim Turner, formerly of the FBI Academy at Quantico, Virginia. Tim came to learn more about emotional intelligence at one of our training sessions. He was able to quickly connect the dots on where emotional intelligence fit in with law enforcement.

Tim went back and carried out the largest study (Turner, 2005) that we've seen looking specifically at the role of emotional intelligence and police officers. As a leadership trainer at the FBI Academy, Tim worked with high-potential police officers who were selected from forces not only throughout the United States but also from around the world. He tested and compared the emotional intelligence test scores of 424 law enforcement leaders who were selected to attend the FBI Academy against a matched set of law enforcement leaders who were not sent. There were many fascinating findings of this study relating emotional intelligence to the backgrounds of the officers— whether they were from rural or urban districts, gender, and so on. Unfortunately, we don't have enough space here to cover all of these groundbreaking results.

One of the most exciting findings was in the differentiation of the "star performer" officers—those who were sent to the Academy. Turner used a complicated statistical procedure (regression analysis) to see which of the many factors best differentiated these groups. One might expect top performers to be less flexible (better at following orders). Or perhaps they were the toughest cops (more aggressive).

Well, we want to dispel those myths of what a high-performing police officer is all about. The most significant factor was social responsibility (Turner, 2005). As we are finding in other studies of top leaders, social responsibility, we believe, will be a defining characteristic of tomorrow's leaders (in much the same way that flexibility characterizes today's leaders). Socially responsible police officers are able to see the greater good—what's best for their division, what's best for their force, what's best for their community, and, yes, what's best for the world.

The second most important defining factor was problem solving. High performers in this area are good at using their emotions when solving problems—defining the problem, generating solutions, and acting on the solution using emotions as opposed to letting them get in the way. Tim had pointed out to us early on that top cops are good problem solvers.

The third area, one that comes up in many of our job studies, is self-actualization. These are the people who really enjoy their work.

They are also good goal-setters—able to set and achieve what they want in life. Our high-performing police officers really love the work they do and have a plan for where they are going both in their career and in life. Finally, and it should not be a surprise, these people excel in their interpersonal relationships. Being successful in this area requires being a good people person. Knowing how to make and keep good relationships is a big part of what makes these leaders successful (Turner, 2005).

● EQ and Sales Talent

We've also profiled sales people for a large, well-known national U.S. electronics chain (Sitarenios, 2003). Unfortunately, we can't divulge the names of the players in this case, but we screened thousands of job applicants—entirely online—to identify people who came close to matching the company's star performers. We see this as the selection method of the future. By creating a formula based on star performers already in the organization, we can use the statistical algorithm to see to what degree applicants come close to this ideal candidate. Applicants are rank ordered, after their skills, availability, location, and various elimination criteria (such as poor language skills) are taken into account. They are then screened, with a brief phone interview to "check" their skills in the areas that the star performer analysis found to be important.

The best applicants, after the phone interview, are then invited for a more in-depth, one- to two-hour interview with the most relevant people in the organization. This process saves not only hundreds of hours in the selection process, but tens of thousands of dollars as well. Just as important, it prevents people from accepting jobs in which they are highly likely to fail—avoiding a waste of their time as well as the humiliation of being let go.

In this case, we looked at cell phone salespeople. We started by testing ninety-one current employees throughout the country with the EQ-i and an online ability test measuring vocabulary and arithmetic. Then individual managers ranked all employees based on a combination of sales, attitude, and attendance to create a performance rating. These ratings were categorized into three groups: top, average, and bottom performers. We then used a complex statistical analysis to examine the relationship between EQ-i responses and performance ratings. We found that self-actualization, empathy, problem solving, and happiness were all positively related to performance in this group. Several other EQ-i components or subcomponents also were significant (Sitarenios, 2003).

These EQ-i factors were extremely effective in differentiating top performers from the other two performance groups, although a bit less effective in distinguishing average from bottom performers. For example, using our formula to predict performance, 8 percent of top performers were correctly identified as top performers and 78 percent of bottom performers were correctly identified as bottom performers. On the other hand, only 13 percent of average performers were incorrectly identified as top performers and 8 percent of bottom performers were wrongly identified as top performers. None of the top performers were classified as bottom performers (Sitarenios, 2003).

The measures of cognitive ability (vocabulary and arithmetic) did not contribute to the predictive model. These results were then used to create a formula that compared all new applicants to the top performers (Sitarenios, 2003). People often worry about cheaters when online testing is used as part of the selection process. The difficulty, however, is that nobody outside of the selection group knows which specific factors are important for this job. Most people who cheat are likely to cheat across the board—on all scales—which would not be helpful in beating the selection formula. Also, the results of cheating likely won't help the cheater get the job. Cheaters may get screened out after the initial screening interview or after the in-depth interview. Even if they fooled everyone in the interviews and got hired, chances are their performance will not be very good or they will end up being unhappy performing a job they really aren't suited for.

The effects of this program led to hiring a much better caliber of salesperson. It also streamlined the selection process, saving a great deal of time and money.

● EQ and Teamwork

What makes a good work team? Are some teams more successful than others? There has been a lot of discussion about the role of emotional intelligence in successful team functioning in the workplace. There have also been studies looking at some of the specific emotional intelligence ingredients that make up good teams. One study looking at this was carried out at Eastern Michigan University by Frye, Bennett, and Caldwell (2006) and colleagues.

The researchers wanted to explore the relationship between the emotional intelligence of self-directed teams and two dimensions of team interpersonal process—team task orientation and team maintenance function. These basically have to do with how well a team focuses on what needs to be done, as opposed to being distracted or off target, and how well the team members keep each other going over time. The EQ-i was administered to all members of thirty-three work teams. Then the average EQ-i score for each of the factors for each of the teams was computed. This study looked at the average scores for each of the teams (Frye et al., 2006).

They used a regression analysis, which allows them to predict which of the EQ-i factors are most important in each of the team areas. They found that the interpersonal relationship factor best predicted the team maintenance factor. In other words, having high interpersonal skills among each of the team members leads to a team that functions well together over time. They also found that both interpersonal relationship and general mood (or the combination of optimism and happiness) predicted how well the team did in team task orientation. Emotional intelligence emerges as an important element in enabling people to work together toward their goals (Frye et al., 2006).

● EQ and Leading a Diverse Team

Increasingly our workplaces are becoming more diverse, with a greater number of people from different backgrounds and cultures needing to work together. How do we manage this diversity? What are the characteristics of people who manage different people well? Emotional intelligence is beginning to play a more important role in diversity training programs.

In a study at the University of North Florida, Conrad (2007) investigated the role of emotional intelligence in intercultural diversity among 70 graduates of Leadership Jacksonville. Using a mixed method design that included testing and interviews, some factors were identified in working successfully with culturally diverse populations.

The emotional intelligence factors that were found to be important in this study included general mood, empathy, the problem-solving aspect of decision making, social responsibility, and interpersonal relationship. The study concludes that leaders seeking to manage diversity would greatly benefit from integrating elements of emotional intelligence into their professional development.

The Role of EQ in Leadership

What impact does emotional intelligence have on leadership? Unfortunately, most of what we've seen has been based on speculation or revisionist science. Wild estimates have been proposed—for example, that emotional intelligence accounts for 80–90 percent of leadership skills. We think these estimates, based on flimsy evidence, can be harmful to the legitimate research into and understanding of the role of emotional intelligence. They run the risk of destroying the credibility of serious researchers in the field. It may be interesting to look at interviews conducted many years ago with leaders of yesterday's companies, but it does not shed much light on what makes today's leaders successful. Also, without standard-ized testing, the reliability of the information is suspect. Interviews and ratings by peers and subordinates often reflect biases. Many of today's 360° (multirater) measures are heavily influenced by a desire to please one's boss (this is especially true of instruments without validity scales), or, at the other extreme, a wish to replace him or her. Moreover, it is difficult to accurately judge the internal emotions of someone with whom you work.

● Young Presidents

Our testing of a large group of members of the Young Presidents' Organization (YPO) (along with some other CEO membership groups we've tested) is the first valid study that looks at the relationship between emotional intelligence and leadership (Stein, Papadogiannis, Yip, & Sitarenios, 2009). This select group of top business achievers has strict rules for membership: to belong, one must be 39 years old or younger and be president or CEO of a company that employs 60 or more people and generates $5 million or more a year in revenue.

One of us (Steven) was invited to speak at a regional meeting of the YPO, which carefully screens its presenters in order to avoid sales pitches and ensure some take-home value to its members. For us, this invitation offered a unique opportunity to collect some very interesting data. After all, it is not easy to get access to groups with such well-defined criteria for success. In exchange for speaking about emotional intelligence, the YPO agreed to let us test willing members with the EQ-i. This would make the presentation more interesting for them and provide useful research material for us. Each member would get his or her own personal scores, and we would incorporate the "group profile" as part of the presentation. To make it even more interesting, we came up with three naturally occurring subgroups that characterized the YPO's membership. Comparing these three groups gave us yet another dimension to explore.

The first group consisted of "Founders." These were the individuals who had started the companies they managed. As young entrepreneurs with an idea for a small business, they had seen their dreams grow, often beyond their wildest expectations. The second group we called "Family Business." These were individuals who, for one reason or another, had taken charge of an enterprise that had been started by a parent, uncle, or other close relative. The third group we referred to as "Professional Managers" or, more colloquially, "Hired Guns." These individuals had demonstrated, perhaps as early as age 25, a great deal of managerial competence. In some cases they would go on to head companies generating more than $50 million per year in revenue (Stein et al., 2009).

Another area of great interest to many of the members was the potential gender differences that we might uncover. How would the EQ scores of successful entrepreneurial men compare to those of equally successful women? Although there were considerably more male members, we still felt that comparing them to the female members would be of great value. What could we learn from the emotional skill sets of these successful businesswomen?

As we began, we had no idea how many of these very busy young executives would have the time to complete our inventory and get back to us in time. As we were competing with their extremely hectic schedules running companies that, in some cases, generated hundreds of millions of dollars in sales, we did not expect a huge return. In most surveys of business people, a return rate of 33 percent is considered quite good. So we were shocked when the responses started to roll in: the return rate was more than 92 percent. And the results were impressive.

The YPO group scored significantly higher than our large sample of general population norms. In fact, they were high in comparison to the hundreds of group scores we have processed. What were the specific emotional skills that set this successful group of entrepreneurs apart?

The first was their high level of flexibility. These individuals are characterized by their ability to see opportunities and grasp them. They are ready and able to move quickly when needed, to take advantage of the opportunities they encounter (Stein et al., 2009).

Another characteristic that stood out in the successful young entrepreneurs was their independence—a crucial component of effective decision-making. We discovered 22-year-olds who had started and continued to manage companies generating more than $20 million in sales. In some cases these individuals far surpassed any of their families or friends in income. They had no role models with whom they could discuss issues and problems. But one of the benefits of the YPO is their "mentoring" program, which gives these 22-year-old millionaires the opportunity to learn from older, more experienced entrepreneurs, who manage $100-million companies. One young millionaire told us he would go to his mentor to discuss business issues, difficulties, and decisions. Although the mentor would freely give advice, the student was, in fact, quite selective about which bits of information to heed. That is the essence of independence: listen to others, weigh the advice, then go out and make your own decisions (Stein et al., 2009).

How did Founders compare with Professional Managers and Family Business? Only one factor differentiated them. The Founders were significantly more assertive than the other two groups. And what about the young female presidents? Interestingly, they performed about the same as their male counterparts in all areas except for two: they scored significantly *higher* in interpersonal relationships and empathy (Stein et al., 2009).

● EI and High-Performing Leaders

Another study in star performers was carried out by an MHS team led by Diana Durek (2005) for a major telecom company. The company wanted to understand the relationship between EQ-i and leadership competencies to enhance training and coaching of leaders in their organization.

In this star performer model, the EQ-i accounted for 48 percent of what differentiated the high- and low-performing leaders. This means that one-half of the skill set required for successful execution of this organization's leadership competencies comprises emotional and social skills. Twenty-four percent of the difference between high and low performers was accounted for by the happiness subscale, 13 percent by the self-regard subscale, 9 percent by self-actualization, 2 percent by interpersonal relationship, and 1 percent by optimism. When we ran a classification test, the resultant model was accurate in predicting star performers 9 out of 10 times (Durek, 2005).

These results had powerful implications for selection and development initiatives in this organization. The EQ-i subscales that account for the difference in performance were incorporated into the competency training, thus strengthening their training results.

We determined that the selection process could be enhanced significantly with the creation of an algorithm that would evaluate a candidate's EQ-i match against high performers in the position, generating a value to predict the likelihood of an individual's becoming a star performer.

So far, the largest and best-designed study looking at emotional intelligence and leadership was carried out by Dr. Marian Ruderman and her colleagues at the Center for Creative Leadership in Greensboro, North Carolina (Ruderman, Hannum, Leslie, & Steed, 2001). The Center for Creative Leadership (CCL) is a world-famous leadership training center with a long history of research into what makes leaders great.

In their study, 302 leaders and senior managers—some quite successful, others struggling—were tested for emotional intelligence with the EQ-i and for their on-the-job (leadership) performance with Benchmarks, a tool designed to get a clear picture of leadership performance from superiors, peers, and subordinates. One finding of Ruderman and her colleagues (2001) was that emotional intelligence accounted for approximately 28 percent of leadership performance. This finding is consistent with a number of other studies we've reported on previously.

● EI and the Pillars of Leadership

Based on their work, we've identified four pillars or competencies that are important for successful leadership. These are (1) being centered and grounded, (2) having the ability to take action, (3) having a participative management style, and (4) being tough-minded. Each of these pillars was significantly related to specific aspects of emotional intelligence as measured by EQ-i (Stein & Book, 2011).

The first pillar of leadership success is *being centered and grounded*. High performers are in control of themselves. They are seen by people around them as having a stable mood, and they don't fly off the handle when things get tough, another way of saying that they have high impulse control. You can predict how these leaders are going to react to things. You don't come in to work, say good morning, and then get berated for something you forgot to do the day before.

Also, the successful leaders were more aware of their strengths and weaknesses. The most dangerous leaders are the ones who propose to know it all. Although it's important to know your strengths and use them wisely, it's equally important to know your weaknesses and not inflict them on everyone around you. We find that not all leaders are willing to invest the time in improving their weaknesses; however, the next best alternative is to surround yourself with people strong in the skills you lack.

Another aspect of this pillar is the ability to balance work life and personal life. Although in the past there has been an overemphasis on the workaholic lifestyle of leaders, we find that balance is associated with better-performing leaders. If you can manage your own life well—managing stress, home life, fitness, diet—then chances are higher that the workplace is well managed.

Successful leaders are also straightforward and self-aware. People know where these leaders stand on issues, as they tend not to be vague or wishy-washy. As well, they are aware of their own feelings and motivators. They are consistent in their approach to issues because they know how they feel and what they believe about issues.

Finally, being centered and grounded helps these leaders to be composed under pressure. They do not flare up or lose control even under difficult circumstances. The most important emotional intelligence skills in this pillar are social responsibility, stress tolerance, impulse control, and optimism.

The second pillar of leadership success is *action taking*, which includes the ability to be decisive. Successful leaders can make decisions, and they have a track record of making good ones. These leaders take into account the views of others, but in the end they make the best decision they can with all available information (Stein & Book, 2011).

Successful leaders don't give up easily once they have decided on a course of action. They realize follow-through is a critical part of the decision-making process. As well, they will evaluate the effectiveness of the decision throughout the process and learn from their mistakes.

This competency was directly related to three factors of emotional intelligence: assertiveness, independence, and optimism.

Participative management style is the third pillar (Stein & Book, 2011). Command and control are no longer in style in business environments. People resent being told what to do with no allowance for their own input, and they certainly do not appreciate being ignored. Successful leaders today focus on winning the hearts and minds of the people around them. Without getting buy-in for their ideas, plans, and tactics, there's little incentive for those around to perform optimally. People want to be involved in the plans and their implementation. As well, they want to feel they have contributed. After all, if people feel they have some ownership of the initiative, they are more likely to want to see it succeed.

The ability to succeed in this aspect of leadership includes good listening and communication skills. Although many leaders know how to present their ideas and directions to others, fewer know how to actively listen to their people to ensure they are on board with decisions. Good leaders are sensitive to what may seem to be minimal objections to ideas and requests. They can draw out the objections and attempt to deal with them, even adjusting plans when flaws are pointed out. Leaders must aim for what is best for the whole organization, not just their own egos.

Great leaders can put people at ease. Bad leaders scare people. When people are at ease, they are more likely to speak their mind, offering suggestions and ideas. Great leaders give people credit for their contributions and make them feel like an important part of the team. Even greater leaders take responsibility for bad decisions and mistakes.

The important work of building consensus begins once the leader has heard everyone out. Successful leaders, after ensuring that they are aware of people's positions, both pro and con, use their skills to get everyone on board with whatever decision is made. If team members feel that they participated in the process, presented their case, and got a fair hearing, they are more likely to go along with the prevailing consensus.

What was surprising about this third pillar of leadership was the nature of its relationship to specific factors of emotional intelligence. Although related to several aspects of emotional intelligence, the strongest relationships were with empathy and social responsibility. Empathic leaders can hear what others are saying and feeling. Leaders who are socially responsible—that is, those who care about their community and those who are less fortunate, and who respect society's rules—are more participatory in their leadership style. These leaders also have better interpersonal relationships and better impulse control, and they are happier.

The fourth pillar of successful leadership is *being tough-minded* (Stein & Book, 2011). These leaders show resiliency following difficult situations. They manage to persevere in the face of obstacles, overcome challenges, and handle pressure well. These people have an air of confidence as they lead the way through difficult times.

The emotional intelligence skills that relate to this competency are self-regard, stress tolerance, and impulse control.

⬤ EQ and the CEO

A group of chief executive officers (CEOs), members of the Innovators Alliance (IA), were tested for emotional intelligence and asked to complete a survey (Stein, et al., 2009). These CEOs are an elite group

Figure 21.1 Leaders and Emotional Intelligence

Note: YPO = Young Presidents' Organization; IA = Innovators Alliance.

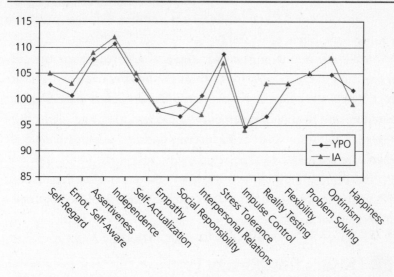

in Canada. Members must be a company CEO or percent; run a company with a minimum cumulative revenue growth rate of 35 percent over three years; generate CDN$2 million or more in annual revenue; employ between 10 and 500 people; and maintain an Ontario-based head office. The sample we tested included 76 IA members, 61 males and 15 females. Their average age was 44, with 50 percent of them 45 years old or younger.

In Figure 21.1 you can see that their results are almost identical to those of the YPO group of leaders. We consistently find that CEOs are very high in independence, assertiveness, and stress tolerance. Interestingly, they scored lower than average in social responsibility and impulse control.

Another analysis we did with the IA group was truly unique. We separated the "top CEOs" from the rest based on what we thought to be the most important measure of success for this group—profitability. So we compared the CEOs of the most-profitable organizations to those of the least-profitable, based on data we collected. We then did a complex statistical analysis to see whether there were any EQ factors that differentiated these groups. We thought that being really good at managing stress would predict business success. Or perhaps the more successful CEOs would be happier than their less-profitable counterparts (Stein et al., 2009).

Well, we were wrong. In fact, there were three factors that differentiated the high performers from the low performers. First, the high performers were more empathic. These leaders were better at listening and reading their employees. Second, they had higher self-regard. They were surer of themselves and had a better handle on their strengths and weaknesses. Finally, they were more assertive. People around them know where they stand and what they expect. They are not about hidden agendas or bullying people into submission (Stein et al., 2009).

● Lessons from Reality TV

Reality TV shows inevitably produce leaders and followers, with some of the leaders flaming out early and others surviving to the next round. Maybe that's why the EQ-i was used as part of the selection process for the reality show *Survivor*, as well as *The Apprentice*, *Big Brother*, and *The Amazing Race*. Dr. Richard Levak of California is the psychologist involved in preselection testing for all of these shows We learned from Dr. Levak that some of the people fired earliest on *The Apprentice* had the highest IQs but the lower EQ scores (Richard Levak, personal communication, November 8, 2005). The participants who managed really well had the higher EQs. In Levak's experience, having a high IQ and a low EQ is like having a powerful sports car with bad steering.

The EQ-i was also used to screen candidates for a Canadian reality TV show called *From the Ground Up*, starring Debbie Travis, a home designer and TV personality. The idea is that a group of young twenty-somethings who have been struggling in life and career may be ripe for working in the trades. The show dispels the myth that you need to be a professional to be successful in the world. The contestants, who were carefully screened, worked on building a house from the ground up. Expert tradespeople mentored the contestants in a variety of different skills required in home construction and design. The winners were selected from the first half of the series by Debbie, and for the last half by votes from Canadians across the country. Suffice it to say, the predictions made using the EQ-i scores were surprisingly accurate regarding the outcomes of the various contestants.

● Leading a Non-Profit

Another study in leadership compared the emotional intelligence scores of leaders in non-profit health and human service agencies to the scores of leaders of for-profit organizations in the business arena. The study, carried out by Michelle Morehouse (2007), evaluated 32 non-profit leaders and 32 business leaders. She found significant differences between these two groups of leaders. There were differences in overall emotional intelligence scores as well as differences in the subscales of stress management and adaptability. These results could be important in training future leaders for the type of organization they will be working in.

● Identifying Future Leaders

We get a lot of questions about identifying high-potential future leaders and managers. We are pleased to report that there are now studies available that have explored this area. One interesting study was carried out at Vrije University in Brussels by Nicky Dries and Roland Pepermans (2007). They looked at 51 high potentials in organizations and matched them to 51 "regular" managers. They were matched based on managerial level, gender and age.

All of these managers were given a battery of tests that included the EQ-i. A number of EQ-i scales differentiated the high-potential managers. These included assertiveness, independence, optimism, flexibility, and social responsibility (Pepermans, 2007). This helps confirm some of our other work looking at successful leadership. Note that social responsibility pops up as one of those factors we predicted would become increasingly important for tomorrow's leaders.

● Emotional Intelligence and Leadership Style

One of the most popular topics for continuing research in emotional intelligence includes gaining a better understanding of successful leadership behaviors. Are good leaders born that way, or can they be created? What leadership behaviors are important for specific types of leaders—business, religious, sports, non-profit, public service, and so on? In one study, looking at leadership in non-profit, faith-based organizations in Colorado, researchers Frye, Bennett, and Caldwell (2006) found that emotional intelligence was strongly related to transformational leadership. In this type of leadership, leaders create a vision of what's to be accomplished and inspire action by others toward this vision. This has been found to be one of the most productive ways of leading others.

The researchers found that the most important EQ-i factors related to transformational leadership were optimism, self-actualization, empathy, problem solving, and assertiveness. These results parallel and support the findings with leaders across a variety of different organizations and industries.

CHAPTER 22

EQ, Lifestyle, Healthy Living, and Relationships

We've saved the best research for last. Can you leverage emotional intelligence to help you be happier, healthier, more satisfied in relationships? You're probably not surprised that the answer is yes.

Is Emotional Intelligence Good for Your Health?

In 1996 Jenny Dunkley, a graduate psychology student in South Africa, carried out a study comparing the EQ-i scores of 58 patients who had recently suffered heart attacks with a control group with no history of heart disease. As she'd expected, the recovering patients scored much lower, particularly on stress tolerance, flexibility, and self-actualization. But to her surprise, they actually scored higher in social responsibility. Perhaps a brush with death served to refocus them on one of the most important and rewarding things in life—generosity toward one's fellow men and women.

But Dunkley didn't stop there. She knew that some of the patients had participated in a program designed to help them better manage stress and others had not. She compared their scores and found significant differences in both the overall scores and every component score except interpersonal relationships and self-regard. Those who'd gone through the program were retested after five weeks of training; they had increased their total score by an average of 9 points, registering the greatest improvements in stress tolerance, self-regard, flexibility, happiness, reality testing, self-actualization, problem solving, and impulse control (Dunkley, 1996).

It's not surprising that there's consistency across research related to the association between emotional intelligence and various aspects of physical and emotional health when people are asked to self-report their health and exercise activities (Schutte, Malouff, Thorsteinsson, Bhullar, & Rooke, 2007). Research with Canadian university students goes further, though; it reveals that it's your exercise *behavior,* not your *attitude* toward exercise that is related to your emotional intelligence. In other words, students of different EI levels expressed similar attitudes toward exercise, but higher EI scores—especially in the self-perception and interpersonal relationship realms—predicted who actually exercised (Saklofske, Austin, Rohr, & Andrew, 2007). In addition, higher emotional intelligence scores are associated with lower levels of alcohol and cigarette consumption among early adolescents (Trinidad & Johnson, 2002). Perhaps it's the ability to resist peer pressure, fueled by higher self-regard, independence, and assertiveness; or perhaps it's simply better impulse control. Either way, the relationship is clear: higher EI is associated with less consumption of alcohol and cigarettes during the early teen years.

A number of studies have looked at the effects that training people to improve their emotional intelligence can have on their health status. One interesting study was carried out in the faculty of medicine and department of psychology at Ondokuz Mayis University in Turkey (Yalcin, Karahan, Ozcelik, & Igde, 2008) The researchers collected data from 184 patients with type 2 diabetes who volunteered to participate in the study. They collected a vast array of information, including health status, psychological well-being, and emotional intelligence.

They selected the 36 patients with the lowest scores on the health status questionnaires. These patients were then randomly assigned to either a treatment group or a control group (with 18 patients in each group). The treatment group went through a 12-week emotional intelligence training. The control group wasn't part of any special intervention. All of the patients were retested at the end of the program and again three and six months later. Only the group that went through the emotional intelligence training increased in their reported quality of life, well-being, and emotional intelligence.

In short, a growing number of studies are finding that patients, even with chronic health problems, can benefit from developing their emotional intelligence. In fact, there have been so many studies of the relationship between emotional intelligence and health that researchers have begun doing major reviews of all the studies in order to summarize their findings. One analysis of the research was published by Nicola Schutte at the University of New England. She and her colleagues (Schutte, Malouff, Thorsteinsson, Bhullar, & Rooke, 2007) analyzed the effects found in 44 studies looking at this connection. They identified significant relationships between emotional intelligence and mental health, psychosomatic health, and physical health.

● Are You Getting the Amount of Exercise You Need?

Would increasing your emotional intelligence help with your exercise plan? What's the role of emotional intelligence in exercise behavior? A study carried out at the University of Calgary in Canada and the University of Edinburgh in the U.K. has looked at the role of personality and emotional intelligence in exercise behavior.

Psychologists Saklofske, Austin, Rohr, and Andrew (2007) tested 497 Canadian university students with a personality test and the EQ-i and had them monitor their exercise behavior. It seems that extroverts and people high in emotional intelligence exercise more frequently. Personality factors were seen as distinct from emotional intelligence skills in terms of their influence of exercise.

● Are You Getting Enough Sleep?

The folks at Walter Reed Army Institute have been doing some very interesting research related to sleep deprivation. What happens when you're overtired? Are you more likely to do things that you wouldn't normally do? William Killgore and his colleagues (Killgore, Killgore, Day, Li, Kamimori, & Balkin, 2007) at Walter Reed looked at what happens when you face a moral dilemma after 53 hours of not sleeping. Twenty-six healthy adults took part in the research. The results are fascinating.

After being deprived of sleep, your response latency increases—it takes longer for you to make a decision—but only when it comes to moral dilemmas that are personally significant. In other words, only those dilemmas that are emotionally important to you are affected. Impersonal dilemmas (those that don't arouse your emotions—or matter that much) and nonmoral dilemmas don't generate the same delays.

Interestingly, emotional intelligence as measured by the EQ-i played a role in determining the willingness of someone deprived of sleep to violate that person's moral beliefs. People with higher emotional intelligence are better able to keep their moral beliefs intact under trying circumstances. This may help us better understand those politicians (who may have lower EQ) who go against their moral beliefs and have extramarital affairs—although they may not be sleep deprived (Killgore, Killgore, et al., 2007).

● EQ and Relationship Bliss

What's the relationship between emotional intelligence and marital or dyadic satisfaction?

To find out, staff at MHS (Stein, 1999b) administered the EQ-i to more than 1,100 people and asked them to rate themselves in this regard. As expected, people who were satisfied with their relationships scored an average 5 points higher than those who weren't. Differences cropped up across all 5 realms of emotional intelligence, as well as among its 16 scales, but which do you suppose played the greatest role in determining whether a person was happy in his or her union? Many of us might name interpersonal relationship skills, empathy, or flexibility. But happiness led the list, followed by self-regard, self-awareness, self-actualization, and reality testing. Only after these did interpersonal relationships per se come into force.

Whenever happiness appears to play a significant role in one of our studies, someone always wonders whether (as in this particular case) satisfactory marriages lead to higher happiness scores or vice versa. We think that happiness is the key because people who score high in this component tend to be happy in a wide variety of situations, through good times and bad (or, as the marriage vows put it, for better or for worse). As we hope you have learned from this book, happiness comes from the inside out.

Self-regard is obviously important in a marriage, dealing as it does with both strengths and weaknesses. Viewing yourself with clarity will help you be less prickly and defensive. Being secure will help you deal constructively with criticism or "constructive feedback" by looking at it honestly and, if it's valid, doing something about it instead of yelling at the messenger. As for self-awareness, it gives you the chance to monitor and control your internal thermometer, making it less likely that you will end up exploding or falling apart because you didn't see the emotion coming. Finally, self-actualization, although it adds spice to every element of our lives, is especially vital when it comes to intimate relationships. Finding meaning and purpose in our most important relationships is vital to their success.

● Dealing with Trauma

One morning in 2001, Steven received an unexpected phone call from Robert Fazio, who shared his story of what had happened to his family. Here's a summary of what Steve learned.

At 9 ~AM on a Tuesday morning the previous week, Rob's brother had called to tell him that their father was okay. Rob, quite puzzled, had replied, "Well, why wouldn't he be?" His brother had immediately told him to turn on the TV. Their father worked in the South Tower of the World Trade Center, and it was September 11, 2001.

Rob switched on the TV in time to see the second plane hit the South Tower. His father had called his mother shortly after the North Tower was hit to tell her that he loved her and that he was safe. Rob and his family had every reason to believe that his father had made it safely out of the tower that day. In fact, it took Rob three weeks to finally accept the fact that his father had not survived the attack.

After dealing with the grief and unanswered questions, Rob eventually learned more about his father's fate. What he learned would change his life and the lives of many other people. Rob discovered from a number of his father's colleagues that he was last seen holding the door open so that others could safely leave the building and return home to their loved ones.

As a result of this, Rob started a nonprofit organization called "Hold the Door for Others" whose mission is to provide resources and create opportunities that connect people and empower them to grow through loss and to achieve their dreams. We were more than happy to help out when Rob asked us to support his research work by looking at family members who lost loved ones on September 11. Specifically, he wanted to look at the importance of emotional intelligence and resilience in predicting people's post-traumatic growth—that is, whether people can successfully grow and move forward with their lives after experiencing a traumatic loss (Fazio & Fazio, 2005).

Their results were fascinating. Specifically, they found a connection between post-traumatic growth and three areas of emotional intelligence: interpersonal, intrapersonal (now known as self-perception and self-expression), and general mood (optimism and happiness). Two of these realms (interpersonal and interpersonal) were mediated by resilience. In other words, people high in these two areas of emotional intelligence were more resilient and therefore more effective in dealing with the trauma (Fazio & Fazio, 2005). And it makes sense that those who can remain positive and persist when facing adversity (the very definition of optimism) will recover better from a trauma like what Robert's family experienced.

● EQ, Cultural Sensitivity, and the Medicine Wheel

The cultural adaptation of emotional intelligence is a topic of great interest. Having given presentations throughout North America, Europe, Africa, Australia and Asia, we have been gratified to see how well the topic fits in with so many cultures. One fascinating example is the work one of us (Steven) has done in Thompson, Manitoba, with the Burntwood Regional Health Authority. Responsible for health care throughout Northern Manitoba up to Hudson's Bay, this group services large groups of First Nations Cree and Metis indigenous to that region.

Karen McClelland, former president of the Regional Health Authority, has a strong commitment to serving the First Nations people in a culturally sensitive way. All new staff are required to undergo an intensive two-day Northern Cultures course, familiarizing employees with the special needs and cultural issues of this northern part of Canada.

Part of the training includes spending time with the vice president of Aboriginal Affairs for the Authority, Lloyd Martin. He is also known by his aboriginal name, OSAWIKEESIK, which means "Blue Sky." In the process we learned that the medicine wheel, which dates back to early Aboriginal culture, is right on track with the "modern" concept of emotional intelligence. For example, Figure 22.1 depicts a version of the medicine wheel as used in the Cree culture. Notice the importance of looking after yourself first—signified by the "Me" in the center. Without the energy to take care of ourselves, we're unable to look after others.

Figure 22.1 Cree Medicine Wheel

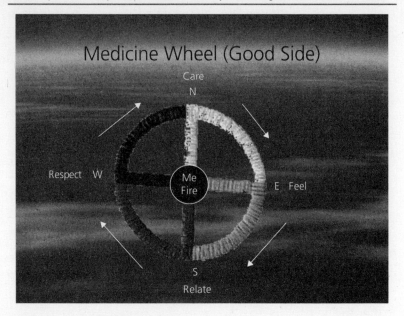

Figure 22.2 Medicine Wheel and EI

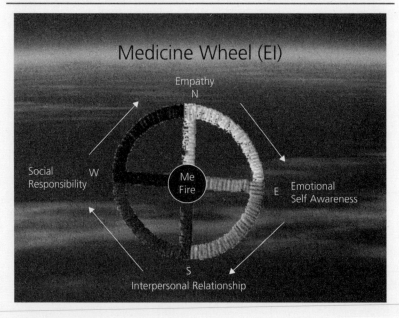

We begin circling the wheel with Care, at the northern point of the wheel. It's important to care for ourselves and others. This leads to our ability to Feel and then to Relate to others. Finally, we learn to Respect those around us.

With just a little translation we create the EI version in Figure 22.2. In this version we also begin at the center with Me, then begin the circle at its northern point with Empathy—understanding others. Moving clockwise, we come to Emotional Self-Awareness—our ability to be aware of our own feelings—which we use to develop Interpersonal Relationships, and finally become Socially Responsible human beings.

CHAPTER 23

What's Next?

A ctually, that's up to you.

We hope that by now you're convinced. Emotional and social intelligence involve widely accepted and applicable principles of human behavior that have been well researched. We know that those who understand themselves and their emotions better (self-perception) are more likely to achieve and be happy with themselves. And they have a better chance of being effective and congruent in their self-expression. But that's not all. To have meaningful professional and personal relationships, you also have to understand and appreciate others and build strong relationships with them. And if you want to be effective in life and work, managing decisions and stress effectively certainly come into the picture.

We've seen how emotional intelligence applies to your work as a student, across cultures, and to occupational groups, work functions, leadership behaviors, relationships, health issues, psychological well-being, and many other facets of human performance. In fact, there's almost no area of life where emotional intelligence does not apply.

So how can you begin to use this information? Being more aware of your emotions gives you much greater control over your life. The exercises in this book and the accompanying student workbook, *The Student EQ Edge: Student Workbook* (Kanoy, Book, & Stein, 2013) will help you explore your emotions and ways in which you can better manage them.

But, as with any new skill, these emotional skills require you to go out into the world and practice them. You won't become an expert in emotional intelligence without practice; in fact, imagine yourself learning to play the piano or a new sport and the practice it takes to become skilled. Practice will reap benefits.

By consolidating the skills—paying attention to your emotions, listening better to others, managing your own emotions, and managing other people's emotions—you'll reap the benefits. But only if you practice! Start listening to your moods, thoughts, and feelings. Pay attention to what they are telling you. Use this information before you act.

Also, start to pay more attention to others you interact with. Listen, watch, and discover where they are really coming from and what they mean to say to you. We often jump to conclusions about what others are thinking and feeling. If you're not sure, then ask.

Never stop practicing the skills you've learned in this book. Remember—emotional intelligence can be learned. And it's never too late to learn.

Alumran, J., & Punamaki, R-L. (2008). Relationship between gender, age, academic achievement, emotional intelligence, and coping styles among Bahraini adolescents. *Individual Differences Research, 6*(2), 104–119.

Aydin, M., Dogan, N. A., Mahmut, K., Oktem, M., & Kemal, M. (2005). The impact of IQ and EQ on pre-eminent achievement in organizations: Implications for hiring decisions of HRM specialists. *International Journal of Human Resource Management, 16*(5), 701–719.

Bachman, J., Stein, S. J., Campbell, K., & Sitarenios, G. (2000). Emotional intelligence in the collection of debt. *International Journal of Selection and Assessment, 8*, 176–182.

Bar-On, R. (1988). *The development of a concept of psychological well-being* (Unpublished doctoral dissertation). Rhodes University, South Africa.

Bar-On, R. (1997). *The Emotional Quotient Inventory (EQ-i): Technical manual.* Toronto, ON: Multi-Health Systems.

Bar-On, R. (2004). The Bar-On Emotional Quotient Inventory (EQ-i): Rationale, description and summary of psychometric properties. In G. Geher (Ed.), *Measuring emotional intelligence: Common ground and controversy* (pp. 111–142). Hauppauge, NY: Nova Science Publishers.

Bar-On, R., Handley, R., & Fund, S. (2005). The impact of emotional and social intelligence on performance. In V. Druskat, F. Sala, and G. Mount (Eds.), *Linking emotional intelligence and performance at work: Current research evidence* (pp. 3–20). Mahwah, NJ: Erlbaum.

Bar-On, R., & Parker, J.D.A. (2000). *Bar-On Emotional Quotient Inventory: Youth version (EQ-i:YV) technical manual.* Toronto, ON: Multi-Health Systems.

Becker, I. M., Ackley, D. C., & Green, R. A. (2003). New study: The value of emotional intelligence in dentistry. *Dentistry Today, 22,* 106–111.

Beidel, D., Turner, S. M., & Morris, T. (2003). *Social Effectiveness Therapy for Children and Adolescents (SET-C): A therapist's guide.* Toronto, ON: Multi-Health Systems.

Berenson, R., Boyles, G., & Weaver, A. (2008). Emotional intelligence as a predictor of college success in online learning. *International Review of Research in Open and Distance Learning, 9*(2), 1–17.

Brunetti, D. (Producer), & Fincher, D. (Director). (2010). *The Social Network* (Motion picture). United States: Columbia Pictures.

Bumphus, A. T. (2009). The emotional intelligence and resilience of school leaders: An investigation into leadership behaviors. *Dissertation Abstracts International Section A. Humanities and Social Sciences, 69*(9), 3401.

Carey, E. (1997, March 5). Older's better emotionally, test says. *Toronto Star.* Retrieved from http://www.lexisnexis.com/en-us/home.page

Chang, K. (2007). Can we teach emotional intelligence? *Dissertation Abstracts International: Section A. Humanities and Social Sciences, 67*(12), 4451.

Charan, R., & Colvin, G. (1999, June 21). Why CEOs fail. *Fortune Magazine.* Retrieved from http://money.cnn.com/magazines/fortune/fortune_archive/1999/06/21/261696/index.htm

Colston, D. (2008). The relationship between emotional intelligence and academic achievement: Implications of birth order based on social rank for nontraditional adult learners. *Dissertation Abstracts International: Section A. Humanities and Social Sciences, 69*(6), 2156.

Conrad, J. E. (2007). The relationship between emotional intelligence and intercultural sensitivity. *Dissertation Abstracts International: Section A. Humanities and Social Sciences, 68*(3), 846.

Costanza, M., & Lawrence, G. (1998). *The real Seinfeld.* New York: Worldwise Books.

Covey, S. R. (2004). *Seven habits of highly effective people.* New York: Free Press.

Csikszentmihalyi, M. (1999, October). If we are so rich, why aren't we happy? *American Psychologist, 54*(10), 821–827.

Csikszentmihalyi, M., Abuhamdeh, S., & Nakamura, J. E. (2005). Flow. In J. A. Elliot & C. S. Dweck (Eds.), *Handbook of competence and motivation* (pp. 598–608). New York: The Guilford Press.

Damasio, A. (1994). *Descartes' error: Emotion, reason, and the human brain.* New York: Grosset/Putnam.

Deniz, M., Tras, Z., & Aydogan, D. (2009). An investigation of academic probation, locus of control and emotional intelligence. *Educational Sciences: Theory and Practice, 9*(2), 623–632.

Diener, E., & Biswas-Diener, R. (2002). Will money increase subjective well-being? *Social Indicators Research, 57*(2), 119–169.

Diener, E., & Seligman, M. E. (2002). Very happy people. *Journal of Psychological Science, 13*(1), 81–84.

Dizdarevic, T. (1996, September 2). "Soft skills" on rise: IT workers can no longer rely on technical expertise. *Computer Reseller News, 699,* 111.

Dries, N., & Pepermans, R. (2007). Using emotional intelligence to identify high potential: A metacompetency perspective. *Leadership & Organization Development Journal, 28*(8), 749–770.

Drucker, P. F. (1999). *Management challenges for the 21st century.* New York: Harper Business.

Drury, L. (2008). Coaches' perceptions of emotional and social intelligence. *Dissertation Abstracts International: Section B. Sciences and Engineering, 69*(6), 3831.

Dulko, J. P. (2008). Application of the emotional intelligence construct to college student binge drinking. *Dissertation Abstracts International: Section B. Sciences and Engineering, 69*(2), 1321.

Dunkley, J. (1996). *The psychological well-being of coronary heart disease patients before and after an intervention program* (Unpublished master's thesis). University of Pretoria, Pretoria, South Africa.

Durando, J. (2010, June 1). BP's Tony Hayward: "I'd like my life back." *USA Today.* Retrieved from http://content.usatoday.com/communities/greenhouse/post/2010/06/bp-tony-hayward-apology/1#.T8JqTtVfFX0

Durek, D. (2005, June). *Return on emotion: Emotional intelligence and leader performance at Telecom NZ.* Paper presented at the Nexus EQ conference, Egmond aan Zee, The Netherlands.

D'Zurilla, T., & Nezu, A. (1999). *Problem-solving therapy: A social competence approach to clinical intervention.* New York: Springer Series on Behavior Therapy and Behavioral Medicine.

Ellis, A. (1955). New approaches to psychotherapy techniques. *Journal of Clinical Psychology, 11,* 207–260.

Ellis, A. (2004). Expanding the ABCs of rational emotive therapy. In A. Freeman, M. J. Mahoney, P. Devito, & D. Martin (Eds.), *Cognition and psychotherapy* (2nd ed., pp. 185–196). New York: Springer.

Fazio, R., & Fazio, L. (2005). Growth through loss: Promoting healing and growth in the face of trauma, crisis, and loss. *Journal of Loss & Trauma, 10*(3), 221–252.

Freud, S. (1915). Repression. *Collected Papers, 4,* 84–97.

Frye, C., Bennett, R., & Caldwell, S. (2006). Team emotional intelligence and team interpersonal process effectiveness. *American Journal of Business: Applying Research to Practice, 21*(1), 49–56.

Gawryluk, J. R., & McGlone, J. (2007). Does the concept of emotional intelligence contribute to our understanding of temporal lobe resections? *Epilepsy & Behavior, 11,* 421–426. doi:10.1016/j.yebeh.2007.06.002.

Gelernter, D. (1998, December 7). Bill Gates: Software strongman. *Time Magazine, 152*(23), 200.

Goleman, D. (1995). *Emotional intelligence: Why it can matter more than IQ.* New York: Bantam.

Gottman, J. (1994). *Why marriages succeed or fail.* New York: Simon & Schuster.

Handley, R. (1997, April). AFRS rates emotional intelligence. *Air Force Recruiter News,* 10–11.

Hansen, R. (2010). A study of school district superintendents and the connection of emotional intelligence to leadership. *Dissertation Abstracts International: Section A. Humanities and Social Sciences, 70*(10), 3920.

Hughes, S. (1998). The effect of mood on the processing, representation, and potency of persuasive communications. *Dissertation Abstracts International: Section B. Sciences and Engineering, 59*(3), 1412.

Iacocca, L. (1998, December 7). Henry Ford. *Time, 153*(23), 76.

Jae, J. H-W. (1997). Emotional intelligence and cognitive ability as predictors of job performance among bank employees (Unpublished master's thesis). Ateneo De Manila University, Philippines.

Jaeger, A. (2004). Examining the relationship between emotional intelligence and college student success. *Dissertation Abstracts International: Section B. Sciences and Engineering, 68*(9), 6301.

Jaschik, S. (2006, October 17). Student volunteerism is up. *Inside Higher Education.* Retrieved from http://www.insidehighered.com/news/2006/10/17/volunteer#ixzz1rf2RFtrX

Jerome, K. (2010). *An examination of the relationship between emotional intelligence and the leadership styles of early childhood professionals* (Unpublished doctoral dissertation). University of Oklahoma, Norman, OK.

Kanoy, K., Book, H., & Stein, S. (2013). *The student EQ edge: Student workbook.* San Francisco: Jossey-Bass.

Killgore, W.D.S., Killgore, D. B., Day, L. M., Li, C., Kamimori, G. H., & Balkin, T. J. (2007). The effects of 53 hours of sleep deprivation on moral judgment. *Journal of Sleep and Sleep Disorders Research, 30*(3), 345–352.

Killgore, W.D.S., & Yurgelun-Todd, D. (2007). Neural correlates of emotional intelligence in adolescent children. *Cognitive Affective & Behavioral Neuroscience, 7*(2), 140–151. doi:10.3758/CABN.7.2.140.

Kohaut, K. M. (2010). Emotional intelligence as a predictor of academic achievement in middle school children. *Dissertation Abstracts International: Section B. Sciences and Engineering, 71*(4), 2688.

Krivoy, E., Weyl Ben-Arush, M., & Bar-On, R. (2000). Comparing the emotional intelligence of adolescent cancer survivors with a matched sample from the normative population. *Medical & Pediatric Oncology, 35*(3), 382.

Kruger, P. (1999, May). A leader's journey. *Fast Company.*

Lerner, J. S., Gonzalez, R. M., Dahl, R. E., Hariri, A. R., & Taylor, S. E. (2005). Facial expressions of emotion reveal neuroendocrine and cardiovascular stress responses. *Biological Psychiatry, 58*(9), 743–750.

Levine, M. (1993). *Effective problem solving* (2nd ed.). Englewood Cliffs, NJ: Prentice Hall.

Logan, D., & Papadogiannis, P. (2007). *GA Performance and EQ-i.* (Technical report #0063). Toronto, ON: Multi-Health Systems.

Lykken, D., & Tellegen, A. (1996). Happiness is a stochastic phenomena. *Psychological Science, 7*(3), 186–189.

Mann, D., & Kanoy, K. (2010, February). *The EQ factor in student retention and success: From theory to practice.* Paper presented at the annual First Year Experience Conference, Denver, CO.

Maslow, A. H. (1987). *Motivation and personality* (3rd ed.). New York: Harper & Row.

Mehrabian, A. (1971). *Silent messages.* Oxford, England: Wadsworth.

Mirsky, S. (1997, April). Separate but EQ. *Scientific American, 276*(4), 25.

Mischel, W., Ayduk, O., Berman, M., Casey, B., Gotlib, I. H., Jonides, J., Kross, E., Teslovich, T., Wilson, N., Zayas, V., & Shoda, Y. (2011). "Willpower" over the lifespan: Decomposing self-regulation. *Social Cognitive and Affective Neuroscience, 6*(2), 252–256.

Mischel, W., Ebbesen, E., & Zeiss, A. (1972). Cognitive and attentional mechanisms in delay of gratification. *Journal of Personality and Social Psychology, 21*(2), 204–218.

Moffitt, T. E., Arseneault, L., Belsky, D., Dickson, N., Hancox, R. J., Harrington, H., Houts, R., Poulton, R., Roberts, B., Ross, S., Sears, M., Thomson, M., & Caspi, A. (2011). A gradient of childhood self-control predicts health, wealth, and public safety. *The Proceedings of the National Academy of Sciences, 108*(7), 2693–2698.

Morehouse, M. (2007). An exploration of emotional intelligence across career arenas. *Leadership & Organization Development Journal, 28*(4), 296–307.

Multi-Health Systems. (2011). *Emotional quotient inventory 2.0 (EQ-i 2.0) user's handbook.* Toronto, Ontario: Multi-Health Systems.

Murphy, S. (1996). *The achievement zone: 8 skills for winning all the time from the playing field to the boardroom.* New York: Putnam.

Myers, D. G., & Diener, E. (1995) Who is happy? *Psychological Science, 6*(1), 10–19.

Nigli, R. (1998). *Executive summary of LEAP program.* Unpublished manuscript. Toronto, ON: YWCA of Metropolitan Toronto.

Nowak, M., & Sigmund, K. (2005). Evolution of indirect reciprocity. *Nature, 437*(7063), 1291–1298.

Palarmis, J., Allred, C. G., & Block, C. (2010). Letting off steam or just steaming? The influence of target and status on attributions and anger. *International Journal of Conflict Management, 21*(3), 260–280.

Parker, J.D.A., Duffy, J., Wood, L. M., Bond, B. J., & Hogan, M. J. (2005). Academic achievement and emotional intelligence: Predicting the successful transition from high school to university. *Journal of First-Year Experience & Students in Transition, 17*(1), 67–78.

Parker, J.D.A., Summerfeldt, L. J., Hogan, M. J., & Majeski, S. (2004). Emotional intelligence and academic success: Examining the transition from high school to university. *Personality and Individual Differences, 36*(1), 163–172.

Perlini, A. H., & Halverson, T. R. (2006). Emotional intelligence in the National Hockey League. *Canadian Journal of Behavioural Science/ Revue Canadienne des Sciences du Comportement, 38*(2), 109–119.

Raths, D. (2006). 100 best corporate citizens for 2006: Celebrating companies that excel at serving a variety of stakeholders well. *Business Ethics, 20*(1).

Rovnak, A. (2007). A psychometric investigation of the emotional quotient inventory in adolescents: A construct validation and estimate of stability. *Dissertation Abstracts International: Section A. Humanities and Social Sciences, 68*(9), 3747.

Ruderman, M., & Bar-On, R. (2003). *The impact of emotional intelligence on leadership*. Unpublished manuscript. Toronto, ON: Multi-Health Systems.

Ruderman, M., Hannum, K., Leslie, J. B., & Steed, J. L. (2001, August). Leadership skills and emotional intelligence. Paper presented at the Applying Emotional Intelligence to Business Solutions and Success Conference, Toronto, ON.

Sadri, E., Akbarzadeh, N., & Poushaneh, K. (2009). Impact of social-emotional learning skills instruction on emotional intelligence of male high school students. *Psychological Research, 11*, 69–83.

Saklofske, D. H., Austin, E. J., Rohr, B. A., & Andrews, J.J.W. (2007). Personality, emotional intelligence, and exercise. *Journal of Health Psychology, 12*(6), 937–948. doi:10.1177/1359105307082458.

Saw, A. (2011). Influences of personal standards and perceived parental expectations on worry for Asian American and White American college students. *Dissertation Abstracts International: Section B. Sciences and Engineering, 72*(6), 3739.

Schulman, P. (1995). Explanatory style and achievement in school and work. In G. Buchanan & M. Seligman (Eds.), *Explanatory style* (pp. 159–171). Hillsdale, NJ: Lawrence Erlbaum.

Schutte, N. S., & Malouff, J. M. (2002). Incorporating emotional skills content in a college transition course enhances retention. *Journal of the First-Year Experience, 14*(1), 7–21.

Schutte, N. S., Malouff, J. M., Thorsteinsson, E. B., Bhullar, N., & Rooke, S. E. (2007). A meta-analytic investigation of the relationship between emotional intelligence and health. *Personality and Individual Differences, 42*(6), 921–933.

Seligman, M. (1991). *Learned optimism: How to change your mind and your life*. New York: Knopf.

Seligman, M., & Schulman, P. (1986). Explanatory style as a predictor of productivity and quitting among life insurance sales agents. *Journal of Personality and Social Psychology, 50*(4), 832–838.

Selye, H. (1976). *The stress of life*. New York: McGraw-Hill.

Shoda, Y., Mischel, W., & Peake, P. (1990). Predicting adolescent cognitive and self-regulatory competencies from preschool delay of gratification: Identifying diagnostic conditions. *Developmental Psychology, 26*(6), 978–986.

Sirois, B. C., & Burg, M. M. (2003). Negative emotion and heart disease: A review. *Behavior Modification, 27*(1), 83–102.

Sitarenios, G. (1998). *Pre-post analysis: American Express Co. employees*. Unpublished manuscript. Toronto, ON: Multi-Health Systems.

Sitarenios, G. (2003). *Electronic Company Wireless Specialist (Ref. Program 135, Position 5): DNA revision.* (Technical Report #0080). Toronto, ON: Multi-Health Systems.

Sitarenios, G., & Stein, S. J. (1998a). *EQ-i ethnicity analysis.* Unpublished manuscript. Toronto, ON: Multi-Health Systems.

Sitarenios, G., & Stein, S. J. (1998b). *Emotional intelligence in the prediction of sales success in the financial industry.* Unpublished manuscript. Toronto, ON: Multi-Health Systems.

Smith, T. W., Glazer, K., Ruiz, J. M., & Gallo, L. C. (2004). Hostility, anger, aggressiveness, and coronary heart disease: An interpersonal perspective on personality, emotion and health. *Journal of Personality, 72*(6), 1217–1270.

Sparkman, L. (2009). Emotional intelligence as a non-traditional predictor of college-student retention and grades. *Dissertation Abstracts International, Section A. Humanities and Social Sciences, 69*(8), 3068.

Stanley, T. J. (2001). *The millionaire mind.* Kansas City, KS: Andrews McMeel Publishing.

Stein, S. (1999a). *Emotional intelligence and nationality: A comparison of Canadians and Americans.* Unpublished manuscript. Toronto, ON: Multi-Health Systems.

Stein, S. (1999b). *Emotional intelligence and relationship satisfaction.* Unpublished manuscript. Toronto, ON: Multi-Health Systems.

Stein, S. (1999c). *The emotional intelligence of broadcast journalists.* Unpublished manuscript. Toronto, ON: Multi-Health Systems.

Stein, S. (2000). *Hockey prospect analysis, Part two* (Unpublished manuscript). Toronto, ON: Multi-Health Systems.

Stein, S. (2010). *Emotional intelligence and nationality revisited: A comparison of Canadians and Americans.* Unpublished manuscript. Toronto, ON: Multi-Health Systems.

Stein, S., & Book, H. (2011). *The EQ edge: Emotional intelligence and your success.* Ontario, ON: Wiley.

Stein, S., Papadogiannis, P., Yip, J., & Sitarenios, G. (2009). Emotional intelligence of leaders: A profile of top executives. *Leadership Organization Development Journal, 30,* 87–101.

Stein, S., & Sitarenios, G. (1997). *Emotional intelligence and elementary and secondary teachers.* (Technical report #0079). Toronto, ON: Multi-Health Systems.

Stein, S., & Sitarenios, G. (1999). *EQ-i: Hockey prospect analysis.* Technical Report #0002. Toronto, ON: Multi-Health Systems.

Stein, S., & Sitarenios, G. (2000). *The emotional intelligence of U.S. fighter pilots. Data base and analysis.* Unpublished manuscript. Toronto, ON: Multi-Health Systems.

Stone, H., Parker, J., & Wood, L. (2005, February). *Report on the Ontario principals' council leadership study.* Unpublished manuscript. Consortium for Research on Emotional Intelligence in Organizations. Retrieved from www.eiconsortium.org

Swift, D. (1999, March 9). Do doctors have an emotional handicap? *The Medical Post, 35*(10), 30.

Taylor, I. (2002, July/August). Canada's top 25 litigators. *LEXPERT,* 64–89.

Trinidad, D. R., & Johnson, C. A. (2002). The association between emotional intelligence and early adolescent tobacco and alcohol use. *Personality and Individual Differences, 32,* 95–105.

Turner, S. M., Beidel, D., & Cooley-Quille, M. (1997). *Social Effectiveness Therapy (SET): A therapist's guide.* Toronto, ON: Multi-Health Systems.

Turner, T. (2005). *Identifying emotional intelligence competencies differentiating FBI National Academy graduates from other law enforcement leaders* (Unpublished dissertation). Curry School of Education, University of Virginia, Charlottesville, VA.

United States House of Representatives. (1998a, March 12). *Military attrition: DOD needs to better analyze reasons for separation and improve recruiting systems* (GAO/T-NSIAD-98-117). Washington, DC: U.S. Government Printing Office.

United States House of Representatives. (1998b, September 9). *The Starr Report.* (Submitted by the Office of the Independent Counsel). Washington, DC: U.S. Government Printing Office.

United States Senate. (1998, January 30). *Military recruiting: DOD could improve its recruiter selection and incentive systems* (GAO/NSIAD-98-58). Washington, D.C.: U.S. Government Printing Office.

Vargas, J. A. (2010, September 20). The face of Facebook. *New Yorker.* Retrieved from http://www.newyorker.com/reporting/2010/09/20/100920fa_fact_vargas

Veenhoven, R. (1984). *Conditions of happiness.* Dordrecht/Boston/Lancaster: Kluwer Academic.

Wagner, P., Moseley, G., Grant, M., Gore, J., & Owens, C. (2002). The relationship between physician, emotional intelligence, and patient satisfaction. *Family Medicine, 34*(10), 750–754.

Wagner, R. K. (1997). Intelligence, training, and employment. *American Psychologist, 52*(10), 1059–1069. doi:10.1037/0003-066X.52.10.1059

Webb, T. (2010, May). BP boss admits job on the line over gulf oil spill. *Guardian*. Retrievedfromwww.guardian.co.uk/business/2010/may/13/bp-boss-admits-mistakes-gulf-oil-spill

Wong, Y. J., Brownson, C., & Schwing, A. (2011). Risk and protective factors associated with Asian American students' suicidal ideation: A multicampus, national study. *Journal of College Student Development, 52*(4), 396–408.

World Values Study Group. (1994). *World Values Surveys, 1981–1994 and 1990–1993* (Data file). ICPSR version. Ann Arbor, MI: Institute for Social Research. Retrieved from http://www.wvsevsdb.com/wvs/WVSData.jsp

Yalcin, B. M., Karahan, T. F., Ozcelik, M., & Igde, F. A. (2008, November/December). The effects of an emotional intelligence program on the quality of life and well-being of patients with Type-2 Diabetes Mellitus. *Diabetes Educator, 34*, 1013–1024. doi:10.1177/0145721708327303.

Zavala, M. A., Valadez, M. D., & Vargas, M. C. (2008). Emotional intelligence and social skills in adolescents with high social acceptance. *Electronic Journal of Research in Educational Psychology, 6,* 319–338.